Praise for
The Concept of Intrinsic Evil and Catholic Theological Ethics

"This book offers an accurate and in-depth analysis of the concept of intrinsic evil. It considers historical instances, systematic articulations, and applications to moral fields, such as sexual ethics. The theme of the moral negativity of an action is related to the notion of the agent as subject of her or his choices. This turn toward the subject does not weaken the question of moral evil and does not weaken the structure of ethical discourse, degrading it to something subjectivist and relativistic. On the contrary, it emphasizes, with vigor and effectiveness, the responsibility of moral action, both in personal and collective agency. For such a perspective it is necessary to have a sensitivity for the human good as a whole and to develop a moral passion that helps to make it concrete in the paths of history. That takes us in a different direction than intrinsic evil, and this book is a powerful help for developing that newer pathway."

—**Antonio Autiero**, University of Münster

"Recent Catholic teaching, especially in *Veritatis Splendor*, has too often used the technical moral theological concept, 'intrinsic evil,' as an authoritarian bludgeon to aggressively suppress theological conversation on, and discernment about, controversial ethical issues, especially in sexual ethics. This invaluable collection of essays by noted scholars critically engages the tradition, and one another, to deconstruct the concept by exploring its historical, philosophical, theological, and ideological roots, and to move the tradition forward with a comprehensive and comprehensible framework for constructing foundational ethical concepts."

—**Todd A. Salzman**, Amelia and Emil Graff Professor of Theology,
Creighton University

The Concept of Intrinsic Evil and Catholic Theological Ethics

Edited by
Nenad Polgar and
Joseph A. Selling

LEXINGTON BOOKS/FORTRESS ACADEMIC
Lanham • Boulder • New York • London

Quoted material in chapter 1 from *The Complete Works of Aristotle: The Revised Oxford Translation* (edited by Jonathan Barnes; Bollingen Series edition, 1984) used with permission of Princeton University Press.

Published by Lexington Books/Fortress Academic

Lexington Books is an imprint of The Rowman & Littlefield Publishing Group, Inc.
4501 Forbes Boulevard, Suite 200, Lanham, Maryland 20706
www.rowman.com

6 Tinworth Street, London SE11 5AL, United Kingdom

British Library Cataloguing in Publication Information Available

Library of Congress Cataloging-in-Publication Data

Names: Polgar, Nenad, editor. | Selling, Joseph A., editor.
Title: The concept of intrinsic evil and Catholic theological ethics / edited
   by Nenad Polgar and Joseph A. Selling.
Description: Lanham : Lexington Books/Fortress Academic, [2019] | Includes
   bibliographical references and index.
Identifiers: LCCN 2019007083 (print) | LCCN 2019010177 (ebook) | ISBN
   9781978703254 (Electronic) | ISBN 9781978703247 (cloth : alk. paper)
Subjects: LCSH: Good and evil--Religious aspects--Catholic Church. |
   Christian ethics--History. | Sexual ethics--History. | Sex--Religious
   aspects--Catholic Church. | Christian ethics--Catholic authors.
Classification: LCC BJ1401 (ebook) | LCC BJ1401 .C596 2019 (print) | DDC
   241/.042--dc23
LC record available at https://lccn.loc.gov/2019007083

∞™ The paper used in this publication meets the minimum requirements of American National Standard for Information Sciences Permanence of Paper for Printed Library Materials, ANSI/NISO Z39.48-1992.

Printed in the United States of America

Contents

The Proliferation of "Intrinsic Evil"

Nenad Polgar and Joseph A. Selling

The concept of intrinsic evil has acquired a foundational status within the official documents of the teaching office of the Catholic Church on ethical issues. Putting aside some early and sporadic references to it,[1] its rise in the official documents of the Church started with the promulgation of Pope Pius XI's encyclical *Casti Connubii* and was closely tied to issues in sexual ethics. After that and up until the start of the most recent pontificate of Pope Francis, one could hardly find an official document on sexual ethics that did not make use of the term by pointing out that some sexual acts are always morally wrong, no matter the circumstances or intention of the agent, and hence "intrinsically evil."[2]

This approach, of course, begs the question precisely why certain acts are considered "always morally wrong." In the past, many of these sexual acts were condemned because they were said to be "contrary to nature," or against the natural law. However, in the minds of many moral theologians the appeal to what is and is not "natural" has been seriously called into question. Having abandoned any direct appeal to "nature," official teaching on sexual activity now simply labels certain activities as "intrinsically evil" which we are subsequently told are "always morally wrong"—without being given any explanation of why that is so.

Perhaps due to its presumed efficiency in dealing with thorny issues in the Church, in his encyclical *Veritatis Splendor* (*VS*) Pope John Paul II ventured to expand the area in which the concept of intrinsic evil could be used. In order to achieve this, he first disentangled the concept from its exclusive use in the area of sexual ethics by pointing out that there are "objects of the human act that are by their nature 'incapable of being ordered to God.'"[3] The Church's moral tradition, he argued, calls these intrinsically evil and this view is not only an important part of the moral doctrine of the Church, but even a Scriptural teaching (*VS*, 80–81). When the encyclical attempts to demonstrate what it means by this, examples of intrinsically evil acts are taken from the pastoral constitution, *Gaudium et Spes* (*GS*), 27, which mentions "genocide, [. . .] voluntary suicide, [. . .] whatever violates the integrity of the human person, such as mutilation, physical and mental torture and attempts to coerce the spirit [. . .],"[4] and so on.

When one takes into account this widening of the area in which the concept can be used, it is perhaps not surprising that the concept worked its way into political discourse, where it started to mark "a Catholic approach" to various issues, especially in the United States. In that sense, the examples include the document of the U.S. bishops on the political responsibility of Catholics, *Forming Consciences for Faithful Citizenship*,[5] the U.S. bishops' objection to a health care program that would finance the use of contraceptives, which "remains a grave moral concern,"[6] and the various individual statements of bishops and other Catholic political commentators who regularly invoke the term intrinsic evil. Of course, the "grave moral concern" refers to a belief that contraception is intrinsically evil. Furthermore, the former document (*Forming Consciences*) detected a number of "acts" which fit the category of intrinsic evil: abortion, euthanasia, human cloning, the destruction of embryos, genocide, torture, racism, targeting noncombatants in war, treating workers as mere means to an end, deliberately subjecting workers to subhuman living conditions, treating the poor as disposable, and redefining marriage to deny its essential meaning.[7]

This Magisterial insistence on the importance and the broadening of the scope of the concept of intrinsic evil becomes clearer when seen in the context of various theological debates that have been going on in the Catholic Church since the Second Vatican Council. These debates[8] within theological ethics have been sanctioned by the Council itself, especially by the Council's document *Optatam Totius*, which stated: "Special attention needs to be given to the development of moral theology. Its scientific exposition should be more thoroughly nourished by scriptural teaching."[9] Although the Council did not elaborate in detail what this development would entail, many theological ethicists understood it as a clear sign of the Council Fathers' dissatisfaction with the old manual tradition of doing theological ethics and, accordingly, they answered the Council's call.

At first, this seemed to imply that only the basis of theological ethics should be widened by updating the discipline, while its conclusions would remain fundamentally the same. However, this amount of catching up[10] made at least some theologians realize that the task of developing theological ethics could not be contained within the framework of finding more and better arguments for the same conclusions, but should instead go much deeper by re-examining methodological presuppositions of the whole discipline. These theologians who were involved in the project of re-examining theological ethics later became known as revisionists. On the other hand, there were those who held that the Council certainly did not give theological ethicists such a broad mandate and that their efforts to renew the discipline, through either terminological or methodological updating, could not relativize in any way the conclusions that had already been reached within the manual tradition and accepted by the teaching office of the Church. These latter theologians became known as traditionalists.

Since these two theological "schools" became so sharply divided on the interpretation of the mandate that the Council gave to theological ethicists, it is perhaps not surprising that they regularly found themselves on opposing sides in almost every debate that has been going on within the discipline of theological ethics for the last fifty years. Through all of this, the (ir)relevance of the concept of intrinsic evil has become a crucial issue that not only has tremendous methodological significance for the future of theological ethics, but is also seen as decisive for the very identity and the mission of the Catholic Church in the field of ethics.

Despite the fact that Pope Francis tried to sidestep the debates that have been going on in the area of theological ethics after the Second Vatican Council by taking a distance from the kind of Magisterial interventions that characterized the pontificate of Pope John Paul II, ironically, the most recent example of the importance of the concept of intrinsic evil is related to the promulgation of his apostolic exhortation *Amoris Laetitia (AL)*. Although the document avoids the concept and tentatively explores a different style of pastoral guidance, it is precisely this that some found objectionable. Thus, shortly after the exhortation was published, a number of cardinals issued five *dubia* or "doubts" about the document in which they summon the Pope to explain himself on certain points that they find unacceptable or even heretical.[11] Three of these five *dubia* invoke the concept of intrinsic evil and *VS*, which leaves no doubt on the angle of approach and mind-set of its authors.

Nevertheless, the pontificate of Pope Francis is also providing an opportunity to explore the issues surrounding the concept of intrinsic evil in a more theologically circumspect way than was possible until recently. Furthermore, there are reasons to believe that this pontificate signals the end of the "Church under siege" paradigm in which the concept found its natural habitat, and announces a new paradigm of discussion and dialogue. Within this new paradigm, the importance of the concept of intrinsic evil for the identity and the mission of the Church has already been brought into question, but its final fate remains to be settled and its comeback is not beyond the imaginable.

THE WORKSHOP AND THE STRUCTURE OF THE BOOK

In February 2016 one of the authors of these lines (Nenad Polgar) received a generous grant from the Austrian Science Fund[12] for a project titled *Origin(s), Meaning, and Relevance of the Concept of Intrinsic Evil* that was to be carried out at the Faculty of Catholic Theology of the University of Vienna, Austria. As the project was entering the final phase, a portion of the grant was used to organize an expert workshop entitled *The Concept of Intrinsic Evil in Catholic Theological Ethics* that was held in Vienna, January 30–31, 2018. Developed in cooperation with Sigrid Müller, the dean of the Faculty of Catholic Theology of the University of Vienna and Joseph A. Selling, professor emeritus at the Faculty of Theology and Religious Studies of the Catholic University Leuven, the workshop aimed at bringing together a number of prominent English- and German-speaking theological ethicists in order to assess the role of the concept of intrinsic evil in theological ethics.

The workshop deliberately avoided following the typical structure of academic conferences in which long papers are read and discussions are kept to a minimum. Instead, all participants were obliged to prepare short position papers well in advance and to read the contributions of all the other participants before the workshop took place so that the two-day meeting could be almost entirely used for critical and constructive discussions. In this way, the organizers hoped, an opportunity would take place to allow different views to be openly discussed so that new insights might be allowed to emerge whereby we could take a step forward in the analysis of the concept of intrinsic evil.

When the workshop ended, the participants were asked to expand their short position papers into chapters of approximately five thousand words, incorporating ideas and perspectives that emerged during the discussions. The chapters in this book represent the reflections of the individual participants in this exercise.

The structure of the book and its chapters largely follow the thematic sessions that were held during the workshop and offer the reader an insight into the lively debate that ensued. This is reflected not only in its division into five parts, each containing two chapters, but also in the fact that a good number of chapters pick up the points made by other authors and provide further reflection on them. After the five parts containing the ten chapters, the concluding chapter draws upon all the contributions and offers some final thoughts.

Part I, "The Origin and Meaning(s) of the Concept of Intrinsic Evil," explores some historical references to this concept and provides the necessary background for a more detailed discussion of the concept in the parts that follow. Writing from a philosophical perspective, Stephan Herzberg's chapter, "Aristotle on Intrinsically Bad Actions," provides an analysis of

Aristotle's concept of the mean as it relates to actions that are "bad in themselves." Herzberg offers a common and substantive reading of the meaning of the notion of acts bad in themselves. Although he uses Aristotle as the starting point, he also poses a hermeneutical question on contemporary interest in the concept of intrinsic evil and traces the development of this contemporary discussion. In the end he comes back to Aristotle in order to show that "The Philosopher" uses this concept (not the term) as a "placeholder" for the morally unthinkable. This being so, it would be unreasonable to expect the concept to have clearly defined boundaries and/or constitutive moral characteristics.

Nenad Polgar's chapter, "The Concept of Intrinsic Evil: An Exploration of Some Theological Sources," pursues this tension between what appears to be a clear contemporary definition of "intrinsic evil" and a somewhat vague notion of "acts that ought never to be done" through a number of theological sources. The main point that he makes is that the older notion of "acts that ought never to be done" cannot strictly be identified with the later concept/term "intrinsic evil." Although this identification seems to underlie the contemporary usage of the concept of intrinsic evil in theological discussions, a clear recognition of the anachronism involved would make the concept much less controversial.

Part II, "The Concept of Intrinsic Evil in Sexual Ethics," engages with the role and the usage of the concept in its primary habitat, Catholic sexual ethics. In that regard, Stephen Pope's chapter, "Intrinsic Evil in Catholic Sexual Ethics: Time to Move On," first briefly sketches some key factors in the ongoing discussion of the usefulness of the notion of intrinsic evil. These "key factors" are established in a brief historical survey of associated ideas in Aristotle, Augustine, and Aquinas, but the bulk of the chapter focuses on the post-conciliar debate within the field of theological ethics. He arrives at five problematic points related to the usage of the concept of intrinsic evil in sexual ethics. On the basis of these points he proposes that theological ethics ought to abandon the usage of the concept and suggests that perhaps Pope Francis has already initiated such a move.

Gunter Prüller-Jagenteufel's chapter, "Intrinsic Evil in Catholic Sexual Ethics: New Insights, New Approaches, New Logic," expands further on the "inherent logic of intrinsic evil" and argues in favor of transforming the basis of the concept from the/a natural law approach to a human dignity approach. Hence, the bulk of the chapter analyzes how the concept of intrinsic evil functions within the natural law approach, where it detects moral evil in human acts, and what kind of distinctions it establishes. This "logic," he suggests, is in itself an argument against adopting or defending this approach. Nevertheless, he disagrees with Stephen Pope and a number of other contributors to this volume that the concept should be abandoned. Instead, he argues for its reinterpretation along the lines of results of an ethical analysis inspired by personalism.

Part III, "The Concept of Intrinsic Evil and *Veritatis Splendor*," moves the discussion on the concept into its "later phase" of application in other areas of Catholic ethics. James Bretzke's chapter, "Intrinsic Evil in *Veritatis Splendor* and Two Contemporary Debates," introduces the reader into the controversy surrounding the promulgation of the encyclical *Veritatis Splendor* and argues that the interpretation of the concept of intrinsic evil lies at the center of this controversy. He identifies a number of ways in which the encyclical's usage of the concept can be interpreted, but favors the "inclusive" interpretation. This interpretation emphasizes that the object of the act cannot be determined on the basis of the act's physical description, but necessarily includes some notion of intention and circumstances; that is, the so-called moral object. Furthermore, he argues that this interpretation not only lies in the background of the encyclical's notion of intrinsic evil, but is also the dominant understanding of the concept of intrinsic evil within the tradition. Nevertheless, he does not argue in favor of his thesis "directly," but instead demonstrates through two other contemporary debates that adopting this thesis might be the best way to overcome the impasse in theological ethics, while showing due respect to the Magisterium and the tradition of the Catholic Church.

Sigrid Müller's chapter, "What Are Intrinsically Evil Acts?" takes issue with a number of points James Bretzke makes in his chapter: first, his statement that "intrinsic evil is used metaphorically and politically, but no one knows what it is"; secondly, the way he understands the specification of a human act in terms of its intention and circumstances; thirdly, the distinction he made between the absolute moral truth founded in God's objective moral order and our understanding of this truth. Müller also offers a concise survey of the work of more prominent German-speaking theologians as a starting point of her own reflection. This leads her to a definition of intrinsically evil acts that takes into account contemporary developments within the field. In the process, she also takes a stand on the three issues of Bretzke's contribution.

Part IV, "The Concept of Intrinsic Evil in Fundamental Theological Ethics," engages directly with methodological issues surrounding the concept of intrinsic evil that were progressively identified in the preceding chapters. Joseph Selling's chapter, "The Naming of Evil in Fundamental Theological Ethics," notes the general dissatisfaction with the usage of the concept of intrinsic evil in theological circles and proposes that one of the reasons why this concept is deficient and confusing is the fact that theological ethicists have not paid enough attention to the terminology that they are using. Hence, his starting point is the proposal of a more coherent terminology for describing various elements within the human act. In the process of developing this, he also points out links between the terminology employed and the method being used. In terms of the latter, he shows that the usage of the concept of intrinsic evil favors a certain conceptualization of human acts that starts with a consideration of their physical objects and only subsequently moves to circumstances and intentions. As opposed to that, he suggests a reversal of that order that would start with an examination of the (circumstantiated) intention of the agent and then move to the (circumstantiated) object of the act. He argues that this is, in fact, a more faithful interpretation of Aquinas's theory of action and he demonstrates the advantages through a number of vivid examples. If adopted, this "new" approach would eliminate the usage of the concept of intrinsic evil as simply unhelpful when it comes to the challenges of describing human acts in a morally adequate way.

Werner Wolbert's chapter, "Intrinsic Evil and the Sources of Morality," takes the issue of terminological (and methodological) confusion within the field of theological ethics a step further. He points out and demonstrates with a number of examples from the moral manuals and ecclesial documents that all the key terms (circumstance, intention, object, and distinctions based on these) involved in the discussion on intrinsically evil acts are ambiguous and/ or homonymous, which often leads to wrong conclusions. These confusions lead him to suggest that the *fontes moralitatis* are not the right context for discussing intrinsically evil acts, even if such a concept can be maintained. Instead, the issues that surround the concept ought to be discussed within the context of normative ethics in general, since what is branded intrinsically evil is an outcome of a process of moral reasoning (on the basis of normative criteria) and not a tool of such an analysis.

Part V, "The Future of the Concept of Intrinsic Evil," analyzes the role of the concept within various ethical perspectives and addresses the question whether the concept will have any role in the further development of the discipline of theological ethics. Andreas Weiß's chapter, "Intrinsic Evil in Different Ethical Perspectives," analyzes the role of the concept in normative ethics, the doctrine of the sources of morality, metaethics, and parenetic speech while paying particular attention to how Bruno Schüller and Peter Knauer approached the issue. After reflecting on the post-conciliar debate on the concept of intrinsic evil, he ends with a note of caution on what might be lost if the Church/theology stopped employing the concept of intrinsic evil. Namely, he believes that the Church's ability to issue "strong moral statements" partly depends on the usage of this (or similar) concept(s) and fears that getting rid of it might mean "throwing out the baby along with the bathwater."

Edward Vacek's chapter, "Pope Francis's Heresy?" offers a reflection on the pontificate of Pope Francis in relation to the concept of intrinsic evil. Vacek focuses on what he reads in *AL* and comments on what the critics are saying about the document. Finding this critique unjustified, he expands more on the three key terms of the apostolic exhortation: mercy, conscience, and conversion. He argues that the way these frame the future debate within theological ethics does not leave room for concepts such as intrinsic evil.

Finally, Polgar and Selling's concluding chapter, "What Is Intrinsic Evil?," recapitulates insights offered by all the preceding chapters and uses these as the starting point for "building a bridge to the future" of theological ethics. The overview of insights reached by the preceding chapters detected some "weak points," that is, aspects of the issue of the concept of intrinsic evil (such as the objective moral order, the human good and evil, hierarchy of goods, change in moral teaching and practice, etc.) that were certainly raised but not sufficiently resolved in the course of the workshop. Thus, this final chapter sketches an outline of morality and theological ethics by elaborating further on these "weak points" and how they relate to the concept of intrinsic evil. The position that the concept of intrinsic evil has no place within this outline of morality and theological ethics comes through, we believe, quite clearly.

The reader will naturally make up his/her own mind about this position. However, if the chapters gathered in this volume manage to demonstrate what is at stake in the controversy surrounding the concept of intrinsic evil, their authors will consider it well worth the effort.

NOTES

1. James Murtagh identified two references to "intrinsic evil" by the Holy Office in the nineteenth century (in 1842 and in 1853) and one reference to it by the Sacred Penitentiary at the beginning of the twentieth century (in 1916) (*Intrinsic Evil: An Examination of This Concept and Its Place in Current Discussions on Absolute Moral Norms* [Rome: Tipografia di Patrizio Graziani, 1973], 29–30).

2. Of course, the meaning of the term (and especially the concept) of intrinsic evil is much more complex than this "working definition" (intrinsically evil acts are always morally wrong no matter the circumstances or intention of the agent) can demonstrate. Some of the contributions in this volume deal with precisely this issue.

3. John Paul II, "Veritatis Splendor," accessed May 13, 2018, http://w2.vatican.va/content/john-paul-ii/en/encyclicals/documents/hf_jp-ii_enc_06081993_veritatis-splendor.html, 80.

4. Ibid.; Second Vatican Council, "Gaudium et Spes," accessed May 13, 2018, http://www.vatican.va/archive/hist_councils/ii_vatican_council/documents/vat-ii_const_19651207_gaudium-et-spes_en.html, 27. It is important to point out that *GS* (27) does not call these acts/ (social) conditions "intrinsically evil." In fact, and contrary to what *VS* implies, the pastoral constitution does not use this kind of vocabulary at all, which already suggests that the constitution itself had a different approach to moral issues.

5. USSCB, "Forming Consciences for Faithful Citizenship—Part I—The U.S. Bishops' Reflection on Catholic Teaching and Political Life," accessed May 13, 2018, http://www.usccb.org/issues-and-action/faithful-citizenship/forming-consciences-for-faithful-citizenship-part-one.cfm.

6. USSCB, "Bishops Renew Call to Legislative Action on Religious Liberty," accessed May 13, 2018,http://usccb.org/news/2012/12-026.cfm.

7. USSCB, "Forming Consciences," 22–23.

8. These debates cover a wide area of issues in theological ethics. Perhaps the most evident ones are those that focus on a specific issue in applied ethics, such as contraception, masturba-

tion, homosexuality, war and peace, biomedical issues, and so forth. However, behind these more evident issues are those related to methodological and anthropological issues in theological ethics, such as the right interpretation of the natural law, foundational sources of moral wisdom (Scripture, tradition, reason, experience) and their interpretation, the role of authority in moral matters, the existence of absolute moral norms, moral decision-making, moral agency, and so forth. All these issues have been fiercely debated in theological ethics since the Second Vatican Council.

9. Second Vatican Council, "Optatam Totius," accessed May 14, 2018, http://www.vatican.va/archive/hist_councils/ii_vatican_council/documents/vat-ii_decree_19651028_optatam-totius_en.html, 16.

10. The tremendous scope of the task that moral theologians were facing in their attempt to update their discipline has been well described by Joseph Selling: "Human and social sciences have progressed nearly as rapidly as the so-called positive or empirical sciences. Insights into psychology and sociology have opened doors into the human psyche and the very decision-making process itself. Anthropology and ethnology have shed light on the construction and evolution of mores, morals and ethical systems. Philosophy and psychology have exposed the intricacies of valuing and value systems that inform decisions that are being made every day" ("The Context and the Arguments of *Veritatis Splendor*," in *The Splendor of Accuracy: An Examination of the Assertions Made by Veritatis Splendor*, eds. Joseph A. Selling and Jan Jans [Kampen: Kok Pharos Publishing House, 1994], 13).

11. Walter Brandmüller, Raymond L. Burke, Carlo Caffarra, and Joachim Meisner, "Seeking Clarity: A Plea to Untie the Knots in *Amoris Laetitia*," accessed May 27, 2018, http://www.ncregister.com/blog/edward-pentin/full-text-and-explanatory-notes-of-cardinals-questions-on-amoris-laetitia.

12. The Austrian Science Fund (*Der Wissenschaftsfonds*) is an Austrian funding organization that supports the ongoing development of Austrian science and basic research at a high international level.

REFERENCES

Brandmüller, Walter, Raymond L. Burke, Carlo Caffarra, and Joachim Meisner. "Seeking Clarity: A Plea to Untie the Knots in *Amoris Laetitia*." Accessed May 27, 2018. http://www.ncregister.com/blog/edward-pentin/full-text-and-explanatory-notes-of-cardinals-questions-on-amoris-laetitia.

John Paul II. "Veritatis Splendor." Accessed May 13, 2018. http://w2.vatican.va/content/john-paul-ii/en/encyclicals/documents/hf_jp-ii_enc_06081993_veritatis-splendor.html.

Murtagh, James. *Intrinsic Evil: An Examination of This Concept and Its Place in Current Discussions on Absolute Moral Norms*. Rome: Tipografia di Patrizio Graziani, 1973.

Second Vatican Council. "Gaudium et Spes." Accessed May 13, 2018. http://www.vatican.va/archive/hist_councils/ii_vatican_council/documents/vat-ii_const_19651207_gaudium-et-spes_en.html.

———. "Optatam Totius." Accessed May 14, 2018. http://www.vatican.va/archive/hist_councils/ii_vatican_council/documents/vat-ii_decree_19651028_optatam-totius_en.html.

Selling, Joseph A. "The Context and the Arguments of *Veritatis Splendor*." In *The Splendor of Accuracy: An Examination of the Assertions Made by Veritatis Splendor*, edited by Joseph A. Selling and Jan Jans, 11–70. Kampen: Kok Pharos Publishing House, 1994.

USSCB. "Bishops Renew Call to Legislative Action on Religious Liberty." Accessed May 13, 2018. http://usccb.org/news/2012/12-026.cfm.

———. "Forming Consciences for Faithful Citizenship—Part I—The U.S. Bishops' Reflection on Catholic Teaching and Political Life." Accessed May 13, 2018. http://www.usccb.org/issues-and-action/faithful-citizenship/forming-consciences-for-faithful-citizenship-part-one.cfm.

The Origin and Meaning(s) of the Concept of Intrinsic Evil

Chapter One

Aristotle on Intrinsically Bad Actions

Stephan Herzberg

THE DOCTRINE OF THE MEAN

At the center of Aristotle's doctrine of moral virtue stands the concept of the mean.[1] To understand what is meant by this concept, we find two starting points in the text: (1) *The analogy from the area of health:* just as an excess as well as a shortage of food destroys health, whereas the right amount produces, maintains, and increases it, so it is regarding the virtues: "For the man who flies from and fears everything and does not stand his ground against anything becomes a coward, and the man who fears nothing at all but goes to meet every danger becomes rash."[2] This is a quantitative understanding of the mean ("nothing in excess") which has led to the misinterpretation of moral virtue as mediocrity. (2) *The concept of the continuum:* each ethical virtue correlates (*peri ti*)[3] to a certain sphere of emotion or action. This sphere is understood as a continuum.[4] In each continuum there is an excess, a shortage, and the mean. To be *properly* adjusted and thus disposed to the right decision means to attain the mean in such an area. Yet since the matter of emotion or action is always embedded into a concrete situation, the relevant mean cannot be the one in relation to the matter "in itself," but the mean "in relation to us."[5] This is not just one, and likewise not the same, in all cases. Such a mean constitutes the essence of virtue: virtue is such that it aims at the mean, finds and chooses it. The mean explains in what the goodness of such a disposition consists. This mean is elucidated by different *normative* parameters:

> I mean moral excellence; for it is this that is concerned with passions and actions, and in these there is excess, defect, and the intermediate. For instance, both fear and confidence and appetite and anger and pity and in general pleas-

3

ure and pain may be felt both too much and too little, and in both cases not
well; but to feel them at the right times, with reference to the right objects,
towards the right people, with the right aim, and in the right way, is what is
both intermediate and best, and this is characteristic of excellence. Similarly
with regard to actions also there is excess, defect, and the intermediate. [6]

The list of these different normative perspectives is repeated as a pattern in
several descriptions of the individual virtues. Here Aristotle names different
aspects that constitute the moral *rightness* of an emotion or of an action: the
relation to specific persons or things (object), the concrete goal (intention),
time, and the manner of the action (circumstances). These different normative aspects are "distinguished"[7] by right reason (*orthos logos; recta ratio*) as
well as "informed,"[8] that is, determined in its specific content. The standard
for this is the prudent person (*phronimos*): "Excellence, then, is a state concerned with choice, lying in a mean relative to us, this being determined by
reason and in the way in which the man of practical wisdom would determine
it."[9]

Moral virtue thus presupposes right reason. With regard to the mean
Aristotle says that there are many kinds of misconduct, but that there is only
one manner of right action (in a concrete situation). It is therefore easy to
miss the goal of the mean, yet difficult to hit it, that is, to act in a way that
satisfies all the morally relevant aspects of the situation.[10] In this respect it is
sometimes necessary to choose the lesser evil.[11] Also, with regard to moral
estimation, there is a range of tolerance (those deviating little from right
action are not reproached).[12]

Thus we may summarize: (1) The concept of the mean has to be understood in a qualitative sense.[13] This concept covers different *normative* parameters that together constitute the *rightness* of an action or emotion and
thus the goodness of a virtue. According to its essence virtue is a mean. (2)
The different normative parameters are grasped by *right reason*; practical
reason refers to the overall character of a situation with its different morally
relevant features. To hit the mean thus means to respond to the moral demands of a situation adequately. (3) By itself the mean is thus *no criterion* of
right action, but presupposes one already. More precisely: How the normative parameters have to be determined in detail has to be clarified *somewhere
else*. (Modern virtue ethics takes the *phronimos* to be such a standard.)[14] The
doctrine of the mean merely serves to *distinguish* the *possible* normative
aspects (in the sense of a classificatory scheme)—no more and no less than
that.[15] (This could be seen a parallel to what Bruno Schüller refers to as the
scholastic doctrine of the *fontes moralitatis*.)[16] (4) The question regarding the
criteria (*horoi*) for the mean or for the right reason (*orthos logos*) respectively, is formulated by Aristotle himself,[17] yet it is impossible to gain an imme-

diate answer from the text.[18] We rarely read about general normative principles or rules, although we must assume that they exist.[19]

THE DOCTRINE OF INTRINSICALLY BAD ACTIONS: A COMMON READING

Aristotle's doctrine of the mean would be incomplete, however, if one were to ignore the passage below, which immediately follows:

> But not every action nor every passion admits of a mean; for some have names that already imply badness, e.g. spite, shamelessness, envy, and in the case of actions adultery, theft, murder; for all of these and suchlike things imply by their names that they are themselves bad, and not the excesses or deficiencies of them. It is not possible, then, ever to be right with regard to them; one must always be wrong. Nor does goodness or badness with regard to such things depend on committing adultery with the right woman, at the right time, and in the right way, but simply to do any of them is to go wrong. It would be equally absurd, then, to expect that in unjust, cowardly, and self-indulgent action there should be a mean, an excess, and a deficiency; for at that rate there would be a mean of excess and of deficiency, an excess of excess, and a deficiency of deficiency. But as there is no excess and deficiency of temperance and courage because what is intermediate is in a sense an extreme, so too of the actions we have mentioned there is no mean nor any excess and deficiency, but however they are done they are wrong; for in general there is neither a mean of excess and deficiency, nor excess and deficiency of a mean.[20]

This doctrine is not merely an appendix but an important clarification of the concept of the mean. We find it in all three of Aristotle's treatises on ethics.[21] Most of the scholars of the last century interpreting Aristotle have either neglected this passage or at least not allocated to it the importance that it deserves (with regard to Aristotle's conception of ethics as a whole).[22]

On a first reading, it seems that Aristotle is telling us merely that some emotions and actions have names that are already linked to a moral evaluation:[23] the word "murder" (as a prominent example of actions) already implies a badness, so that the course of action denoted by it is always, that is, under all circumstances, bad (and therefore forbidden). Such actions and emotions are precisely not a morally neutral "matter" (of emotion or action), within which one would then have to search for a "mean." Rather, we are already dealing with *kinds* of emotion and action that are already fixed in their moral quality.[24] The question regarding the "mean" does not find application, since we are dealing with an already *formed*, that is, specified matter of action.[25] (There are activities which do not allow for the mean *any longer*. So they are no exceptions from the doctrine of the mean, but are the *result* of its application.[26]) There is no act of murder which could become morally transformed as a result of a certain intention or due to specific circumstances. To ask for the mean in cases like these would be the same as if one were to expect that there is a mean, an excess, or a deficiency in the case of unjust, cowardly, or intemperate actions. If this were so, Aristotle explains, there would be a mean in the case of excess and deficiency, an excess of excess and a deficiency of deficiency. Yet this is impossible, since from an axiological point of view the "mean" already is an extreme.

The function of this passage therefore seems to be, as Hardie says, none other than a logical one: Aristotle draws our attention to the fact that some words denote no neutral matter of action, but rather an already-formed kind[27] within such an area (e.g., adultery).[28] The simple message here is that we have to take a close look at our moral language. In it we find many hybrid concepts that have an evaluative as well as a descriptive component.

THE NEW INTEREST IN INTRINSICALLY
BAD ACTIONS: A SUBSTANTIAL READING

The phrase intrinsically bad/evil came to prominence outside of Aristotelian scholarship. First to be mentioned here is of course Catholic moral theology that invokes Aristotle as an early witness of the *intrinsece malum*.[29] Yet also among philosophers there is a renewed interest in this expression: (1) In her famous article "Modern Moral Philosophy," Elizabeth Anscombe had already drawn attention to certain types of activities that are bad in themselves and thus always and everywhere forbidden, solely because of their kind and completely independent of their consequences.[30] It makes no sense to ask whether actions that are *per se* unjust in Aristotle's sense can be morally right under certain circumstances. The *intrinsece malum* becomes the core of a nonconsequentialist foundation of morality. (2) The neo-Kantian Robert Louden points out that there are such things as *intolerable actions* that are bad *per se* and which demand a categorical prohibition. An ethical theory must be able to integrate such types of action. It must be able to evaluate actions while at the same time disregarding the character of the agent. However, it is precisely this which an agent-based virtue ethics, in which the decisions of the virtuous person are the criterion for what is morally right and wrong, cannot do.[31] (3) Yet those interpreters of Aristotle who oppose a strictly particularistic interpretation of his ethics continue to point out that for Aristotle there are universal prohibitions.[32]

This newly awakened interest is based on a stronger, substantial reading of the passage in question. According to this reading, Aristotle does not *only* want to point to a logical and semantic problem, but he also wants to formulate norms for concrete types of action. The decisive point here is the following: Aristotle says that certain names for actions denote an already misformed matter of action. Does he want to say by this that "adultery" merely denotes an "excess," that is, a misformation in the area of "sexual intercourse" so that the "mean" is not applicable and that actions qualifying as adulterous are false always and everywhere? "Adultery" would in this case mean nothing but "morally wrong sexual intercourse" or "unjust sexual intercourse." Exactly why it would be misformed, that is, what constitutes an act of adultery, would remain an *open question*. Or does Aristotle want to say by this that "adultery" denotes a certain type of activity which represents something quite specific, that is, as sexual intercourse with a person other than one's own spouse? In that case, the mean would not be applicable any more, with the result that what is classified as "adultery" would be wrong always and everywhere. "Adultery" would then have the meaning "sexual intercourse with a person other than one's spouse" which subsequently would always be wrong.

In this first reading the descriptive component is underdetermined. It is left an open question which feature it is that is responsible for the misformation of the relevant matter of action: what exactly is it that makes an activity a morally wrong one? Contrary to this, commentators adopting the second reading, clearly state that the name "adultery" denotes a type of activity which, *due to its nature*, represents a misformation and is therefore immoral. According to them, Aristotle is precisely not leaving the descriptive component unspecified (in the sense of a merely generic description), but he uses a specific definition. This definition contains the characteristic which makes this kind of action wrong always and everywhere ("intercourse with a person other than one's spouse"), that is, which explains why a certain type of action is *per se* linked to a certain moral quality. It is the false *pros hous* which makes this type of activity bad.

What are the reasons for reading our passage in such a substantial way? (1) Aristotle is not just saying that some actions are named in such a way that this immediately implies an evaluation, but he also mentions the reason for this:

> But not every action nor every passion admits of a mean; for some have names that already imply badness, e.g. spite, shamelessness, envy, and in the case of actions adultery, theft, murder; for all of these and suchlike things (καὶ τὰ τοιαῦτα)[33] owe their names (λέγεται)[34] to the fact, that they are themselves bad (τῷ αὐτὰ φαῦλα εἶναι), and not the excesses or deficiencies of them.[35]

In the *Eudemian Ethics* Aristotle also says:

> Nor must we forget that some of the faults mentioned cannot be taken to depend on the manner of action, if manner means excess of passion: e.g. the adulterer is not so called from his excessive intercourse with married women;

'excess' is inapplicable here, but the act is simply in itself wicked; the passion and its character are expressed in the same word.[36]

In both passages Aristotle connects the *de dicto* level with the *de re* level: All of the actions mentioned and others of this kind have their *names* because of the fact that they *themselves* are, that is, as that, *which* they essentially *are*, bad or wicked (*phaulos, mochthêria*), and not their excess or insufficiency. These actions owe their naming not to *special* circumstances (e.g., especially frequent acts of adultery, the way it is committed), but to their *nature* itself.[37] (2) It is possible to show independently of this passage that the concept "adultery," for example, is precisely determined in its descriptive component. In several places Aristotle talks of adultery as an unjust action and of a corresponding prohibition, respectively.[38] It is therefore not controversial what is to be understood by adultery: "As to adultery, let it be held disgraceful, in general, for any man or woman to be found in any way unfaithful when they are married and called husband and wife. If during the time of bearing children anything of the sort occur, let the guilty person be punished with a loss of privileges in proportion to the offence."[39]

Aristotle is convinced in principle that it is necessary to formulate definitions of what theft, maltreatment, adultery, and so forth, each exactly are: he holds that in legal and moral controversies it is often not contentious *that* someone has done something describable in value-neutral terms. What is controversial is the question as to how this act is to be further specified morally. Aristotle points out the need to establish definitions of unjust acts.[40] If such definitions are available, it is possible to decide by reference to objective criteria whether a certain act is an instance of theft, maltreatment, adultery, and so forth. This puts us in a position "to bring the just to light."

At this point the suspicion might arise that the "substantial" reading ends up as a crude form of physicalism: that an action is wrong solely because of the description that can be given to it. Against this the following has to be stated: In the types of action identified here as 'in themselves bad' we are not dealing with purely physical descriptions of activities, but with an action that, in its moral content, as to *what* it is (τί), is already clearly determined. Yet only that description of an action, under which it is *intended* by the agent, determines "what" it is.[41] Morally relevant is only that which someone *intends* to do, the *intended* manner of action (*finis proximus; obiectum actus*). That is the reason why some defend themselves by saying that although they have had sexual intercourse, they did not commit adultery since they acted out of ignorance or were forced.[42] In the case of adultery this specification results from the parameter of relation: from the answer to the question: "vis-à-vis which persons"? (πρὸς οὕς; *ad quos*). It refers to the person, toward whom a certain action is directed and in whom one intends to produce a certain effect.[43]

Therefore it is crucial that in some cases (like adultery, theft, murder) *a certain parameter* from the ensemble of normative parameters already suffices for the moral specification of the action (e.g., to knowingly have sexual intercourse with a person other than one's spouse). In this case all other parameters (e.g., time, frequency, the manner it is carried out, further intentions) play no part any more. Thus, the *nature* of this type of action is defined precisely as an action that is carried out vis-à-vis the wrong person. We are dealing with a *complex* matter of action that is formed already in a certain respect.

OPEN QUESTIONS

However, why it is that this or that aspect of an activity is crucial for its moral specification, Aristotle does not explain any further. The direction in which we have to look for a reason in Aristotle is given by the concept of justice: actions like adultery, theft, or murder are first of all unjust *in a general sense*, in as far as they violate fundamental laws. The laws which aim at the common good or common happiness[44] call for actions in accordance with a specific virtue (e.g., not to desert one's post, commit adultery or outrage).[45] General justice requires that all contribute to the benefit of common happiness and desist from everything that endangers it. This means, first of all, not to endanger or diminish the basic goods of others which are essential to a good life (life itself, bodily integrity, property). Actions like those listed above do massive damage to such goods and thereby destroy fundamental moral relations which are essential for the common good.

The question regarding the epistemological status of exceptionless norms is likewise left open by Aristotle. How does one arrive at the judgment that adultery is *absolutely* or *always* wrong, that is, under all circumstances? How can such absolute moral truth be justified? With regard to this there are at least three positions. (1) One might think that such a judgment is arrived at by way of induction. That adultery is absolutely wrong and thus always to be avoided would be an *empirical generalization* based on all cases observed so far. In all these cases adultery has caused great suffering for those affected and the community, and adultery is therefore, as far as is known, wrong and to be avoided.[46] (2) However, the judgment, that adultery is wrong and as such always to be avoided can also be understood as a genuinely *universal*. A *universal* has the characteristic of being valid "always and everywhere."[47] This type of action has the moral quality of a *malum*, independent of its *specific* instantiation. This means that further circumstances cannot change anything about its quality, they can only add "aggravating" or "mitigating" aspects. Such a *universal* represents a "synthetic a priori." In this case it is impossible to avoid some form of intuitionism.[48] (3) Beyond these alterna-

tives one could make a link to Aristotle's methodological remark that ethics—as a practical science—can only arrive at statements which are true
"roughly and in outline" (*pachylôs kai typô*) or valid only "for the most part"
(*hôs epi to poly*).[49] By saying this, one does not deny in any way that ethics is
capable of formulating genuine universal judgments, that is, universal
norms.[50] One is merely saying that on this level ethics needs to be content
with normative outlines,[51] the more detailed elaboration and concretization
regarding the situation is subject to prudence.[52] The concrete situation is
judged in the light of these unchanging normative elements. "For the most
part" does not imply that moral rules are true in a statistical sense only; it
describes "the normal case."[53] This remark does not serve to separate ethics,
regarding its fundamental claim to knowledge, from the other sciences. However, it does distinguish it regarding its subject and method.

HOW TO DEAL WITH THE CATEGORY OF
WHAT IS "INTRINSICALLY BAD"?

If the "substantial reading" set out above is correct, we are confronted by the
question of how Aristotle deals with such a category in the context of his
moral theory. Each universalist ethics—in Aristotle one might speak of a
context-sensitive universalism[54]—knows certain "exculpation principles," in
order to mitigate certain extreme cases which can result from the application
of universal norms.

In the context of his doctrine of "mixed actions" Aristotle distinguishes
between four types of cases.[55] In the first two types the justification lies in
the proportion between the *extra*-moral badness accepted and the desired
good: (1) If the action is in proportion with the noble end, one is praised.
However, (2) if this proportion does not exist, one is reproached. The other
two types of cases concern actions which are *morally* wrong. (3) Here someone is carrying out actions which are forbidden to do, but where the person is
subject to conditions "which go beyond human nature and which nobody
could endure." The person afflicted in this way can be shown understanding
(*syngnômê*). The action, which is wrong, is condemned, but not the person.[56]
The person has done nothing resulting from a bad attitude, but because they
were under immense moral pressure and were overstrained by it *as a human
being*. (4) Yet, according to Aristotle, there are "probably" (*isôs*) some actions which one should never do, even if coerced, but "ought rather to face
death after the most fearful sufferings." Someone doing such a thing cannot
expect to find understanding, since what they are doing is simply abhor-
rent.[57] (As an example Aristotle mentions matricide; nowadays we might
rather think of cases of sexual violence or torture.) Such actions are inexcus-
able and cannot be justified by anything. Anybody doing something like this

will corrupt oneself as a person. "Bestimmte Handlungen *sind* als solche Mißlingen des Lebens"[58] ("Certain actions *are* as such a failure of life").

The distinction between (3) and (4) is instructive for the way we can deal with the category of what is "bad in itself": There are morally wrong actions which are excusable in certain circumstances (i.e., they are wrong and remain so),[59] and there are those things which one should never do, under no circumstances whatsoever, even if this would cost one's own life. Yet Aristotle adds this class with an *isôs* (= "probably, possibly"). Philosophical ethics needs such a placeholder for the morally unthinkable. There are actions that, when carried out, are not just a disturbing factor in the structure of one's life, but which destroy one's soul irrevocably.

NOTES

1. I thank Manfred Weltecke for translating my text into English. For a comprehensive study of the mean in Aristotle's ethics, see, Christof Rapp, "What Use Is Aristotle's Doctrine of the Mean?" in *The Virtuous Life in Greek Ethics*, ed. Burkhard Reis (Cambridge: Cambridge University Press, 2006), 99–126.

2. *Nicomachean Ethics* (EN) II 2, 1104a20–22. Translations are taken from Jonathan Barnes, ed., *The Complete Works of Aristotle. The Revised Oxford Translation* (Princeton, NJ: Princeton University Press; Bollingen Series edition, 1984).

3. EN III 9, 1115a5.

4. EN II 5, 1106a26.

5. EN II 5, 1106a28.

6. EN II 5, 1106b16–24.

7. EN II 2, 1104b23.

8. EN II 6, 1107a1.

9. EN II 6, 1106b36–1107a2.

10. EN II 5, 1106b28–33.

11. EN II 9, 1109a34–35: "[S]ince to hit the mean is hard in the extreme, we must as a second best, as people say, take the least of the evils."

12. EN II 9, 1109b18–19.

13. Rapp, "Doctrine of the Mean," 121–25.

14. Robert B. Louden, "On Some Vices of Virtue Ethics," *American Philosophical Quarterly* 21, no. 3 (1984): 228–29.

15. This "clarifying" function is also emphasized by Rapp, "Doctrine of the Mean," 123, 126.

16. Bruno Schüller, "Die Quellen der Moralität," *Theologie und Philosophie* 59, no. 4 (1984): 546, 558.

17. EN VI 1, 1138b23, b34.

18. In the older German literature this was dealt with under the keyword *Normproblem*. See, for example, Franz Dirlmeier, trans., *Aristoteles. Nikomachische Ethik*, 10th ed. (Berlin: Akademie Verlag, 1999), 441.

19. For a more detailed discussion, see Dorothea Frede, "Auf Taubenfüßen. Über Natur und Ursprung des ΟΡΘΟΣ ΛΟΓΟΣ in der Aristotelischen Ethik," in *Beiträge zur Aristotelischen Handlungstheorie*, eds. Klaus Corcilius and Christof Rapp (Stuttgart: Franz Steiner Verlag, 2008), 107–8.

20. EN II 6, 1107a8–27.

21. EE II 3, 1221b17–27; MM 1186a36–b3.

22. See, for example, William D. Ross, *Aristotle*, 5th ed. (London: Methuen, 1923, 1949), 196; Harold H. Joachim, *Aristotle. The Nicomachean Ethics* (Oxford: Clarendon Press, 1951),

90–91; Donald J. Monan, *Moral Knowledge and Its Methodology in Aristotle* (Oxford: Clarendon Press, 1968), 87–88; William F. R. Hardie, *Aristotle's Ethical Theory* (Oxford: Clarendon Press, 1968), 137–38.

23. See also EE II 3, 1221b22–23.

24. In what follows I will ignore emotions and concentrate on actions.

25. Joachim, *Nicomachean Ethics*, 91: "Some things, popularly regarded as mere πάθη or πράξεις (as mere materials of action), are really formed πάθη, formed πράξεις: i.e., conduct already characterized as morally bad. The moment you name them you are expressing by the name not bare material but material formed and wrongly formed. [. . .] No doubt what he means is that the things which are called by the name of the πάθος or πρᾶξις are in fact συνειλημμένα: conjoint inclusive composites, including the form."

26. See also Christopher C. W. Taylor, *Aristotle. Nicomachean Ethics. Books II–IV* (Oxford: Clarendon Aristotle series, 2006), ad loc.

27. EE II 3, 1221b10.

28. Hardie, *Aristotle's Ethical Theory*, 137–38: "He is making a purely logical point which arises from the fact that certain words are used to name not ranges of action or passion but determinations within a range with the implication, as part of the meaning of the word, that they are excessive or defective, and therefore wrong. [. . .] In our vocabulary for referring to actions and passions there are words which name misformations; and, in such cases, there is no sense in asking what is the right formation of the object named. This, and no more than this, is what Aristotle means when he says that 'not every action nor every passion admits a mean.'"

29. See, for example, John M. Finnis, *Moral Absolutes. Tradition, Revision, and Truth* (Washington, DC: The Catholic University of America Press, 1991), 31–32; Eberhard Schockenhoff, *Naturrecht und Menschenwürde. Universale Ethik in einer geschichtlichen Welt* (Mainz: Matthias Grünewald, 1996), 199.

30. Gertrude E. M. Anscombe, "Modern Moral Philosophy," in *Human Life, Action and Ethics. Essays by G. E. M. Anscombe*, eds. Mary Geach and Luke Gormally (Essex: Imprint Academic, 2005), 181–82.

31. Louden, "On Some Vices of Virtue Ethics," 230–31.

32. See, for example, Christopher Kaczor, "Exceptionless Norms in Aristotle? Thomas Aquinas and Twentieth-Century Interpreters of the *Nicomachean Ethics*," *Thomist* 61, no.1 (1997): 33–62.

33. "The Online Liddell-Scott-Jones Greek-English Lexicon," accessed May 14, 2018, http://stephanus.tlg.uci.edu/lsj/#eid=1&context=lsj, translates τοιοῦτος as "of such kind, nature or quality."

34. Here I follow Ingram Bywater, ed. *Aristotelis Ethica Nicomachea* (Cambridge: Cambridge University Press, 2010), who reads—with the codex Laureantianus—λέγεται (see also Aristotle, *Nicomachean Ethics*, trans. Christopher Rowe, comm. Sarah Broadie [Oxford: Oxford University Press 2002]: "for all these, and others like them, owe their names to the fact that they themselves—not excessive versions of them, or deficient ones—are bad"; see also Aristotle, "Nicomachean Ethics," trans. by W. D. Ross rev. by J. O. Urmson, in *The Complete Works of Aristotle: The Revised Oxford Translation*, rev. by Jonathan Barnes, vol. 2 [Princeton, NJ: Princeton University Press, 1984]). On the other hand, Bekker and Susemihl read ψέγεται with the *codex Marcianus* ("Alle diese und ähnliche Dinge werden ja deshalb getadelt [. . .]." Aristoteles, *Nikomachische Ethik*, 10th ed., trans. and comm. by F. Dirlmeier [Berlin: Akademie Verlag, 1999]; see also Aristoteles, *Die Nikomachische Ethik*, trans. and comm. by Olof Gigon [München: Dt. Taschenbuchverlag, 1991]).

35. EN II 6, 1107a8–14.

36. EE II 3, 1221b18–23.

37. In his commentary Aquinas speaks of actions which are *secundum se mala* (In Eth. 2,7 n. 329).

38. EN V 3, 1129b21 f.; V 5, 1131a6; V 7, 1132a3; V 15, 1138a25 f.

39. Pol. VII 16, 1335b38–1336a2.

40. Rhet. I 13, 1373b38–1347a9: "Now it often happens that a man will admit an act, but will not admit the prosecutor's label for the act nor the facts which that label implies. He will admit that he took a thing but not that he stole it; that he struck someone first, but not that he

committed outrage; that he had intercourse with a woman, but not that he committed adultery. [. . .] Here therefore we must be able to distinguish what is theft (κλοπή), outrage (ὕβρις), or adultery (μοιχεία), from what is not, if we are to be able to make the justice of our case clear."

41. EN III 2, 1111a4. Someone discloses information but is not aware that it is a secret (1111a9 f.). A further example is, when someone wants to demonstrate how a slingshot works and sets it off accidentally (a10 f.). In these cases the agent is likewise ignorant of 'what' the action is. It is a case of something that happens by mistake (1135b12–19).

42. EE II 3, 1221b23–26.

43. Regarding such an interpretation of ἐφ' οἷς and πρὸς οὓς compare the translations of *Ross/Urmson* ("with reference to the right objects, towards the right people"), *Broadie/Rowe* ("at the things one should, in relation to the people one should"), and *Taylor* ("and about the things one should, and in relation to the people one should").

44. EN V 3, 1129b17–19.

45. EN V 3, 1129b19–24.

46. For such an inductive interpretation see Richard Kraut, "Aristotle on Becoming Good: Habituation, Reflection, and Perception," in *The Oxford Handbook of Aristotle*, ed. Christopher Shields (Oxford: Oxford University Press, 2012), 551: "When he says, for example, that adultery is always wrong, he need not be taken to mean that each particular act of adultery is to be avoided because it would violate a general principle for the regulation of human behavior. For the direction of explanation may go from the particular cases to the general rule, rather than the other way round. In other words, the universal generalization that all adultery is wrong may rest on the fact that, without exception, each particular act of adultery has brought about so much harm. [. . .] Noticing how destructive each act of infidelity is, we generalize, and say that this sort of behavior is always to be avoided. It is not because there is a rule against adultery that it is wrong whenever it occurs; rather, it does great harm whenever it occurs, and that is why we can correctly formulate an exceptionless generalization about its wrongness." However, one has to object that phrases like "so much harm," "destructive," "great harm" are not precise enough. Is this about extra moral goods? What exactly does the destructiveness consist in?

47. An. Post. I 31, 87b32 f. On the concept of the "scientific universal" see also An. Post. I 4.

48. Theo G. Belmans, *Der objektive Sinn menschlichen Handelns. Die Ehemoral des hl. Thomas* (Vallendar-Schonstatt: Patris Verlag, 1984), 168. According to Belmans, these absolute prohibitions cannot be understood as *a posteriori* generalizations, but represent a genuine kind of *a priori* truths without which no moral perception and no moral judgment could originate.

49. EN I 1, 1094b19–22.

50. EN V 10, 1135a8.

51. On this point, see, Otfried Höffe, *Praktische Philosophie—Das Modell des Aristoteles*, 2nd ed. (Berlin: Akademie Verlag 1996), 166, 172.

52. EN II 7, 1107a29–31: "For among statements about conduct those which are general apply more widely, but those which are particular are more true."

53. Christoph Horn, "Epieikeia: The Competence of the Perfectly Just Person in Aristotle," in *The Virtuous Life in Greek Ethics*, ed. Burkhard Reis (Cambridge: Cambridge University Press, 2006), 159: "This implies that regularities can be formulated even if one has to keep in mind that there are relevant exceptions."

54. Ibid., 158.

55. EN III 1, 1110a19–29.

56. Friedo Ricken, *Allgemeine Ethik*, 5th ed. (Stuttgart: Kohlhammer, 2013), 111–12.

57. Significantly, in his commentary Aquinas says that some actions are "so very bad" (quaedam operationes sunt adeo malae), that there is nothing that could justify carrying them out. See Thomas Aquinas, *In decem libros ethicorum Aristotelis ad Nicomachum exposito* (Taurini: Marietti, 1934), 3, 2 n.395.

58. Robert Spaemann, *Grenzen. Zur ethischen Dimension des Handelns* (Stuttgart: Klett-Cotta, 2001), 51.

59. Maybe this thought—together with the advice to take the least of the evils (EN II 9, 1109a35)—is Aristotle's way to deal with the problem of "dirty hands."

REFERENCES

Anscombe, Gertrude E. M. "Modern Moral Philosophy." In *Human Life, Action and Ethics. Essays by G.E.M. Anscombe*, edited by Mary Geach and Luke Gormally, 169–94. Essex: Imprint Academic, 2005.

Aquinas, Thomas. *In decem libros ethicorum Aristotelis ad Nicomachum exposito*. Taurini: Marietti, 1934.

Aristoteles. *Die Nikomachische Ethik*. Translated and commentary by Olof Gigon. München: Dt. Taschenbuchverlag, 1991.

———. *Nicomachean Ethics*. Translated by Christopher Rowe, commentary by Sarah Broadie. Oxford: Oxford University Press, 2002.

———. *Nikomachische Ethik*. 10th ed. Translated and commentary by Franz Dirlmeier. Berlin: Akademie Verlag, 1999.

Barnes, Jonathan, ed. *The Complete Works of Aristotle. The Revised Oxford Translation*. Princeton, NJ: Princeton University Press; Bollingen Series edition, 1984.

Belmans, Theo G. *Der objektive Sinn menschlichen Handelns. Die Ehemoral des hl. Thomas*. Vallendar-Schönstatt: Patris Verlag, 1984.

Bywater, Ingram, ed. *Aristotelis Ethica Nicomachea*. Cambridge: Cambridge University Press, 2010.

Finnis, John M. *Moral Absolutes. Tradition, Revision, and Truth*. Washington, DC: The Catholic University of America Press, 1991.

Frede, Dorothea. "Auf Taubenfüßen. Über Natur und Ursprung des ΟΡΘΟΣ ΛΟΓΟΣ in der Aristotelischen Ethik." In *Beiträge zur Aristotelischen Handlungstheorie*, edited by Klaus Corcilius and Christof Rapp, 105–21. Stuttgart: Franz Steiner Verlag, 2008.

Hardie, William F. R. *Aristotle's Ethical Theory*. Oxford: Clarendon Press, 1968.

Höffe, Otfried. *Praktische Philosophie—Das Modell des Aristoteles*. 2nd ed. Berlin: Akademie Verlag, 1996.

Horn, Christoph. "Epieikeia: The Competence of the Perfectly Just Person in Aristotle." In *The Virtuous Life in Greek Ethics*, edited by Burkhard Reis, 142–66. Cambridge: Cambridge University Press, 2006.

Joachim, H. H. *Aristotle. The Nicomachean Ethics*. Oxford: Clarendon Press, 1951.

Kaczor, Christopher. "Exceptionless Norms in Aristotle? Thomas Aquinas and Twentieth-Century Interpreters of the *Nicomachean Ethics*." *Thomist* 61, no. 1 (1997): 33–62.

Kraut, Richard. "Aristotle on Becoming Good: Habituation, Reflection, and Perception." In *The Oxford Handbook of Aristotle*, edited by Christopher Shields, 529–57. Oxford: Oxford University Press, 2012.

Louden, Robert B. "On Some Vices of Virtue Ethics." *American Philosophical Quarterly* 21, no. 3 (1984): 227–36.

Monan, J. Donald. *Moral Knowledge and Its Methodology in Aristotle*. Oxford: Clarendon Press, 1968.

"The Online Liddell-Scott-Jones Greek-English Lexicon." Accessed May 14, 2018. http://stephanus.tlg.uci.edu/lsj/#eid=1andcontext=lsj.

Rapp, Christof. "What Use Is Aristotle's Doctrine of the Mean?" In *The Virtuous Life in Greek Ethics*, edited by Burkhard Reis, 99–126. Cambridge: Cambridge University Press, 2006.

Ricken, Friedo. *Allgemeine Ethik*. 5th ed. Stuttgart: Kohlhammer Verlag, 2013.

Ross, W. David. *Aristotle*. 5th ed. London: Methuen, 1923, 1949.

Schockenhoff, Eberhard. *Naturrecht und Menschenwürde. Universale Ethik in einer geschichtlichen Welt*. Mainz: Matthias Grünewald, 1996.

Schüller, Bruno. "Die Quellen der Moralität." *Theologie und Philosophie* 59, no. 4 (1984): 535–59.

Spaemann, Robert. *Grenzen. Zur ethischen Dimension des Handelns*. Stuttgart: Klett-Cotta, 2001.

Taylor, C. C. W. *Aristotle. Nicomachean Ethics. Books II–IV*. Oxford: Clarendon Aristotle series, 2006.

Chapter Two

The Concept of Intrinsic Evil

An Exploration of Some Theological Sources

Nenad Polgar

One of the highly contested issues of the long-lasting debate between neo-manualists/traditionalists and revisionists was on the existence of a class of acts that are intrinsically evil. Even a cursory glance at this debate that went on for decades after the Second Vatican Council is bound to leave one perplexed when it comes to settling this issue.[1] For some, the issue was finally "settled" with the promulgation of the encyclical *Veritatis Splendor*[2] (*VS*), but the questionable nature of this settlement is strongly indicated by the fact that the issue erupted again after the promulgation of the Apostolic Exhortation *Amoris Laetitia*[3] (*AL*). The difference, however, is that this time it was not disobedient theologians who were causing trouble again, but the Pope himself. Hence, the guardians of orthodoxy tried to summon him to account by publishing five *Dubia* to which, in their mind, the Pope ought to respond in order to justify himself.[4] Three of these *Dubia*—the second, fourth, and fifth—raised the issue of intrinsic evil and, thus, confirmed that the whole controversy surrounding this concept was not about defying the authority in the Church; nor could one expect it to be resolved through its exercise.

Instead, the events that unfolded after the promulgation of *AL* under-scored the fact that the issue was never actually settled among theologians and that its perplexity needs to be revisited. This perplexity extends to, or is even deepened by, a study of theological sources on this issue.[5] Namely, any search for straightforward continuity or an uninterrupted and unchanging doctrine in this regard will certainly leave one disappointed. In order to make sense, then, of both the contemporary debate and the testimony of theological sources, one would do well to take a step back and think carefully about what is involved in this issue.

In this chapter I will attempt to demonstrate that the concept of intrinsic evil is incoherent and that, because of this, it ought to be avoided in theological and other discourses. To do this, I will argue historically that the incoherency of the concept is largely due to the fact that those who used it did not clearly distinguish between the elements that need to be taken into account for the decision that there are some kinds of acts one should never do (IE 1), and the judgment or label of "intrinsic evil" itself (IE 2). In effect, this led to the emergence of too many (and sometimes contradictory) meanings of the concept of intrinsic evil. Toward the end of the chapter I argue that this confusion of meanings ought to play the decisive role in the evaluation of its usefulness in theological and other discourses.

THEOLOGICAL SOURCES ON "INTRINSIC EVIL"

Before proceeding with a short historical exploration of the concept of intrinsic evil, it is worth pointing out that demonstrating its incoherency has an added effect on contemporary theological debates. Namely, if the study of theological sources reveals multiple contradictory meanings of the concept of intrinsic evil, then contemporary theological debates cannot simply be about defending the *doctrine* of intrinsic evil. Since the contrary claim, that the concept of intrinsic evil is a part of the moral doctrine of the Catholic Church, has been repeatedly put forward,[6] the existence of multiple meanings of the concept of intrinsic evil necessitates from its defenders, at the very least, a specification concerning which of these meanings ought to be considered *the* traditional one and why.[7]

At the very outset of probing into the historical or traditional roots of the concept of intrinsic evil, one is faced with the problem that the term itself does not appear in theological (or any other) literature until the fourteenth century. This, of course, does not mean that no earlier theologian discussed any of the ideas associated with the later concept, but it does advise caution in making too hasty conclusions about the origins of the concept. Namely, one of the requirements of detecting the origins of the concept is to establish clearly its meaning today, and since this is a disputed matter,[8] one can easily get caught up in a vicious circle and explore theological writings only insofar as they contribute to the thesis one wants to defend.

In order to avoid at least this crude form of anachronism, I propose a distinction between elements of the idea that there are (or might be) some kinds of acts one should never do[9] (IE 1), and the concept or label of intrinsic evil itself (IE 2). Bearing in mind this distinction, one could, in theory, try to track and discern the historical roots of IE 1 throughout the whole Christian tradition, while the IE 2 ought to be limited to the explicit references to the concept from the fourteenth century onward. Hence, theologians like Augustine, Lombard, Aquinas, or Scotus should not be discussed in the context of IE 2.

At the very least, this approach will immediately eliminate claims that the concept of intrinsic evil is a Scriptural teaching or taught by some of the aforementioned theologians,[10] unless one is able to provide an impressive argument to back up such a claim on the basis of a hidden continuity that has not been unearthed until now. On a more realistic note, the distinction between IE 1 and IE 2, besides being historically more accurate and enhancing clarity, emphasizes the fact that there *might be* a significant difference between the judgment that one should never do such and such an act (along with an explanation of how one arrived at that judgment) and that an act is "simply intrinsically evil," however one wants to define this term. Although it would be interesting to explore this point further with particular examples,[11] in the rest of this chapter I will focus on the interplay between IE 1 and IE 2 in order to demonstrate that the fact that this distinction was not recognized is one of the main reasons that led to the incoherence of IE 2.

Although Aquinas never referred to the concept of intrinsic evil (IE 2), he certainly did hold that some kinds of acts should never be done (IE 1). In order to substantiate this, one only needs to refer to texts such as *Summa Theologiae*, I–II, q. 20, a. 2,[12] *Quodlibet*, 9, q. 7, a. 2,[13] or *De Malo*, q. 2, a. 3, ad 1.[14] Since, as these texts show, there are acts that are not morally blameworthy on account of the end the agent is intending, one can be tempted to conclude that Aquinas held that these acts are blameworthy "in themselves" or in their material aspect (IE 2), especially in light of the *De Malo* reference to the "external act." If this is correct, one could easily present Aquinas's concept of *secundum se* evil as an immediate predecessor of the concept of intrinsic evil as understood by John Paul II in *VS*, 78. Furthermore, this interpretation would allow one to defend the view that Aquinas argued for a separate moral evaluation of ends (intentions) and means (objects).

Such an interpretation would, however, be premature for a number of reasons. First, it disregards Aquinas's general theory of human acts (*Summa Theologiae*, I–II, qq. 1–21) which insists on the intention toward the end as the starting point of the specification and evaluation of any human act. This is confirmed, second, in the *De Malo* reference that mentions adultery, murder, and theft as examples of *secundum se* evil external acts, which would all need a consideration of other elements of the act (apart from what is done) in order to not only reach a moral judgment on a particular act, but also to specify it as a kind of act. Third, Aquinas's statement that there are acts that ought not to be done on account of their object can also mean that the intention is not the only relevant element of ethical evaluation, something most medieval and contemporary theologians would agree on. Fourth, Aquinas's teaching on the Decalogue and divine dispensations, as John Dedek showed, is the reason that prompted Durandus of Saint Pourçain to develop the concept of intrinsic evil, because he believed that Aquinas did not take sufficiently into account the morally determinative character of material acts.[15] These reasons are not meant to deny that Aquinas held that some acts ought never to be done (IE 1); they are merely advising caution in specifying the basis of his position and its precise meaning.

With a different approach than Aquinas, Scotus is much more straightforward when it comes to acts that ought never to be done (IE 1). He distinguishes between natural law in the strict and the extended sense; the former incorporates only necessary moral principles, while the latter contains all the other moral principles that are part of the current moral order.[16] He also distinguishes between generic and specific goodness. Generic goodness specifies the object of the act in terms of its suitability or appropriateness in relation to right reason, while specific goodness specifies the object further in terms of its purpose (end) and other circumstances and, again, in relation to right reason. Scotus further adds that there is only one act that ought never to be done (IE 1) on the basis of its generic goodness and this is the act of hatred of or disrespect for God, precisely because it violates natural law in the strict sense.[17] However, in this case Scotus is not talking about an act being wrong in its material specificity, but about turning against the only absolute value.[18] This shows that for Scotus *secundum se* evil signifies an act that is, once properly specified, morally contradictory, and he managed to identify only one such act. Apart from disassociating generic goodness from the material aspect of an act, Scotus's approach to evaluation of human acts is more resistant to generating abstract classes of acts (that easily lead to instances of IE 2), since his concept of specific goodness necessitates contextualization of acts before their moral evaluation.

The first theologian who coined the term intrinsically evil and, more importantly, tied it to the material specificity of the Decalogue commandments was Durandus of Saint Pourçain, a fourteenth-century Dominican monk.[19] He rejected the common opinion at the time, shared by both Aquinas and Scotus, that the *ratio debiti* of the Decalogue commandments is tied to their formal element or to the fact that they are done *ex libidine*. If this is the case, he argues, what would be the point of materially specifying acts beyond their formal element through a number of commandments. His explanation was that the *ratio debiti* resides intrinsically in the material acts specified in most commandments of the second tablet of the Decalogue and thus, God cannot dispense from them, but only intervene in order to change the nature of these acts.[20]

Durandus's understanding of the concept of intrinsic evil surely resonates with some of its contemporary understandings that associate this concept with acts that ought never to be done, no matter the intention, circumstances, or consequences, and/or acts that are intrinsically evil on the basis of their material specificity. Although the fact that he ought to be credited with the invention of the concept of intrinsic evil is surely disappointing for those who would like to associate it with more renowned names such as Augustine or Aquinas, Durandus's contribution is not without merit. Namely, by introducing the concept of intrinsic evil, Durandus (probably unintentionally) made the distinction between IE 1 and IE 2, and this had a potential to bring some clarity and coherency to the theological discussion on acts that ought never to be done. If this understanding of the concept endured throughout subsequent theological sources, we would have had a different, more meaningful discussion on the concept today. Unfortunately, this was not the case, and by the sixteenth century and even more so later on, there were multiple and often contradictory understandings of the concept in theological sources. This, effectively, neutralized the potential of this concept (IE 2) to be a more coherent and clear focal point of discussions on IE 1. Hence, the issues surrounding this older notion of IE 1—how are these acts specified, on which basis are they condemned, what role should this condemnation have in ethical analysis, and so forth—became the issues surrounding the concept of intrinsic evil.

The first signs of this development are already noticeable in the writings of Francisco Suárez in the sixteenth century. Given his claim that the natural law is immutable in its most general principles and its concrete conclusions,[21] it is not surprising to discover that Suárez offers the same solution as Durandus when it comes to the problem of divine dispensations. On the basis of this, one would expect his notion of intrinsic evil to resemble that of Durandus, but the study of his works confirms this expectation only partially. Suárez writes about the concept of intrinsic evil (*actus intrinsece mali*)[22] in a somewhat systematic way while taking into account positions of earlier theologians (IE 1) and trying to make sense of them. In my opinion, he fails in this latter task, which makes his own position and the concept of intrinsic evil (IE 2) incoherent, because it aims at incorporating too many diverse views in one single concept.

In order to demonstrate the viability of this, as he calls it, traditional concept, Suárez makes three related claims. First, he argues that there are some acts that are evil on the basis of their object. Second, and contrary to Durandus, he rejects the opinion that these objects are evil because evil is joined to or inherent in their *physical entity*. Third, he seems to partially confirm Durandus's position by differentiating between intrinsically evil acts that are evil because of a direct and *physical tendency* and those that tend toward evil indirectly.[23] By merging IE 2 with some elements of IE 1 in this way, Suárez argues that the category of intrinsically evil acts spans from those acts that tend directly and physically toward intrinsically evil objects, through those whose objects are deformed, but could change, and all the way to acts that are intrinsically evil because they are instances of acting against right reason. Because of this widening of the concept, it becomes impossible to discern what the defining characteristics of intrinsically evil acts are for Suárez, beyond stating that they are instances of acts against right reason, that is, they are morally wrong.

Finally, the issue of intrinsically evil acts is raised again during the manualist era that had been ushered in by the Council of Trent and the Jesuits' work on the *Ratio studiorum* (developed in the period from 1580 until 1593), to which Suárez contributed as well. Since this period spans more than 350 years, there is no point in trying to even summarize the variety of views on intrinsic evil that found their way into manuals of moral theology.[24] Instead, I will simply list some of the more frequently occurring ones, especially in the later stage of the manualist era. Thus, for manualists, intrinsically evil can signify: (1) morally bad,[25] (2) contrary to right reason,[26] (3) contrary to (human/rational) nature,[27] (4) a confirmation of intrinsic morality,[28] (5) (physical?) object minus circumstances and end,[29] (6) moral object (including relevant end and circumstances/conditions),[30] and (7) contrary to right.[31] These are still followed by more nuanced distinctions such as the one between absolutely intrinsically evil acts, conditionally intrinsically evil acts, and occasionally intrinsically evil acts[32] or between strictly intrinsically evil and conditionally intrinsically evil acts.[33]

Of course, some of these meanings can be combined with each other, and there is nothing wrong as such with introducing additional distinctions within the concept.[34] Nevertheless, such combinations cannot explain exhaustively the variety of views, and the distinctions do become problematic when they reconfigure the outer boundary of the concept and start merging IE 1 and IE 2, which leads to incoherency. Furthermore, manualists' definitions of intrinsically evil acts have to be tested on their examples of such acts in order to determine whether these satisfy the conditions of their definitions. If one then takes into account that these lists have increased exponentially until the end of the manualist period, and that describing examples of intrinsically evil acts demands surgical precision and a fair amount of philosophical work (in order to maintain a coherent concept)—neither being the strong points of manualist writers—these lists themselves become an argument against the viability of the concept of intrinsic evil.

A SKETCH OF THE CONCEPT

The preceding historical exploration has shown that the concept of intrinsic evil owes its longevity to its ability to move back and forth along the spectrum whose two poles are marked by IE 1 and IE 2 (as Durandus defined it) and to be identified, in terms of its meaning(s), with just about any point on that spectrum. This outcome was the price the concept paid for wanting to enlist major voices of the tradition among the ranks of its supporters, i.e., for multiple and still ongoing attempts to equate IE 1 with IE 2.

There was, of course, much to be gained by promoting this broad understanding of the concept of intrinsic evil in terms of adding force to authoritative pronouncements of the Church on moral issues. Additionally, and when needed, the concept could have been narrowed down in its meaning to one of the points along the aforementioned spectrum, while still implicitly maintaining that it was precisely this meaning that the tradition gave it. This illusion, however, dispersed as soon as theologians undertook a closer look at the concept as a part of the post-conciliar renewal of theological ethics. At that moment, the strength of the concept and the secret of its longevity became its weakness, due to the mutually contradictory and overly broad meanings associated with it.

One way of dealing with this problem, for those who wanted to retain the concept, was again to attempt *somewhat* to disassociate IE 1 from IE 2 by maintaining that the concept of intrinsically evil acts refers to those classes of acts that are always morally wrong no matter the intention, circumstances, or consequences.[35] This would seemingly bracket out those elements of an act that ought not to be considered when one uses the concept and to exclude from consideration, for instance, fully-formed act-descriptions and formal descriptions of acts (murder is unjust killing, intrinsically evil act is contrary to right reason, inordinate, etc.). However, this interpretation necessarily raises the question—What is left of an act when one strips it of circumstances, consequences, and intentions?

Obviously, here, one cannot aim at a coherent position without introducing concepts such as the *object* or the *act itself* in order to differentiate between the essential and the accidental in an act, precisely in terms of the act's circumstances, consequences, and, perhaps, intentions. In that sense, the object in terms of which the act is specified here (and then designated as intrinsically evil) can be either a physical or a moral object. The former possibility is identical with Durandus's understanding of IE 2 and is the more coherent of the two. However, no contemporary theological ethicist would opt for this possibility, since it exposes one to the charge of physicalism. The latter possibility, on the other hand, neutralizes the potential of clarifying the concept of intrinsic evil by adding "no matter the intention, circumstances, or consequences," since the distinction between essential and accidental intentions, circumstances, and consequences is settled precisely in the process of specifying moral objects.[36]

If, consequently, the contemporary understanding of the concept of intrinsic evil presupposes the concept of moral object, then its role within ethical analysis is to express (more or less successfully) evaluative conclusions and not to be a tool of such an analysis. Hence, what the concept of intrinsic evil means in a particular context depends on how that analysis was conducted and/or what one wanted to condemn. Furthermore, insofar as these meanings vary significantly, they also hide unspecified presuppositions, epistemological and anthropological claims, background beliefs, and so on.

These problems have immediate implications for the concept's usefulness in contemporary theological ethics. Although one could argue that the concept can be reinterpreted so that it would designate acts that are incompatible with human dignity, the human person integrally and adequately considered, or some such criterion, one still has to deal with its theological and pastoral baggage. Namely, any usage of the concept seems to necessitate a long explanation of what is meant by it and how it is used. Historical and pastoral experience, however, appears to signal that most ethicists would opt for something that makes their job easier in that regard instead of complicating it even further.

Of course, the question of usefulness could be pursued further because what might not be useful in the context of ethical discourse could be useful in pastoral, political, or some other context, and vice versa. Since no one can police the language, perhaps the problems associated with the theological usage of the concept of intrinsic evil are simply moot when it comes to its usage in other contexts. At the same time, some other arguments, such as the concept's tendency to express moral judgments in absolute terms, can play a role and even act as a reason to insist on its usage. Admittedly, such reasons might prompt us to disagree on the merits of the concept's usage in these other contexts and, perhaps, theologians would not be able to do much about it anyway. Nevertheless, my reservation against its usage in these other contexts is that it is difficult to know where to draw the line between exhortation, teaching, and doing a moral analysis, or between (in)forming conscience and replacing conscience. Consequently, my fear is that by using the concept of intrinsic evil, we are already setting the stage, and possibly limits, of moral development of those we are talking to.

CONCLUSION

The study of theological sources confirms that the claim that there are acts that "ought never to be done" and the concept of "intrinsic evil" *are* grounded in tradition. However, there is no one, distinctive sense of the claim/concept that is present throughout the theological sources. Since this is the case, the theological discussion on the concept of intrinsic evil cannot be about mounting a defense of a doctrine, but, at best, about the methodological usefulness of one or a number of these meanings for contemporary ethical discourse or other discourses. A clear recognition of only this last point would suffice for having, finally, a coherent theological discussion on the concept of intrinsic evil.

NOTES

1. In order to keep this reference manageable, I will only mention two books that provide a good overview and point to further sources: Bernard Hoose, *Proportionalism: The American Debate and Its European Roots* (Washington, DC: Georgetown University Press, 1987); Christopher Kaczor, ed., *Proportionalism: For and Against* (Milwaukee, WI: Marquette University Press, 2000).

2. John Paul II, "Veritatis Splendor," accessed May 27, 2018, http://w2.vatican.va/content/john-paul-ii/en/encyclicals/documents/hf_jp-ii_enc_06081993_veritatis-splendor.html, 71–83.

3. Francis, "Amoris Laetitia," accessed May 27, 2018, https://w2.vatican.va/content/francesco/en/apost_exhortations/documents/papa-francesco_esortazione-ap_20160319_amoris-laetitia.html.

4. The five *Dubia* are a part of the letter sent to Pope Francis by four cardinals: Walter Brandmüller, Raymond L. Burke, Carlo Caffarra, and Joachim Meisner, "Seeking Clarity: A Plea to Untie the Knots in *Amoris Laetitia*," accessed May 27, 2018, http://www.ncregister.com/blog/edward-pentin/full-text-and-explanatory-notes-of-cardinals-questions-on-amoris-laetitia.

5. For two opposing views on what one can find in the Christian tradition in relation to this issue, see Garth L. Hallett, *Christian Moral Reasoning: An Analytic Guide* (Notre Dame, IN: University of Notre Dame Press, 1983), 107–22; Garth L. Hallett, *Greater Good: The Case for Proportionalism* (Washington, DC: Georgetown University Press, 1995), 1–19. For an opposing view, see William E. May, *Moral Absolutes: Catholic Tradition, Current Trends, and the Truth* (Milwaukee, WI: Marquette University Press, 1989), 2–19; John M. Finnis, *Moral Absolutes: Tradition, Revision, and Truth* (Washington, DC: The Catholic University of America Press, 1991), 58–83.

6. See John Paul II, "Veritatis Splendor," 79-81; Brandmüller, Burke, Caffarra, and Meisner, "Seeking Clarity," Dubia 4–5; Germain Grisez, "Revelation versus Dissent," in *Considering Veritatis Splendor*, ed. John Wilkins (Cleveland, OH: The Pilgrim Press, 1994), 3–4.

7. Of course, the fact that something has been repeated often in the tradition is not, by itself, a reliable guide to what ought to be considered a part of the tradition. As Margaret Farley argues: "If, in fact, tradition means only whatever has always, or for a long time, been taught or practiced, then inequality between men and women would have to remain part of the ongoing tradition" (*Just Love: A Framework for Christian Sexual Ethics* [New York: Continuum International Publishing Group, 2006], 186–87). For a more detailed overview of the issue, see Brian V. Johnstone, "What Is Tradition? From Pre-Modern to Postmodern," *Australian eJournal of Theology* 5 (2005): 1–22.

8. For more on this, see other contributions in this book.

9. Although a mouthful, I prefer this descriptive notion to the notion of "always morally wrong acts," since the latter is dependent on the contemporary distinction between goodness and rightness of the moral act.

10. Both of these claims (the former explicitly, the latter implicitly) are defended in John Paul II, "Veritatis Splendor," 76–81.

11. One of the issues worth exploring in this regard is the example of lying and whether there is any difference between, for instance, Augustine's categorical condemnation of lying, Aquinas's stance on lying, and Francisco Suárez's position that lying is intrinsically evil. While a superficial evaluation might use this example as an extraordinary sign of the continuity within the tradition, a more careful deliberation would point out, I believe, very different reasons why the three authors condemned lying. On that basis, it seems legitimate to ask whether they were even expressing the same judgment.

12. "There are some actions which neither a good end nor a good will can make good."

13. "Some acts have a deformity inseparably linked to them, such as fornication, adultery, and the like. These acts can in no way be done well."

14. "Some sins involve external acts that are not *secundum se* evil but evil insofar as they proceed from a perverted intention or will [. . .]. And some sins involve external acts that are *secundum se* evil, as is obvious in the case of theft, adultery, murder, and the like."

15. John F. Dedek, "Intrinsically Evil Acts: An Historical Study of the Mind of St. Thomas," *Thomist* 43, no. 3 (1979): 405.

16. Allan B. Wolter and Frank A. William, *Duns Scotus on the Will and Morality* (Washington, DC: The Catholic University of America Press, 1997), 195; *Ordinatio* b. IV, dist. 17.

17. Wolter and William, *Duns Scotus*, 48–49; *Quodlibet*, q. 18, a. 1.

18. Scotus argues that generic goodness puts an act in the category of moral acts. This suggests that determining the generic goodness of the act takes into consideration not only that the act is intentional (otherwise it could not be a *moral* act), but also the contents of the intention (otherwise one could not know *what kind* of an act it is). In other words, determining generic goodness means specifying the act's moral object (such as giving alms). Why is he, then, claiming that this suffices for the moral evaluation only in the case of hatred of God, but not for any other act determined in its generic goodness? I believe the answer to this question lies in his distinction between natural law in the strict sense and the extended sense. Namely, while the act of hatred of God properly belongs to the former category, all other acts belong to the latter. Thus, circumstances of specific goodness could not qualify the act of hatred of God further, while this is, at least theoretically, possible for any other act.

19. John F. Dedek, "Intrinsically Evil Acts: The Emergence of a Doctrine," *Recherches de Théologie Ancienne et Médiévale* 50 (1983): 219–24. Of note are also his other two studies that demonstrated that a general consensus among medieval theologians opposed Durandus's position: "Moral Absolutes in the Predecessors of St. Thomas," *Theological Studies* 38, no. 4 (1977): 654–80; "Intrinsically Evil Acts: An Historical Study of the Mind of St. Thomas," 385–413.

20. Dedek, "Intrinsically Evil Acts: The Emergence," 219–24.

21. Suárez's notion of natural law and his view of human nature cannot be adequately explained here. For my purposes it will suffice to point out that in developing his understanding of natural law Suárez insists that it is immutable and universal in its first principles and in its most concrete conclusions. The role of practical reason is, therefore, limited to deducing conclusions from a relevant precept of the natural law in a given situation. These judgments, in Suárez's view, presuppose only knowledge of human nature, more general precepts of natural law, and relevant circumstances of a given situation. Hence, the truth of a conclusion is identified with the correctness of a syllogism. For a more detailed treatment of Suárez's understanding of natural law, see Francisco Suárez, "De Legibus ac Deo Legislatore," in *Selections from Three Works*, ed. Thomas Pink (Indianapolis, IN: Liberty Fund, 2015), 151–355; Paul Pace, "Suárez and the Natural Law," in *A Companion to Francisco Suárez*, eds. Victor M. Salas and Robert L. Fastiggi (Leiden: Brill, 2015), 274–96; James Gordley, "Suárez and Natural Law," in *The Philosophy of Francisco Suárez*, eds. Benjamin Hill and Henrik Lagerlund (Oxford: Oxford University Press, 2012), 209–29.

22. The term appears in his treatise *De Bonitate et Malitia Humanorum Actuum* but also in *De Legibus ac Deo Legislatore*. Francisco Suárez, *Opera Omnia*, vol. 4 (Paris: Vivès, 1856), tract. 3, disp. 7, sect. 1. n. 13, 375; *Opera Omnia*, vol. 5, b. 2, chap. 7, n. 5, 113.

23. Suárez, *Opera Omnia*, vol. 4, tract. 3, disp. 7, sect. 1, n. 6, 373–75. Unfortunately, I cannot go into the details of Suárez's defense of these three claims, but only briefly present the results.

24. The general avoidance of manualist writers toward methodological issues in moral theology is, perhaps, of some benefit here insofar as most of them did not bother to reflect critically on various meanings of the concept of intrinsic evil that they were employing and, thus, these various meanings could exist side by side, even in the work of a single author.

25. This is evident in many authors, since they define morally bad acts and intrinsically evil acts in a similar way. For example, Henry Davis gives the following two definitions: "contrary to rational nature, viewed in all its relations" and "opposed to human nature" (*Moral and Pastoral Theology: Human Acts, Law, Sin, Virtue*, vol. 1 [London: Sheed and Ward, 1935],

35). I leave it to the reader to determine which of the two refers to morally bad and which to intrinsically evil.

26. Thomas Slater, *A Manual of Moral Theology: For English Speaking Countries*, vol. 1 (London: St. Pius X Press Inc., 2012), 21.

27. Benedictus H. Merkelbach, *Summa Theologiae Moralis ad Mentem D. Thomae et ad Normam Iuris Novi: De Principiis*, vol. 1 (Paris: Typis Desclee de Brouwer, 1947), 113.

28. To some extent this understanding underlies all definitions of intrinsically evil that manualists specify. Some of them do not move much further than that in explaining what they mean by this term.

29. No manualist defines intrinsically evil in terms of a physical object, but this understanding is quite evident in some of them as they discuss concrete examples. For instance (when it comes to pollution): Dominic M. Prümmer, *Handbook of Moral Theology* (Cork: The Mercier Press Limited, 1956), 235.

30. Jean P. Gury, *Compendium Theologiae Moralis*, vol. 1 (Lugundi: J. B. Pelagaud et socios, 1857), 27–28.

31. Arthur Preuss, *A Handbook of Moral Theology: Introduction*, vol. 1 (St. Louis, MO: B. Herder Book Co., 1918), 266.

32. Gury, *Compendium*, vol. 1, 27–28.

33. Hieronymus Noldin and Albert Schmitt, *Summa Theologiae Moralis: De Principiis Theologiae Moralis*, vol. 1 (Ratisbonae: Typis et sumptibus Fel. Rauch, 1925), 76–77.

34. For instance, one manualist points out that not all intrinsically evil acts are bad to the same degree, which is a kind of distinction that works well with the concept (Slater, *A Manual of Moral Theology*, vol. 1, 21).

35. I used "somewhat" here to point out the fact that this understanding of the concept of intrinsic evil is reminiscent of Durandus's understanding (exclusion of intention), but those who support it still maintain that this understanding can be found throughout the tradition.

36. For more on this, see Werner Wolbert's contribution in this volume.

REFERENCES

Brandmüller, Walter, Raymond L. Burke, Carlo Caffarra, and Joachim Meisner. "Seeking Clarity: A Plea to Untie the Knots in *Amoris Laetitia*." Accessed May 27, 2018. http://www.ncregister.com/blog/edward-pentin/full-text-and-explanatory-notes-of-cardinals-questions-on-amoris-laetitia.

Davis, Henry. *Moral and Pastoral Theology: Human Acts, Law, Sin, Virtue*, vol. 1. London: Sheed and Ward, 1935.

Dedek, John F. "Intrinsically Evil Acts: The Emergence of a Doctrine." *Recherches de Théologie Ancienne et Médiévale* 50 (1983): 191–226.

———. "Intrinsically Evil Acts: An Historical Study of the Mind of St. Thomas." *Thomist* 43, no. 3 (1979): 385–413.

———. "Moral Absolutes in the Predecessors of St. Thomas." *Theological Studies* 38, no. 4 (1977): 654–80.

Farley, Margaret A. *Just Love: A Framework for Christian Sexual Ethics*. New York: Continuum International Publishing Group, 2006.

Finnis, John M. *Moral Absolutes: Tradition, Revision, and Truth*. Washington, DC: The Catholic University of America Press, 1991.

Francis. "Amoris Laetitia." Accessed May 27, 2018. https://w2.vatican.va/content/francesco/en/apost_exhortations/documents/papa-francesco_esortazione-ap_20160319_amoris-laetitia.html.

Gordley, James. "Suárez and Natural Law." In *The Philosophy of Francisco Suárez*, edited by Benjamin Hill and Henrik Lagerlund, 209–29. Oxford: Oxford University Press, 2012.

Grisez, Germain. "Revelation versus Dissent." In *Considering Veritatis Splendor*, edited by John Wilkins, 1–8. Cleveland, OH: The Pilgrim Press, 1994.

Gury, Jean P. *Compendium Theologiae Moralis*, vol. 1. Lugundi: J. B. Pelagaud et socios, 1857.

Hallett, Garth L. *Christian Moral Reasoning: An Analytic Guide*. Notre Dame, IN: University of Notre Dame Press, 1983.

———. *Greater Good: The Case for Proportionalism*. Washington, DC: Georgetown University Press, 1995.

Hoose, Bernard. *Proportionalism: The American Debate and Its European Roots*. Washington, DC: Georgetown University Press, 1987.

John Paul II. "Veritatis Splendor." Accessed May 27, 2018. http://w2.vatican.va/content/john-paul-ii/en/encyclicals/documents/hf_jp-ii_enc_06081993_veritatis-splendor.html.

Johnstone, Brian V. "What Is Tradition? From Pre-Modern to Postmodern." *Australian eJournal of Theology* 5 (2005): 1–22.

Kaczor, Christopher, ed. *Proportionalism: For and Against*. Milwaukee, WI: Marquette University Press, 2000.

May, William E. *Moral Absolutes: Catholic Tradition, Current Trends, and the Truth*. Milwaukee, WI: Marquette University Press, 1989.

Merkelbach, Benedictus H. *Summa Theologiae Moralis ad Mentem D. Thomae et ad Normam Iuris Novi: De Principiis*, vol. 1. Paris: Typis Desclee de Brouwer, 1947.

Noldin, Hieronymus, and Albert Schmitt. *Summa Theologiae Moralis: De Principiis Theologiae Moralis*, vol. 1. Ratisbonae: Typis et sumptibus Fel. Rauch, 1925.

Pace, Paul. "Suárez and the Natural Law." In *A Companion to Francisco Suárez*, edited by Victor M. Salas and Robert L. Fastiggi, 274–96. Leiden: Brill, 2015.

Preuss, Arthur. *A Handbook of Moral Theology: Introduction*, vol. 1. St. Louis, MO: B. Herder Book Co., 1918.

Prümmer, Dominic M. *Handbook of Moral Theology*. Cork: The Mercier Press Limited, 1956.

Slater, Thomas. *A Manual of Moral Theology: For English Speaking Countries*, vol. 1. London: St. Pius X Press Inc., 2012.

Suárez, Francisco "De Legibus ac Deo Legislatore." In *Selections from Three Works*, edited by Thomas Pink, 151–355. Indianapolis, IN: Liberty Fund, 2015.

———. *Opera Omnia*, vol. 4 and 5. Paris: Vivès, 1856.

Wolter, Allan B., and Frank A. William. *Duns Scotus on the Will and Morality*. Washington, DC: The Catholic University of America Press, 1997.

Part II

The Concept of Intrinsic Evil
in Sexual Ethics

Chapter Three

Intrinsic Evil in Catholic Sexual Ethics

Time to Move On

Stephen J. Pope

"Intrinsically evil" is a classification used in Roman Catholic moral theology to designate a class of acts that are prohibited without exception. This essay will briefly sketch some key factors in the contemporary theological and ethical discussion of the usefulness of this concept. I would like to suggest that the concept of intrinsic evil carries such significant liabilities that we ought, as much as possible, to drop this term from our moral lexicon.

BACKGROUND

Aristotle agreed with his fellow ancient Greeks that some acts, for example, murder or adultery, should never be done.[1] Aquinas follows suit and says that some acts are "wrong in themselves" (*malum in se*). He defines the sin of lust as "seeking venereal pleasure in a way that is not in accordance with right reason."[2] He differentiates sins of lust according to two kinds of objects. The first category encompasses all those acts that violate right reason by their inconsistency with the end of the sexual act. This can happen in a variety of ways, from fornication (leading to the neglect of children) to masturbation and sodomy. A second category of acts violate reason by their treatment of other people, for example, incest, adultery, rape, and seduction. Aquinas found most objectionable the species of lust whose sexual acts in some way or other contradict not only the order of reason but also the order of nature, for example, deliberate "pollution," masturbation, sodomy, bestiality, and any other sexual activity that does not involve vaginal intercourse.

29

Citing Augustine (*De Bono Conjugalii*, viii), Aquinas maintained that "unnatural vice" is the greatest sin among the species of lust.[3] This judgment is based on a ranking of sinfulness according to two criteria: (1) the particular way in which an agent acts against right reason and (2) the kind of harm he or she does to other persons. The worst transgressions of the order of reason involve acts that violate the order "determined by nature." Aquinas explains: "Wherefore just as in speculative matters the most grievous and shameful error is that which is about things the knowledge of which is naturally bestowed on man, so in matters of action it is most grave and shameful to act against things as determined by nature."[4] Since acts of unnatural vices transgress the most fundamental purpose of sexual acts, this kind of sin is the most gravely wrong.[5] Since injustice magnifies the wrongfulness of an act, rape is worse than incest, incest worse than adultery, and adultery worse than "simple fornication."

Cultural anthropologists reading Aquinas might understand him to be attempting to provide intellectual coherence to a medieval ethic that was in turn based on elements of the purity code enshrined in Leviticus and other Biblical texts. Mary Douglas argued that ancient cultures organized their particular social orders by separating the sacred from the profane, pure from the impure, the clean from the unclean.[6] Societies identify conducts that are polluting and categorize them as taboo in order to establish boundaries between acceptable and unacceptable conduct. Communities give their members a sense of control and security by maintaining boundaries and controlling or eliminating anomalies. Individuals whose behavior does not conform to their particular community's purity code are often seen as dangerous aberrations that threaten the well-being of the wider community. A society's rituals, religion, and morality provide social reinforcement and symbolic support for its purity code.[7]

When we look at Aquinas's sexual ethics in this light, it is easy to see that the conduct he identifies as "against nature" always involves some kind of deviation from the purity norm of heterosexual, procreative intercourse (misplacement of semen is even called "pollution"). The more the behavior deviates from the heterosexual, procreative norm, the greater the gravity of the sin. Aquinas's ranking of sins against nature is arranged according to degree of departure from the natural order. Masturbation is morally worse than incest, "contraceptive acts" worse than rape, and "sodomy" worse than unjustifiable torture. Aquinas regards what is "natural" as reflecting the will of the Creator, and he takes for granted the widely accepted taboos of his day that simply forbid what is "unnatural." He describes every sexual sin against nature as an injury done to God, the author of nature (even though he knew in a strict sense God *per se* cannot be injured).

VATICAN II AND BEYOND: CONCEPTUAL
PROBLEMS WITH "INTRINSICALLY EVIL ACTS"

Aquinas himself did not use the phrase "intrinsic evil," but the framework sketched above was adapted and developed by subsequent generations of moral theologians who applied the phrase to acts that can never be considered ethically permissible. [8] This concept provided the kind of clarity made possible by a legal conception of morality, but it also brought significant liabilities. Progressive moral theologians after the Second Vatican Council called for a personalist and Biblical conception of Christian morality. Instead of analyzing discrete physical acts, they turned to persons-in-relations; instead of focusing only on isolated individuals, they paid attention to interpersonal and social contexts; instead of external acts, they were concerned with intentions, motivations, and virtues; instead of conformity to moral law, they insisted on forming consciences. [9] *Humanae Vitae* used personalist language (e.g., sex has a unitive end) but continued the act-centered analysis of neoscholastic physicalism.

Progressive moral theologians like Bernard Häring, Louis Janssens, Josef Fuchs, and others put pressure on the natural law justification for the notion of intrinsic evil. [10] John Paul II's "Theology of the Body" attempted to provide a new way of justifying the official natural law norms taught by Paul VI. [11] The pope insisted that the concept of intrinsic evil belongs to the bedrock of Catholic morality and even significantly expanded its use. [12] His most intellectually sophisticated allies supported his endorsement of the concept through their "new natural law" theory. Their account of practical reason holds that it is always wrong directly to attack a basic good. They argue that it is always wrong to directly attack the good of marriage, defined as a form of friendship oriented to procreation. Married couples who use artificial birth control are said *a priori* to "attack" the good of marriage (regardless of the actual state of their marriages). [13]

The notion of intrinsic evil has a number of significant problems. The current list of acts the Magisterium identifies as "intrinsically evil" is eclectic, selective, and theologically and ethically unhelpful. The contemporary catalogue includes acts like murder and adultery that the Church has traditionally prohibited, types of acts the Church did not pay much attention to until the very recent past (sexual abuse and domestic violence), types of acts that the Church used to accept but now condemns (enslavement and torture), and kinds of acts that the Church came to condemn in the modern period ("pornography production"). [14] The list of intrinsically evil acts includes some acts that are condemned in Scripture but not particularly prevalent today (sex with animals) and condemns acts accepted in Scripture and still common in some parts of the world (polygamy). [15]

The concept itself, moreover, has significant problems. First, it is used with an odd selectivity that suggests it is no longer used with care, precision, and rigor. The Magisterium, for example, condemns as intrinsically evil acts of injustice to widows and orphans but not injustice to the poor, wrongdoing to employees but not wrongdoing to employers, injustice to foreigners but not injustice to compatriots.

Second, the current list of intrinsic evils is an incoherent hodgepodge marked at times by puzzling specificity and at other times by extreme generality. The Magisterium prohibits specific classes of acts like sodomy, adultery, and rape and also prohibits a wide category of acts involving sexual abuse. Its condemnation of racism as intrinsically evil marks a radical departure from how the notion was used in the past. Neither an act nor a species of acts, racism can refer to individual actions, moral attitudes, cultural values, institutional practices, and public policies. It can be manifested in potentially countless acts, from telling a joke to outright lynching. In describing racism as intrinsically evil, the Magisterium expanded the concept in a way that makes it equivalent to racial injustice.

Third, what counts as "intrinsically evil" is still primarily sexual in nature. In fact, the largest category of acts the Magisterium defines as intrinsically evil are sexual. They include adultery, "homosexual acts," masturbation, "pedophilia acts," polygamy, pornography production, pornography use, prostitution, rape, sex with animals, sexual abuse, sodomy, and the use of artificial contraception. Each of these involve moral species of acts that the Church has deemed always wrong on the dual grounds that they violate the natural law and contradict the will of God (two traits that characterize all forms of serious wrongdoing). While also condemning evil done in the form of economic injustice, environmental destruction, military aggression, and forced migration, the magisterium's predominant focus on sexual matters, coupled with its repeated use of the language of "intrinsic evil," can be misleadingly taken to imply that sexual sins are the most grave form of human wrongdoing.

Fourth, the language of intrinsic evil has had the effect of distorting degrees of moral gravity. The language can be taken to imply moral equivalence among all the various ways of acting under this description, so that sexual abuse, for example, is no worse than using artificial birth control. To be fair, the Magisterium recognizes gradations of wrongdoing among various modalities among intrinsically evil acts, so they should not be read as morally equivalent. But if intrinsic evil has now come to mean "really bad," then Catholics can hardly be blamed for assuming that acts that are not listed as intrinsically evil are not as morally bad as those that are so listed. This logic might lead people to assume that the Church regards artificial contraception as worse than kidnapping and masturbation as worse than arson.

Fifth, the phrase "intrinsic evil" has been co-opted for partisan political purposes that misleads the public about Catholic social ethics.[16] This is particularly a problem in the United States, where conservative Catholic moralists and bishops argue that Catholics should not vote for politicians (Catholic or not) who support policies which permit or advance intrinsically evil acts, including abortion, stem cell research, the "contraceptive mandate" (in Obamacare), and same sex marriage. Some bishops have taken these norms to have an absolute priority over all other ethical considerations, including policies regarding the death penalty, war, and climate change. Even here, the ideological use of this concept by conservative Catholic political activists excludes attention to other intrinsically evil acts condemned by the Church such as torture, injustice to foreigners, racism, and violations of just war norms.[17] Ordinary Catholics can have the impression that pro-life and sexual norms are at the heart of Catholicism and that all the other norms are merely aspirational. Yet the American bishops do not take this position in their document *Forming Consciences for Faithful Citizenship*.[18] They teach that while a Catholic may not vote for a candidate because he or she supports a policy that promotes a specific kind of intrinsically evil act like abortion or euthanasia, each of us must consider how the competing candidates' respective policies would affect the common good overall. As Bishop McElroy of San Diego points out, "Voters will often find themselves in situations where one candidate supports an intrinsically evil position, yet the alternative realistic candidates all support even graver evils in the totality of their positions."[19]

A CONTEMPORARY PROPOSAL: ABANDONING THE LANGUAGE OF INTRINSIC EVIL

Some theologians want to keep the notion of intrinsic evil but expand its range to include social evils like racism.[20] They would like to see the strongly deontological emphasis that is usually applied to discrete acts applied much more broadly to structural evils. But if the concept is as deeply flawed and misleading as suggested here, then its wider use would both add to our confusion and lend credibility to a notion that it has outlived its usefulness.

Some of the items the Magisterium identifies as intrinsically evil seem to function in an analytic way, that is, they are defined in a way that necessarily entails immorality. This is true, for example, of terms like "murder" and "racism." Labeling an act as intrinsically evil is valuable when the act in question is *always* unjustly harmful to self or others. Such a label carries very strong deontological force and usually renders deliberation about the moral quality of the behavior in question as unnecessary, obtuse, and wasteful. Once an act has been identified as "rape," for example, we do not then go on to ask whether it might be ethically justifiable under the circumstances. The Magisterium wants to associate similar emphatic, deontological force to all the items listed as intrinsically evil. The problem is that many of the other terms are not analytic in their moral meaning—for example, to mention the most clear-cut case, most adults acknowledge that artificial contraception can be used in ways that are either responsible or irresponsible and therefore do not assume that all "contraceptive acts" are gravely wrong.

Today most people agree that adultery and sexual abuse of all kinds, including rape, are always wrong. In different ways, each of these kinds of acts involve one or more persons demonstrably violating the dignity and disrespecting the freedom of another person or other persons. Common sense and empirical evidence indicate that these kinds of harm are real. The Church is right to condemn them. But while adultery, pedophilic acts, and rape are clearly unjustly harmful, it is not so obvious that other items on the list of intrinsic evils—for example, masturbation and "sodomy"—always involve demonstrable harm.[21] Rather than supporting the generalization that all such acts harm self or others, ordinary experience tells us that a faithful sexual relationship can be life-giving for some same-sex couples. In an analogous way, evidence from psychological studies do not support the generalization that masturbation is always self-destructive.[22] Nor does evidence from ordinary testimonies and social scientific studies indicate that same-sex relations are always selfish, hedonistic, and manipulative (as new natural lawyers insist).[23]

The moral realism of the Catholic tradition takes seriously well-founded and empirically supported generalizations about human flourishing. What is evil for people in any concrete situation is what unjustly undermines their overall flourishing, and what is good for them in any concrete situation is what contributes to their overall flourishing. Defenders of intrinsic evil language think *abstractly*, but the human good is always *concrete*. We need to think about what is good, better, or best for this specific person or these specific people situated in this particular context at this particular time and place. This approach comports with virtue ethics and the "ethic of growth" suggested by Roger Burggraeve and others.[24] The term "intrinsic" is fundamentally detached from concrete historicity and meant to function as a transhistorical norm. But when thinking about a young adult who is gay, for example, we need to help him think about what kind of life he wants to lead, what kinds of people he wants to be his friends, what kinds of moral ideals appeal to him, and how his concrete choices can reflect his own priorities, deepest values, and greatest aspirations. What is concretely evil for him is anything that creates an obstacle to his integrity, compassion, and responsibility.

Knowledge about human behavior generated from the psychological, social, and cultural sciences should make us self-critical about the dominant background assumptions regarding human sexuality that we have inherited from our tradition. Instead of simple, clearly defined, and binary, human sexuality is complex, ambiguous, and at times amorphous. Epistemological critical realists should want to know more about these and other kinds of complexities so that their ethical standards can be appropriate to who we really are. The virtue of epistemic humility should lead us to acknowledge our own lack of understanding of sexuality and to be reluctant to cast absolute judgments about behaviors taken out of context.

POPE FRANCIS: PASTORAL INITIATIVE

Pope Francis has not given prominence to the language of intrinsic evil in his pastoral, moral, and social ministry. He encourages Catholics to regard themselves as first and foremost loved by God in Christ and called into fuller, more mature life in relation to Christ and his community. As Christians, we must seek to form our consciences in terms of this relationship and the appropriate virtues, particularly mercy.[25] This program was pursued in Pope Francis's apostolic exhortation *Amoris Laetitia*, including its controversial treatment of the question of whether Catholics in sexually active second unions may receive the Eucharist.[26]

Critics of course accuse *Amoris Laetitia* of "confusing the faithful" not only when it comes to divorced and civilly remarried couples but also for not condemning artificial contraception, adultery, and same-sex unions.[27] A variety of prominent moral theologians have responded to these criticisms.[28] In a recent interview, Fr. Antonio Spadaro explained that the pope does not believe in a "one-size-fits-all" approach to morality. "We must conclude that the pope realizes that one can no longer speak of [. . . a] rule that is absolutely to be followed in every instance." Suggesting that "it's no longer possible to judge people on the basis of a norm that stands above all," Spadaro underscores the concreteness of human good and evil.[29]

In a similar vein, Cardinal Schönborn comments that our norms are only truly "objective" when they take into account the particularities of concrete relationships in all their complexity: "To a greater degree than in the past, the objective situation of a person does not tell us everything about that person in relation to God and in relation to the Church. This evolution compels us urgently to rethink what we meant when we spoke of objective situations of sin." Spirituality is the context for moral judgment. Whether or not we live in "irregular situations," the cardinal insisted, we all need to cultivate a discerning conscience.[30]

CONCLUSION

This chapter argued that the notion of "intrinsic evil" has so many conceptual problems that it would be better for it to be dropped from the vocabulary of moral theology and, indeed, the moral teachings of the Magisterium. The category is employed in an oddly selective, and often imprecise way, as noted in the use of this language to condemn racism. Invocation of this language, moreover, can misleadingly suggest that any act that is intrinsically evil is more gravely evil than other kinds of wrongdoing. Thus, for example, the use of artificial contraception is worse than the deliberate economic exploitation of migrant laborers. Treating sexual sins as the most common locus of intrinsically evil acts can create the impression that the Church is more worried about sexual misbehavior than structural injustices that damage or destroy the lives of millions of people every year. In some countries, notably the United States, politically engaged bishops and Catholic public intellectuals who invoke the language of intrinsic evil routinely do so in ways that lend support to one political party and warn Catholics of the grave defects of the other. Assessed in terms of the principles of Catholic social teaching, the policies of both major parties suffer from grave moral defects. For these reasons, Catholic leaders and intellectuals would do well to move beyond the language of intrinsic evil.

Methodological shifts in both Church teaching and moral theology are usually accomplished slowly and after extensive research, debate, and deliberation. Sometimes the changes are proclaimed, but more often they just happen slowly and without announcement. In the case of the language of intrinsic evil, the intellectual work has been done, the concept has outlived its usefulness, and it is time for moral theologians to stop employing it. Perhaps the strategy of avoidance will not work and it will continue to be invoked. But it might be the case that Pope Francis is doing in a fairly quiet, pastoral way what decades of theological argumentation could not accomplish: dropping the concept so that we can move on to more fruitful approaches to moral learning and teaching.

NOTES

1. Aristotle, "Nicomachean Ethics," accessed May 10, 2018, http://classics.mit.edu/Aristotle/nicomachaen.html, 1107a8–12.

2. Thomas Aquinas, "Summa Theologiae," accessed May 10, 2018, https://dhspriory.org/thomas/summa/index.html, II–II, q. 154, a. 1.

3. Ibid., q. 154, a. 12.

4. Ibid.

5. Ibid.

6. See Mary Douglass, *Purity and Danger: An Analysis of Pollution and Taboo* (New York: Frederick A. Praeger, 1966).

7. Moral psychologist Jonathan Haidt traces ways in which the conflict between more conservative cultures and modern cultures revolves around contests over the relevance of purity codes to public life (along with tensions over loyalty, honor, and authority). See Jonathan Haidt, *The Righteous Mind: Why Good People Are Divided by Politics and Religion* (New York, NY: Pantheon Books, 2012).

8. On intrinsic evil in modern moral theology, see John F. Dedek, "Intrinsically Evil Acts: The Emergence of a Doctrine," *Recherches de Théologie Ancienne et Médiévale* 50 (1983): 191–226. Manualist treatments include Henry Davis, *Moral and Pastoral Theology: Human Acts, Law, Sin, Virtue*, vol. 1 (London: Sheed & Ward, 1935); Thomas Slater, *A Manual of Moral Theology: For English Speaking Countries*, vol. 1 (London: St. Pius X Press Inc., 2012); and Arthur Preuss, *A Handbook of Moral Theology: Introduction*, vol. 1 (St. Louis, MO: B. Herder Book Co., 1918). For a helpful analysis, see Nenad Polgar, "The Concept of Intrinsic Evil: An Exploration of Some Theological Sources," in this volume.

9. See James M. Gustafson, "The Focus and Its Limitations: Reflections on Catholic Moral Theology," in *Moral Theology: Challenges for the Future*, ed. Charles E. Curran (New York: Paulist Press, 1990), 179–90.

10. See Bernard Häring, "Dynamism and Continuity in a Personalistic Approach to the Natural Law," in *Norm and Context in Christian Ethics*, eds. Gene H. Outka and Paul Ramsey (New York: Scribners, 1968): 199–218; Josef Fuchs, S.J., "An Ongoing Discussion in Christian Ethics: 'Intrinsically Evil Acts,'" in *Christian Ethics in a Secular Arena*, trans. Bernard Hoose and Brian McNeill (Washington, DC: Georgetown University Press, 1984), 71–90; Louis Janssens, "Ontic Evil and Moral Evil," *Louvain Studies* 4 (1972): 115–56.

11. See Stephen J. Pope, "Pope Paul VI," in *Christianity and Family Law: An Introduction*, ed. John Witte, Jr. (New York: Cambridge University Press, 2017), 344–62. On changes and developments within the Catholic moral tradition, see John T. Noonan, Jr., "Development in Moral Doctrine," *Theological Studies* 52, no. 4 (1993): 662–77; and *A Church That Can and Cannot Change* (Notre Dame, IN: University of Notre Dame Press, 2005).

12. John Paul II, "Veritatis Splendor," accessed January 3, 2018, http://w2.vatican.va/content/john-paul-ii/en/encyclicals/documents/hf_jp-ii_enc_06081993_veritatis-splendor.html, 80.

13. See John Finnis, *Natural Law and Natural Rights* (Cambridge: The Clarendon Press, 1980); and *Moral Absolutes: Tradition, Revision, and Truth* (Washington, DC: Catholic University of America Press, 1991); Germain Grisez, *The Way of the Lord Jesus, Volume I: Christian Moral Principles* (Chicago: Franciscan Herald Press, 1983).

14. The *Catechism of the Catholic Church* describes pornography as a "grave offence" to God. The Holy See, "Catechism of the Catholic Church," accessed March 15, 2018, http://www.vatican.va/archive/ENG0015/_INDEX.HTM#fonte, 2354. Some bishops have described it as "intrinsically evil," for example, Bishops of Kansas, "Moral Principles for Catholic Voters," accessed May 15, 2018, https://www.catholicculture.org/culture/library/view.cfm?recnum=7243.

15. Bernard Hoose examines similar problems in Pope John Paul II's use of this concept in *Veritatis Splendor* ("Circumstances, Intentions and Intrinsically Evil Acts," in *The Splendor of Accuracy: An Examination of the Assertions Made by Veritatis Splendor*, eds., Joseph A. Selling and Jan Jans [Grand Rapids, MI: Eerdmans, 1994], 136–52).

16. Cathleen M. Kaveny, "Intrinsic Evil and Political Responsibility: Is the Concept of Intrinsic Evil Helpful to the Catholic Voter?" *America Magazine*, October 27, 2008, https://www.americamagazine.org/issue/673/article/intrinsic-evil-and-political-responsibility. For a more developed argument, see *Law's Virtues: Fostering Autonomy and Solidarity in American Society* (Washington, DC: Georgetown University Press, 2012).

17. David Cloutier, "'Intrinsic Evil' and Public Policy: A Partisan Abuse of the Church's Moral Teachings," *Commonweal Magazine*, October 31, 2012, https://www.commonwealmagazine.org/%E2%80%98intrinsic-evil%E2%80%99-public-policy.

18. USCCB, "Forming Consciences for Faithful Citizenship," accessed May 15, 2018, http://www.usccb.org/issues-and-action/faithful-citizenship/upload/forming-consciences-for-faithful-citizenship.pdf, 37.

19. Robert W. McElroy, "Reclaiming Our National Politics to Protect the Human Person," *America Magazine*, February 15, 2016, https://www.americamagazine.org/politics-society/2016/02/04/reclaiming-our-national-politics-protect-human-person.

20. Bryan N. Massingale, "Has the Silence Been Broken? Catholic Theological Ethics and Racial Justice," *Theological Studies* 75, no. 1 (2014): 151.

21. In 1973 the American Psychological Association (APA) removed homosexuality from its *Diagnostic and Statistical Manual of Mental Disorders III-R* (1987). The APA position is summarized this way: "Empirical evidence and professional norms do not support the idea that homosexuality is a form of mental illness or is inherently linked to psychopathology" (Gregory M. Herek, "Facts about Homosexuality and Mental Health," accessed May 15, 2018, http://psychology.ucdavis.edu/rainbow/html/facts_mental_health.html). We should note that some moralists might argue that non-heterosexual sexual activity can harm self, others, or the wider community. There is, however, no well-established empirical evidence supporting this claim.

22. The *Diagnostic and Statistical Manual of Mental Disorders V* (2013) of the American Psychiatric Association does not classify masturbation as a mental or behavioral disorder. In some cases, of course, masturbation can be associated with significant psychological distress. Giovanni Castellini et al., "Psychological, Relational, and Biological Correlates of Ego-Dystonic Masturbation in a Clinical Setting," *Sexual Medicine* 4, no. 3 (2016): 156–65.

23. John Finnis asserts that all "homosexual conduct" is "radically incapable of participating in, actualizing, the common good of friendship." It "can do no more than provide each partner with an individual gratification and indeed dis-integrates each of them precisely as acting persons" ("Law, Morality, and Sexual Orientation," *Notre Dame Law Review* 69, no. 5 [1994]: 1066–67).

24. Roger Burggraeve, "From Responsible to Meaningful Sexuality: An Ethics of Growth as an Ethics of Mercy for Young People in this Era of AIDS," in *Catholic Ethicists on HIV/AIDS Prevention*, ed. James F. Keenan (New York: Continuum, 2000), 303–16.

25. See David E. DeCosse, "Conscience, Catholicism, and Politics," *Theological Studies* 78, no. 1 (2017): 171–92.

26. Francis, "Amoris Laetitia," accessed May 18, 2018, https://w2.vatican.va/content/dam/francesco/pdf/apost_exhortations/documents/papa-francesco_esortazione-ap_20160319_amoris-laetitia_en.pdf, 8.

27. In a letter released to the public on November 14, 2016, four cardinals charged *Amoris Laetitia* 300–305 with causing confusion and "doctrinal anarchy": Edward Pentin, "Four Cardinals Formally Ask Pope for Clarity on 'Amoris Laetitia,'" *National Catholic Register*, November 14, 2016, http://www.ncregister.com/daily-news/four-cardinals-formally-ask-pope-for-clarity-on-amoris-laetitia. See also Thomas G. Weinandy, O.F.M., Cap., "Fr. Thomas G. Weinandy explains his critical letter to Pope Francis," *The Catholic World Report*, November 1, 2017, https://www.catholicworldreport.com/2017/11/01/fr-thomas-g-weinandy-explains-his-critical-letter-to-pope-francis/; Thomas Reese, "Papal Loyalists Become Dissidents," *National Catholic Reporter*, November 8, 2017, https://www.ncronline.org/news/opinion/signs-times/papal-loyalists-become-dissidents; Austen Ivereigh, "Jesuit Close to Pope Says Attacks on 'Amoris' Are 'Part of the Process,'" *Crux*, December 4, 2016, https://cruxnow.com/interviews/2016/12/04/jesuit-close-pope-says-many-attacks-amoris-result-bad-spirit/.

28. For a helpful overview, see James F. Keenan, S.J., "Receiving *Amoris Laetitia*," *Theological Studies* 78, no. 1 (2017): 193–212.

29. Interview with Spadaro by Joshua J. McElwee, "Bishops Deliberate Whether One Rule Applies to All Divorced People after 'Amoris Laetitia,'" *National Catholic Reporter*, October 6, 2017, https://www.ncronline.org/news/parish/bishops-deliberate-whether-one-rule-applies-all-divorced-people-after-amoris-laetitia.

30. Antonio Spadaro, "The Demands of Love: A Conversation with Cardinal Schönborn about 'The Joy of Love,'" *America*, August 15–22, 2016, http://www.americamagazine.org/issue/demands-love.

REFERENCES

Aquinas, Thomas. "Summa Theologiae." Accessed May 10, 2018. https://dhspriory.org/thomas/summa/index.html.

Aristotle. "Nicomachean Ethics." Accessed May 10, 2018. http://classics.mit.edu/Aristotle/nicomachaen.html.

Bishops of Kansas. "Moral Principles for Catholic Voters." Accessed May 15, 2018. https://www.catholicculture.org/culture/library/view.cfm?recnum=7243.

Burggraeve, Roger. "From Responsible to Meaningful Sexuality: An Ethics of Growth as an Ethics of Mercy for Young People in this Era of AIDS." In *Catholic Ethicists on HIV/AIDS Prevention*, edited by James F. Keenan, 303–16. New York: Continuum, 2000.

Castellini, Giovanni, et al. "Psychological, Relational, and Biological Correlates of Ego-Dystonic Masturbation in a Clinical Setting." *Sexual Medicine* 4, no. 3 (2016): 156–65.

Cloutier, David. "'Intrinsic Evil' and Public Policy: A Partisan Abuse of the Church's Moral Teachings." *Commonweal Magazine*, October 31, 2012. https://www.commonwealmagazine.org/%E2%80%98intrinsic-evil%E2%80%99-public-policy.

Davis, Henry. *Moral and Pastoral Theology: Human Acts, Law, Sin, Virtue*, vol. 1. London: Sheed and Ward, 1935.

DeCosse, David E. "Conscience, Catholicism, and Politics." *Theological Studies* 78, no. 1 (2017): 171–92.

Dedek, John F. "Intrinsically Evil Acts: The Emergence of a Doctrine." *Recherches de Théologie Ancienne et Médiévale* 50 (1983): 191–226.

Douglass, Mary. *Purity and Danger: An Analysis of Pollution and Taboo*. New York: Frederick A. Praeger, 1966.

Finnis, John. "Law, Morality, and Sexual Orientation." *Notre Dame Law Review* 69, no. 5 (1994): 1049–76.

———. *Moral Absolutes: Tradition, Revision, and Truth*. Washington, DC: Catholic University of America Press, 1991.

———. *Natural Law and Natural Rights*. Cambridge: The Clarendon Press, 1980.

Francis. "Amoris Laetitia." Accessed May 18, 2018. https://w2.vatican.va/content/dam/francesco/pdf/apost_exhortations/documents/papa-francesco_esortazione-ap_20160319_amoris-laetitia_en.pdf.

Fuchs, Josef, S.J. "An Ongoing Discussion in Christian Ethics: 'Intrinsically Evil Acts.'" In *Christian Ethics in a Secular Arena,* translated by Bernard Hoose and Brian McNeill, 71–90. Washington, DC: Georgetown University Press, 1984.

Grisez, Germain. *The Way of the Lord Jesus, Volume I: Christian Moral Principles*. Chicago: Franciscan Herald Press, 1983.

Gustafson, James M. "The Focus and Its Limitations: Reflections on Catholic Moral Theology." In *Moral Theology: Challenges for the Future*, edited by Charles E. Curran, 179–90. New York: Paulist Press, 1990.

Haidt, Jonathan. *The Righteous Mind: Why Good People Are Divided by Politics and Religion*. New York: Pantheon Books, 2012.

Häring, Bernard. "Dynamism and Continuity in a Personalistic Approach to the Natural Law." In *Norm and Context in Christian Ethics*, edited by Gene H. Outka and Paul Ramsey, 199–218. New York: Scribners, 1968.

Herek, Gregory M. "Facts about Homosexuality and Mental Health." Accessed May 15, 2018. http://psychology.ucdavis.edu/rainbow/html/facts_mental_health.html.

The Holy See. "Catechism of the Catholic Church." Accessed March 15, 2018. http://www.vatican.va/archive/ENG0015/_INDEX.HTM#fonte.

Hoose, Bernard. "Circumstances, Intentions and Intrinsically Evil Acts." In *The Splendor of Accuracy: An Examination of the Assertions Made by Veritatis Splendor*, edited by Joseph A. Selling and Jan Jans, 136–52. Grand Rapids, MI: Eerdmans, 1994.

Ivereigh, Austen. "Jesuit Close to Pope Says Attacks on 'Amoris' Are 'Part of the Process'." *Crux*, December 4, 2016. https://cruxnow.com/interviews/2016/12/04/jesuit-close-pope-says-many-attacks-amoris-result-bad-spirit/.

Janssens, Louis. "Ontic Evil and Moral Evil." *Louvain Studies* 4 (1972): 115–56.

John Paul II. "Veritatis Splendor." Accessed January 3, 2018. http://w2.vatican.va/content/johnpaul-ii/en/encyclicals/documents/hf_jp-ii_enc_06081993_veritatis-splendor.html.

Kaveny, Cathleen M. "Intrinsic Evil and Political Responsibility: Is the Concept of Intrinsic Evil Helpful to the Catholic Voter?" *America Magazine*, October 27, 2008. https://www.americamagazine.org/issue/673/article/intrinsic-evil-and-political-responsibility.

———. *Law's Virtues: Fostering Autonomy and Solidarity in American Society*. Washington, DC: Georgetown University Press, 2012.

Keenan, James F., S.J. "Receiving *Amoris Laetitia*." *Theological Studies* 78, no. 1 (2017): 193–212.

Massingale, Bryan N. "Has the Silence Been Broken? Catholic Theological Ethics and Racial Justice." *Theological Studies* 75, no. 1 (2014): 133–55.

McElroy, Robert W. "Reclaiming Our National Politics to Protect the Human Person" *America Magazine*, February 15, 2016. https://www.americamagazine.org/politics-society/2016/02/04/reclaiming-our-national-politics-protect-human-person.

McElwee, Joshua J. "Bishops Deliberate Whether One Rule Applies to All Divorced People after 'Amoris Laetitia.'" *National Catholic Reporter*, October 6, 2017. https://www.ncronline.org/news/parish/bishops-deliberate-whether-one-rule-applies-all-divorced-people-after-amoris-laetitia.

Noonan, John T. Jr. *A Church That Can and Cannot Change*. Notre Dame, IN: University of Notre Dame Press, 2005.

———. "Development in Moral Doctrine." *Theological Studies* 52, no. 4 (1993): 662–77.

Pentin, Edward. "Four Cardinals Formally Ask Pope for Clarity on 'Amoris Laetitia.'" *National Catholic Register*, November 14, 2016. http://www.ncregister.com/daily-news/four-cardinals-formally-ask-pope-for-clarity-on-amoris-laetitia.

Pope, Stephen J. "Pope Paul VI." In *Christianity and Family Law: An Introduction*, edited by John Witte, Jr., 344–62. New York: Cambridge University Press, 2017.

Preuss, Arthur. *A Handbook of Moral Theology: Introduction*, vol. 1. St. Louis, MO: B. Herder Book Co., 1918.

Reese, Thomas. "Papal Loyalists Become Dissidents." *National Catholic Reporter*, November 8, 2017. https://www.ncronline.org/news/opinion/signs-times/papal-loyalists-become-dissidents.

Slater, Thomas. *A Manual of Moral Theology: For English Speaking Countries*, vol. 1. London: St. Pius X Press Inc., 2012.

Spadaro, Antonio. "The Demands of Love: A Conversation with Cardinal Schönborn about 'The Joy of Love.'" *America*, August 15–22, 2016. http://www.americamagazine.org/issue/demands-love.

USCCB. "Forming Consciences for Faithful Citizenship." Accessed May 15, 2018. http://www.usccb.org/issues-and-action/faithful-citizenship/upload/forming-consciences-for-faithful-citizenship.pdf.

Weinandy, Thomas G., O.F.M., Cap. "Fr. Thomas G. Weinandy explains his critical letter to Pope Francis." *The Catholic World Report*, November 1, 2017. https://www.catholicworldreport.com/2017/11/01/fr-thomas-g-weinandy-explains-his-critical-letter-to-pope-francis/.

Chapter Four

Intrinsic Evil in Catholic Sexual Ethics

New Insights, New Approaches, New Logic

Gunter Prüller-Jagenteufel

As a participant of the workshop on the topic of "intrinsic evil" held in Vienna in January 2018, I was asked to respond to the paper presented by Stephen J. Pope. Having agreed with just about everything I found in the paper, I felt that I might expand somewhat on the inherent logic of the classic notion of "intrinsic evil" and how this logic which is intrinsically rooted in an ethics of natural law could be transformed into a more open and relevant approach based on human dignity.

If we look at the list of "intrinsically evil acts" that is presented in *Veritatis Splendor* (*VS*), 80, we immediately realize that in the original context of *Gaudium et Spes* (*GS*) this list is not presenting intrinsically evil acts, but rather "infamies" that "poison human society" and are a "supreme dishonor to the Creator." While the notion of "intrinsic evil" refers to the logic of an ethical argument which makes sense only in the context of a deontological system of moral law, *GS* speaks about "whatever insults human dignity."

Of course, *VS* also speaks about the dignity of the human person, but Pope John Paul II is focusing considerably less on human freedom and autonomy but rather more on the "natural inclinations" that can be derived from the bodily nature of the person. This indissoluble connection between (physical) nature and person[1] is one of the basic foundations of Karol Wojtyła's ethics since the early 1960s. This idea—the very basis of the approach later called the "theology of the body"—leads to an ethics of natural law with a personalistic overcoat rather than to true personalism. Hence it has not remained uncriticized by theologians. However, *VS*, 47 explicitly rejects any theological critique that would call John Paul's ethics "physicalism and naturalism" and emphatically affirms the idea that the "particular spiritual and bodily structure" of the human person makes for the "primordial moral requirement of loving and respecting the person." The bodily nature reveals "certain fundamental goods, without which one would fall into relativism and arbitrariness" (*VS*, 48). VS, 47 presents its own list of disputed acts that ought to be considered "intrinsically evil": "contraception, direct sterilization, autoeroticism, pre-marital sexual relations, homosexual relations and artificial insemination."

Of course, we have to question the logic of the idea that we either have to accept all of these as intrinsically evil acts or descend into relativism and arbitrariness. We have to stand firm in our position that to ask critically in which way and to what degree the bodily constitution of the human being is morally relevant does not mean to reject any such connection altogether.[2]

THE LOGIC OF "INTRINSIC EVIL" IN SEXUAL ETHICS

Since the idea of "intrinsic evil" is logically linked with deontological ethics, let us first look into the problem from a purely formalistic, logical perspective. The question is—according to the traditional doctrine of the *fontes moralitatis*—how does one determine the "object" (*finis operis*) of an act in contrast to the intention of the person performing it (*finis operantis*) and the circumstances (*circumstantiae*). The rightness of an act is constituted by all of these, while any defect in one of these constitutes its wrongness.[3] The notion of "intrinsically evil" acts indicates that a certain act is evil in itself, the wrongfulness being embedded in the "object," so that neither intention nor circumstances could in any way alter the negative ethical judgment.

At this point we encounter our first problem in the ethical analysis of an act. What exactly defines the "object" and what are mere "circumstances"? We are in the middle of a hermeneutical circle and how to define "object" and "circumstance" is a matter of deliberate definition—which of course is rooted in human experience.[4] This consideration is to be found already in Aristotle's ethics: Our verbal definition of an act always includes certain circumstances. "Adultery," for example, is defined as sexual intercourse where at least one of the partners is married to another person. So "extramarital" is obviously not considered just a circumstance but is intrinsically relevant for the verdict that a certain sexual act is adulterous.

Another example might help to clarify this even further: How do we define "rape"?

1. We could say rape is "sexual intercourse without the consent of the partner." Obviously the consent is not a mere circumstance but intrinsically relevant for the rightness or wrongfulness of the act because an

act against the sexual self-determination of a person is always a violation of their human dignity.

2. If on the other hand we consider the consent as just circumstantial, we could come to a different conclusion, especially when the consent is assumed as given, an assumption that used to be taken for granted among spouses. That is the reason why there was no such thing as "rape in matrimony" in Austrian law until the 1970s—and the same is true for most Western countries.

3. But what if we realize that "rape" is something completely different, something we cannot truly understand by looking at it from the perspective of sexuality? What if we recognize that rape has to be understood from the perspective of power and violence? Then we come to a completely different definition, such as: "Rape is a violent act (mostly committed by men) breaking the free will and self-determination of another person (mostly women and minors) by sexual means." So the "object" of the act is physical or mental violence against the self-determination of another person. Obviously such an act is "intrinsically evil."

So how we define the "object" of an act is by no means trivial but needs careful deliberation based on human experience.

THE LOGIC OF THEOLOGICAL REASONING

If we go one step further, from philosophical to theological thinking, intrinsic evil denotes an act that is always contrary to God's will, no matter what the intention or circumstances are. In tradition we can find three reasons that would justify such a judgment.[5]

An act is evil because . . .

1. God forbade it (*ex lege divino positivo*); or
2. the human person has no right to freely decide in a certain area because this area is reserved for God's decision making; such an act would therefore violate God's own and exclusive right; or
3. it is contrary to nature (*contra naturam*).

These three notions are linked, and moral theologians have worked hard to figure out why certain acts that are forbidden by God are said to be "against human nature."

ad 1: biblical arguments

For example, adultery, divorce, homosexuality, masturbation, and so forth. All of these are explicitly forbidden in the Bible and are also considered as contrary to nature, be it the nature of human sexuality or the nature of matrimony (which is, of course, not a natural but a cultural entity; but that leads us to other problems altogether).

ad 2: theological arguments regarding reserved rights

The argument that a human being must not do what is exclusively God's prerogative is mostly considered in life-and-death matters such as suicide, euthanasia, and so on. Since God is the supreme lord over life and death, no human decision to end life is possible. It always would violate God's exclusive right to give and take life. The notion of God as the one and only life-giver links this argument to sexual ethics, especially in the area of contraception and medically assisted procreation.

We could also adjust the argument following Augustine's view on sexuality. In his perspective sexual pleasure is bad—in fact it is a punishment for original sin—because it deprives man of reason and freedom. So essentially sexual pleasure is evil because it is in itself disordered and unnatural (considering that the "nature" of man is "rational").[6] But the evidently evil act of sexual intercourse can be "excused" because of certain "goods" (*bona excusantia*), the goods that make marriage a respectable state: offspring (*bonum prolis*), fidelity (*bonum fidei*), and sacramentality (*bonum sacramenti*)— without probing deeper Augustine's concept of "sacrament." To pursue these three goods in holy matrimony grants human persons a right that they originally do not have. So obviously these goods change the "object" of the act from "fornication" to "marital intercourse," which can, even in Augustine's eyes, be tolerated.

ad 3: natural law

In contrast to Augustine, Thomas Aquinas considers sexual desire and pleasure as something natural, given the natural inclination toward procreation (*finis primarius*), marital fidelity, and sacramentality. As long as sexuality is "ordered" toward these goals, it is good; other than that it is considered "disordered" and therefore evil. So masturbation, homosexuality, and contraception are forbidden.

The scholastics (including neoscholastics) differentiate sexual sins further:

• in line with nature (*intra naturam*): every sexual act that is open to procreation;

- contrary to nature (*contra naturam*): every act that excludes procreation.

The big problem arises if we consider sins *contra naturam* to be, in principle, significantly graver than those *intra naturam*, which has been the case in tradition and sometimes still is the case. If that were true we would have to consider an act of masturbation or consensual intercourse between same-sex partners distinctly worse than an act of rape or sexual abuse of minors (given the act is heterosexual and the minors are old enough for conception)—which is evidently absurd.

LOGICAL AND HERMENEUTICAL PROBLEMS OF NATURAL LAW ARGUMENTS

Natural law arguments presuppose that each and every act against "nature" is an act against "God's will." This idea presupposes that nature is a perfect expression of God's intentions, as stated in *Humanae Vitae*, 11:

> God has wisely ordered laws of nature and the incidence of fertility in such a way that successive births are already naturally spaced through the inherent operation of these laws. The Church, nevertheless, in urging men to the observance of the precepts of the natural law, which it interprets by its constant doctrine, teaches that each and every marital act must of necessity retain its intrinsic relationship to the procreation of human life.

Bruno Schüller explains what "natural law" consists of by referring to the highly influential moral theologian Franz Hürth (1880–1963): the will of the creator is incorporated into the human organs and their natural function, therefore any intervention is frustrating the divine plan.[7] Schüller puts it this way: "The presented type of argument is based on the idea, that through the works of nature God himself speaks directly, while through the works of men it is only man who speaks, without any link to God."[8] But that kind of thinking overlooks the hermeneutics of our perception of nature. While Aquinas holds fast—as do the Stoics—that *secundum naturam* is quite the same as *secundum rationem*, because human reason has to determine the intrinsic teleology of nature, neoscholastics supposedly try to recognize nature from the fact itself. This, of course, inevitably leads to an ontological fallacy.

But how are we to determine the intrinsic teleology of "nature"? Theologians and secular ethicists alike question the "assumption of an unambiguous and obvious teleology of nature" that could be considered "authoritative and normative" for ethical considerations.[9] Further, the idea of "natural law" itself is prone to ideology, as critics have expressed long before Vatican II:

"Like a harlot, natural law is at [the] disposal of everyone. The ideology does not exist that cannot be defended by an appeal to the law of nature."[10]

PERSONALIST ARGUMENTS

It seems fitting that John Paul II, in his theological works as professor of ethics as well as in his documents as bishop and pope, tried to reframe natural law norms into personalist ones. I deliberately use the term "reframed" and not "transformed," because under close scrutiny we realize that Karol Wojtyła's idea of person in his argument is rather superficial. The underlying physical nature plays by far the stronger part in his argument. John Paul II considers the "nature" of sexuality essentially as "total personal self-giving" (*Familiaris Consortio*, 11) which includes the bodily expression of the person. Therefore, every act outside this totality does not meet the essential purpose of human sexuality and is therefore intrinsically evil.

Although John Paul II may appear to present a different point of view, his logic is essentially the same as that of natural law, especially because the ideal is not seen as an aim to strive for but a norm to be fulfilled. This means to stress the idea of the "theology of the body" to the extreme ("totality") which is at least questionable logic. The claim of this "theology of the body" seems theologically and logically unsound because there is neither proof nor convincing arguments, only the *allegation* that each and every sexual encounter between two persons ought to be an expression of "total self-giving." The experience of the vast majority—I daresay, all—married couples contradicts this idea: Of course, sexual intercourse is an expression of love, but under human conditions this love is always finite and ambiguous, never "totally" pure. So the weight of "totality" makes this idea rather an ideology than a theology.

"INTRINSIC EVIL" IN A NEW APPROACH TO SEXUALITY

We have mentioned that from *Gaudium et Spes* to *Veritatis Splendor* the ethical approach and its fundamental principles have changed: from human dignity back to the pre–Vatican II idea of natural law, although in a personalist disguise. Stephan Goertz comes to the point: "In *Veritatis splendor* the absolute in morals has changed its place. No longer is the freedom and dignity of the human person an absolute end but the absolute condenses in single rules that push everything situational and circumstantial of moral action into the background."[11]

I will try to show that new concepts of sexual ethics based on the idea of human dignity and human rights are not inferior in comparison with the traditional ones that build on natural law. They are by no means relativist and even lead to a new concept of "intrinsically evil" acts. Some of these coincide with the traditional ones, some of them do not. But nevertheless, they prove to be consistent and of high moral standards.

One well-known example is Margaret Farley's book *Just Love*[12] which convincingly sums up the mainstream of modern theological thinking on sexuality and matrimony. The basic principle for Farley's approach is the personal relationship between equal partners, so sexual relations are linked to questions of honesty, justice, and power relations as well as love, mutual dedication, and commitment. Farley's starting point in her deliberations is not the philosophical concept of a determined "nature" of sexuality but human experience from an intercultural and interreligious background. Thereby the notions of "natural" or "according to God's will" turn out to be matters of hermeneutics; there is no self-evident "natural" sexual behavior: "The supposed bedrock of evidence that experience provides disappears in the endless circles of social construction."[13]

If the supposed self-evident "nature" of human sexuality is obviously a socio-historic construct, the question has to be raised, "Whose experience counts when experiences differ?"[14] But Farley does not stop by deconstructing traditional moral judgments. She reconstructs a consistent "framework" for sexual ethics on a new basis, meaning to say: just and loving sexual relationships. According to her approach those are determined by the following criteria:[15]

(1) Do no unjust harm:

The basic principle of *non nocere* applies to any human action except in situations of self-defense or accepting necessary negative side effects in the pursuit of a greater good. As obvious as it may seem, there are many physical, psychological and social consequences that have to be considered in sexual relationships—and more often than not are neglected.

(2) Always pay attention to the free consent of the partners:

While as self-evident as the first criterion this is by far the most crucial one. The whole discussion about sexual violence, abuse, and misconduct shows the frequent neglect of this criterion.

(3) Mutuality:

In any human relationship it is important that giving and receiving are somehow in balance. Anything else is not only unjust but also destroying the relationship in the long run.

(4) Equality:

While partners never are the same, their basic equality has to be honored since it is intrinsically linked to the criterion of mutuality and is rooted in the fundamental equality of all human beings. This is even more necessary be-cause the ecclesial magisterium focuses now primarily on the quite new notion of "complementarity" which in fact obscures this basic criterion. In fact, it is the so-called nature of the woman that is used as an excuse to openly violate it.

(5) Mutual commitment:

For sexual relationships to flourish, it is important that both partners are committed to the "joint venture" of their life together. Asymmetries in that area, especially constant neglect of commitment by one of the partners, is damaging not only the relationship but also the partner.

(6) Fruitfulness:

Every sexual relationship, even more, every human relationship, needs to be fruitful, which means to grow to something greater than just the sum of its parts. While traditional Church teaching focused on children alone, this task stands also for childless couples[16] and same-sex partners: The relationship will prove satisfying if it engages in some greater "project."

(7) Social justice:

Partners in any sexual relationship also have to consider the basic princi-ples of social justice. Logically self-evident, since justice always has to be observed, it is often overlooked because sexual relationships are widely con-sidered as something private. While they may be intimate, they are by no means private but considerably affect the social sphere. That is why this criterion has to be mentioned explicitly. This is true also vice versa: since partnerships and families are affected by the state of social justice, just and loving relationships that prove to be fruitful also for society are dependent on what this society can provide for them—not only materially but also non-materially.

On that ethical basis Farley's approach leads to a new set of criteria for "intrinsically evil" behavior. For example, any form of violence or deceit is intrinsically immoral. So also is adultery, not because of "natural" reasons but because it violates the marital commitment. Even more, the abuse of power to coerce or seduce someone into a sexual relationship and sexist behavior in general clearly falls under the "new" verdict of "intrinsic evil." So we can see quite clearly that a truly person-based, culturally sensitive, and socially aware ethical approach does not lead to relativism. On the contrary: to take human autonomy, cultural and social traditions, and so on, into ac-count in one's ethical argument leads to clear and unambiguous ethical judg-ments, especially in the hottest topics of today: sexual abuse and misconduct.

On the other hand, some relationships that traditionally have been consid-ered "intrinsically evil" do not show up on that list as long as they coincide with the mentioned criteria. So, for example, premarital or same-sex relations are not considered "intrinsically disordered" but rather evaluated according to personalist criteria.

To sum it up in the words of Todd A. Salzman and Michael G. Lawler: "For any sexual act to be truly human, it must exhibit [. . .] equality between the partners, equal freedom for both partners, free mutuality between the partners, and the mutual commitment of both partners."[17] In such a personalist concept of sexual ethics, the logic and meaning of "intrinsic evil" is not that much different from the traditional one. But the concrete judgment applies to a different class of acts, namely those that violate the personal dignity of one or both partners involved.

Here are two examples:

(1) Adultery

The grave sin of adultery never really fit into the framework of natural law since matrimony is not a "natural" but mainly a cultural entity. Even the idea of "natural marriage," derived from the book of Genesis, proves to be a questionable concept. The exact definition of adultery differs between the Old Testament tradition and the later Christian concept which is also connected to the rejection of polygamy in Christian times (while polygamy had been not uncommon in the Old Testament times). So adultery was rather connected to the sacramentality of marriage, not so much to the nature of human sexuality. From the perspective of just and loving relationships, on the other hand, it is quite easy to determine that adultery is an intrinsically evil act. It clearly breaks the marital vow toward the other partner.[18]

(2) Rape and sexual violence

According to natural law, sexual coercion has not been considered "intrinsically" evil but rather evil because of the circumstances. The free will of the partner—usually, of course, the female one—was one of those circumstances. That a person within a marital relationship could be raped and abused was hardly part of moral reasoning. On the other hand, contraception and all kinds of circumstantial activities (sometimes even kissing) were considered evil because they did not serve the purpose of procreation but rather the bodily pleasure which was at least questionable. If, on the other hand, we evaluate rape and coercion according to the criteria of just and loving relationships, it is unequivocally clear that any form of violent or coercive behavior is wrong—always and under any circumstances—because such actions violate the basic rights of the human person to integrity and freedom, including sexual self-determination.

So far from being relativist or even consequentialist, such a new understanding of sexual ethics is not only deeply rooted in the human person but also leads to clear, definite, and unambiguous moral guidelines and judgments, including a viable concept of "intrinsic evil"—not any longer linked to a metaphysics of natural law but to an anthropology of autonomy and mutual responsibility. While Joseph A. Selling's caution[19] vis-à-vis the concept of intrinsic evil still stands—that it "short-circuits" ethical deliberations and therefore serves as a discussion stopper—I do not consider this problematic. Rather I think such a notion is helpful to clarify: under no circumstances whatsoever can we tolerate the violation of the fundamental dignity of another human person.

NOTES

1. John Paul II, "Familiaris Consortio," accessed May 10, 2018, http://w2.vatican.va/content/john-paul-ii/en/apost_exhortations/documents/hf_jp-ii_exh_19811122_familiaris-consortio.html, 32. While the English translation reads "the deepest interaction of nature and person," the Latin original says "nexu omnino intimo naturae ac personae," which literally translates as "connection," "union." This connection is characteristic for Karol Wojtyła's ethics and leads rather to an ethics of natural law with a personalistic overcoat than to a true personalism.

2. Werner Wolbert, "Die 'in sich schlechten Handungen' und der Konsequentialismus," in *Moraltheologie im Abseits? Antwort auf die Enzyklika 'Veritatis splendor'* ed. Dietmar Mieth (Freiburg i. Br./Basel/Wien: Herder, 1994), 89–91.

3. The classical teaching reads: "Bonum ex integra causa, malum ex quocumque defectu."

4. Please note that "deliberate" is clearly distinguished from "arbitrary." Deliberate means well-considered, so we can dismiss any reproach of "relativism."

5. Bruno Schüller, *Die Begründung sittlicher Urteile. Typen ethischer Argumentation in der Moraltheologie*, 2nd ed. (Düsseldorf: Patmos, 1980), 171–263.

6. Stephan Ernst, "Argumentationsmodelle in der theologischen Sexual- und Beziehungsethik," in *Zukunftshorizonte katholischer Sexualethik*, ed. Konrad Hilpert (Freiburg i. Br./Basel/Wien: Herder, 2011), 163–64.

7. Schüller, *Die Begründung*, 221–22.

8. Ibid., 233: "Hinter dem dargelegten Argumentationstyp steht die Vorstellung, durch die Werke der Natur spreche Gott unmittelbar selbst, durch die Taten der Menschen hingegen spreche der Mensch und nicht Gott."

9. Ernst, "Argumentationsmodelle," 167: "Vor allem aber wird die Voraussetzung einer eindeutigen und klar erkennbaren Teleologie der Natur, die ethisch maßgeblich und normierend ist, in Frage gestellt."

10. Alf Ross, *On Law and Justice* (London: Stevens & Sons, 1958), 261.

11. Stephan Goertz, "Autonomie kontrovers. Die katholische Kirche und das Moralprinzip der freien Selbstbestimmung," in *Nach dem Gesetz Gottes. Autonomie als christliches Prinzip (Katholizismus im Umbruch 2)*, eds. Stephan Goertz and Magnus Striet (Freiburg i. Br./Basel/Wien: Herder, 2014), 175: "Das Absolute in der Moral hat in Veritatis splendor wieder einmal seinen Ort gewechselt. Nun ist nicht mehr die Freiheit und Würde des Menschen absoluter Zweck, nun gerinnt das Absolute in einzelnen normativen Sätzen, die alles Situative, alle Umstände des Handelns in den Hintergrund drängen."

12. Margaret A. Farley, *Just Love. A Framework for Christian Sexual Ethics* (New York/London: Continuum, 2006).

13. Ibid., 192.

14. Ibid., 193.

15. Ibid., 215–32. Farley refers to these criteria as "norms"; I personally prefer the term "criterion" since it provides a frame for assessing the ethical rightness of a concrete relationship, not just single "acts."

16. Gunter M. Prüller-Jagenteufel and Veronika Prüller-Jagenteufel, "Geschenktes Leben?! Theologisch-spirituelle Erkundungen zum unerfüllten Kinderwunsch," *Diakonia* 32 (2001): 259–65.

17. Todd A. Salzman and Michael G. Lawler, *Sexual Ethics. A Theological Introduction* (Washington, DC: Georgetown University Press, 2012), 86.

18. Eberhard Schockenhoff, *Naturrecht und Menschenwürde. Universale Ethik in einer geschichtlichen Welt* (Mainz: Matthias-Grünewald-Verlag, 1996), 229.

19. Joseph A. Selling, *Reframing Catholic Theological Ethics* (Oxford: Oxford University Press, 2016), 20–22.

REFERENCES

Ernst, Stephan. "Argumentationsmodelle in der theologischen Sexual- und Beziehungsethik." In *Zukunftshorizonte katholischer Sexualethik*, edited by Konrad Hilpert, 162–82. Freiburg i. Br./Basel/Wien: Herder, 2011.

Farley, Margaret A. *Just Love. A Framework for Christian Sexual Ethics*. New York/London: Continuum, 2006.

Goertz, Stephan. "Autonomie kontrovers. Die katholische Kirche und das Moralprinzip der freien Selbstbestimmung." In *Nach dem Gesetz Gottes. Autonomie als christliches Prinzip (Katholizismus im Umbruch 2)*, edited by Stephan Goertz and Magnus Striet, 151–97. Freiburg i. Br./Basel/Wien: Herder, 2014.

John Paul II. "Familiaris Consortio." Accessed May 10, 2018. http://w2.vatican.va/content/john-paul-ii/en/apost_exhortations/documents/hf_jp-ii_exh_19811122_familiaris-consortio.html.

Paul VI. "Humanae Vitae." Accessed May 11, 2018. https://w2.vatican.va/content/paul-vi/en/encyclicals/documents/hf_p-vi_enc_25071968_humanae-vitae.html.

Prüller-Jagenteufel, Gunter M., and Veronika Prüller-Jagenteufel. "Geschenktes Leben?! Theologisch-spirituelle Erkundungen zum unerfüllten Kinderwunsch." *Diakonia* 32 (2001): 259–65.

Ross, Alf. *On Law and Justice*. London: Stevens and Sons, 1958.

Salzman, Todd A., and Michael G. Lawler. *Sexual Ethics. A Theological Introduction*. Washington, DC: Georgetown University Press, 2012.

Schockenhoff, Eberhard. *Naturrecht und Menschenwürde. Universale Ethik in einer geschichtlichen Welt*. Mainz: Matthias-Grünewald-Verlag, 1996.

Schüller, Bruno. *Die Begründung sittlicher Urteile. Typen ethischer Argumentation in der Moraltheologie*. 2nd ed. Düsseldorf: Patmos, 1980.

Selling, Joseph A. *Reframing Catholic Theological Ethics*. Oxford: Oxford University Press, 2016.

Wolbert, Werner. "Die 'in sich schlechten Handungen' und der Konsequentialismus." In *Moraltheologie im Abseits? Antwort auf die Enzyklika "Veritatis splendor,"* edited by Dietmar Mieth, 88–109. Freiburg i. Br./Basel/Wien: Herder, 1994.

Part III

The Concept of Intrinsic Evil
and *Veritatis Splendor*

Chapter Five

Intrinsic Evil in *Veritatis Splendor* and Two Contemporary Debates

James T. Bretzke, S.J.

Twenty-odd years ago, while teaching moral theology at the Jesuit School of Theology-at-Berkeley, I joined a few other theologians in a private colloquium with the bishops from the Western Region of the United States. The gathering was chaired by the then Archbishop of San Francisco, William Levada,[1] who exhorted us all to rely heavily—if not exclusively—on the *Catechism of the Catholic Church* in both our academic courses and pastoral catechesis. In the discussion, I raised a question about the accessibility of some of the concepts employed in the *Catechism*. I questioned whether these would be adequately understood by our various target audiences. As an illustration I hypothesized that if we were to go to San Francisco's downtown Union Square (a sort of small public park surrounded by chic stores) and asked ten people at random what "intrinsic evil" meant, the answers would range from an honest "no idea" to "really, really, really bad."

A quarter century after the publication of Pope John Paul II's 1993 Encyclical on Fundamental Moral Theology, *Veritatis Splendor* (*VS*) and the 1992 *Catechism of the Catholic Church* (*CCC*), the miasma surrounding *intrinsece malum in se* has not cleared much—if at all. Elsewhere I have argued that "intrinsic evil" functions metaphorically like a shibboleth, that is, a term that was not common to all and often used to identify and separate one cultural tribe from another, somewhat the way in which the initial "th-" sound is difficult for non-native English speakers to pronounce correctly as in "that" instead of the "dat" non-natives might end up saying.[2] In fact, it seems that we probably can trace significant variants in how intrinsic evil is defined, described, understood, and/or applied in Church documents and by various popes, bishops, priests, theologians—not to mention all the people in the pews and park benches.

In addition to reaffirming the validity of the Church's long-standing moral tradition on objective moral evil, *VS* was certainly intended, at least in part, to resolve some of these differing interpretations discernible in the employment of the term intrinsic evil. The initial theological responses to *VS* were both vigorous and varied.[3] A closer re-examination now, a generation later, that looks at both the text and context of the term as it is actually used in *VS* may shed some light to discern a possible bridge over the initial polarizing divide in both the Church and larger society. In this chapter I will apply my research to two "test cases"—one theoretical, and the other in the area of concrete application. The theoretical case focuses on the five *Dubia* of four Cardinals published in the wake of Pope Francis's Post-Synodal Apostolic Exhortation on Marriage and the Family *Amoris Laetitia*. The concrete application case returns to the much controverted case over the decision by the bishop of Phoenix, Arizona, to revoke the Catholic designation of St. Joseph's Hospital after it came to light in 2010 that the hospital's ethics board agreed to terminate a nonviable pregnancy to save the life of the mother.

THE FIVE *DUBIA* OF THE FOUR CARDINALS REGARDING *VERITATIS SPLENDOR* AND *AMORIS LAETITIA*

Theory, of course, logically precedes and to some extent must ground every concrete application. For this reason it is crucial to investigate carefully exactly what *VS* actually does, and does not, say on intrinsic evil. The importance of moral theory was grasped by many in the wake of the two Synods on the Family in 2014 and 2015 and the resulting Post-Synodal Apostolic Exhortation *Amoris Laetitia*[4] (*AL*) promulgated by Pope Francis in April 2016. *Roma locuta, causa finita* (Rome has spoken, the case is closed) certainly did not prevail in this case, and later the same year four retired cardinals publicized five *Dubia*, or "questions" they had earlier presented to Pope Francis, but which he did not answer in the form they requested.[5] Two of the *Dubia* (1 and 3) dealt with questions regarding the state of grace or sin for those living in irregular marriages. The other three *Dubia* focused on one or another aspect of the interpretation of *VS*:

1. It is asked whether, following the affirmations of *Amoris Laetitia* (nn. 300–305), it has now become possible to grant absolution in the sacrament of penance and thus to admit to Holy Communion a person who, while bound by a valid marital bond, lives together with a different person *more uxorio* without fulfilling the conditions provided for by *Familiaris Consortio* n. 84 and subsequently reaffirmed by *Reconciliatio et Paenitentia* n.

34 and *Sacramentum Caritatis* n. 29. Can the expression "in certain cases" found in note 351 (n. 305) of the exhortation *Amoris Laetitia* be applied to divorced persons who are in a new union and who continue to live *more uxorio*?

2. After the publication of the post-synodal exhortation *Amoris Laetitia* (cf. n. 304), does one still need to regard as valid the teaching of St. John Paul II's encyclical *Veritatis Splendor* n. 79, based on Sacred Scripture and on the Tradition of the Church, on the existence of absolute moral norms that prohibit intrinsically evil acts and that are binding without exceptions?

3. After *Amoris Laetitia* (n. 301) is it still possible to affirm that a person who habitually lives in contradiction to a commandment of God's law, as for instance the one that prohibits adultery (cf. Mt 19:3–9), finds him or herself in an objective situation of grave habitual sin (cf. Pontifical Council for Legislative Texts, Declaration, June 24, 2000)?

4. After the affirmations of *Amoris Laetitia* (n. 302) on "circumstances which mitigate moral responsibility," does one still need to regard as valid the teaching of St. John Paul II's encyclical *Veritatis Splendor* n. 81, based on Sacred Scripture and on the Tradition of the Church, according to which "circumstances or intentions can never transform an act intrinsically evil by virtue of its object into an act 'subjectively' good or defensible as a choice"?

5. After *Amoris Laetitia* (n. 303) does one still need to regard as valid the teaching of St. John Paul II's encyclical *Veritatis Splendor* n. 56, based on Sacred Scripture and on the Tradition of the Church, that excludes a creative interpretation of the role of conscience and that emphasizes that conscience can never be authorized to legitimate exceptions to absolute moral norms that prohibit intrinsically evil acts by virtue of their object?

Much ink has been spilled since the release of the *Dubia* regarding various ecclesial and/or pastoral dimensions of this singular, and rather extraordinary, initiative on the part of the four cardinals. Surprisingly very little attention has been devoted to looking at the substance of the *Dubia* themselves which deal most explicitly with contested interpretations of *VS.* [6] The Second *Dubium* deals most explicitly with the notion of intrinsic evil in asking whether *VS*, 79's teaching still holds "on the existence of absolute moral norms that prohibit intrinsically evil acts and that are binding without exceptions." The Fourth *Dubium* inquires whether it is still true that "circumstances or intentions can never transform an act intrinsically evil by virtue of its object into an act 'subjectively' good or defensible as a choice"? The Fifth *Dubium* concerns the interpretation of conscience in light of *VS*, and I have addressed this particular issue elsewhere. [7]

A key point in interpreting *VS* is to recall that it claims only to be restating the Catholic moral tradition, and therefore, we must use that well-established moral tradition in understanding what *VS* affirms. The classic expression for "intrinsic evil" is *intrinsice malum in se*. The Latin *in se* (in itself) is crucial inasmuch as it *explicitly* connotes due consideration of the circumstances in which the agent finds him/herself, as well as the agent's moral intention (*finis operantis*) for a particular moral object chosen (*finis operis*) in the context of these circumstances. In other words, the "in itself" must refer to the actual situation in which the moral object is found in the concrete. As the late German moral theologian Klaus Demmer, MSC, noted, this *in se* requires a hermeneutical process of interpretation concerning the intention and circumstances even though the accent is still maintained on the gravity of the action itself. This hermeneutical process then keeps us from the moral conundrum of positing morally evil actions totally abstracted from the agent, who is always and only a social, contextualized being.[8] While *VS* does not contradict Demmer's insight neither does it really embrace it, and I believe this lacuna leads in part to so many problematic uses of "intrinsic evil" by both proponents and critics of *VS* alike.[9] Saying much the same thing in line within the moral tradition, I tell my students that an "intrinsically evil act" can never be a different species of moral act, such that absolutely *no* consideration, explicit or implicit, of circumstances and the accompanying moral intention (*finis operantis*) is required to come to a moral evaluation of the act as a whole (the *finis operis*).[10] In this context, then, let us consider carefully *VS*, 80 and its crucial modifier "ulterior" in the description of the core relationship among circumstances, intention, and moral object:

> These are the acts, which, in the Church's moral tradition, have been termed "intrinsically evil" (*intrinsece malum*): they are such *always and per se,* in other words, on account of their very object, and quite apart from the *ulterior intentions of the one acting and the circumstances* [*aliorum adiunctorum ratione habita,* emphasis added]. Consequently, without in the least denying the influence on morality exercised by circumstances and especially by intentions, the Church teaches that "there exist acts which *per se* and in themselves, independently of circumstances, are always seriously wrong by reason of their object." (*VS*, 80)

Of course, what *VS* is seeking to emphasize is that it is never possible to transform a morally evil object (*finis operis*) somehow into a morally good act. Murder is always intrinsically evil, even if the person murdered might have been a serial pedophile.[11] Moreover, *pace* Cardinals Burke et al., neither does *AL* advance a contrary position. Genuine adultery remains intrinsically evil, but just what constitutes "genuine" or continued "adultery" may in fact vary according to particular intentions and circumstances, as I believe Pope Francis has clearly suggested in this key passage:

> For this reason, a pastor cannot feel that it is enough simply to apply moral laws to those living in "irregular" situations, as if they were stones to throw at people's lives. This would bespeak the closed heart of one used to hiding behind the Church's teachings, "sitting on the chair of Moses and judging at

times with superiority and superficiality difficult cases and wounded families."
(*AL*, 305)

The Magisterium traditionally rightly holds to a hermeneutics of continuity. Therefore, to interpret *VS* accurately we need to look at its past context (such as Vatican II) as well as refinements given in subsequent papal teaching, such as Pope Francis's *AL*. In this passage above from *AL*, I believe the Pope is implicitly connecting the abstract "objective moral order" articulated in *VS* with Vatican II's treatment of conscience in documents such as *Gaudium et Spes* (*GS*, 16) and *Dignitatis Humanae* (*DH*, 3). The doubting cardinals' *Miramur* asks whether we still are to hold, in accord with *VS*, that moral truth is absolute, or whether we give in to a moral relativism that permits every individual conscience to make up its own truth. We can reply with an honest reassurance that moral truth remains absolute, but conscience remains the privileged place where the individual meets God to discern best how to obey that moral truth. [12] Moral truth also will inherently have a personal dimension as it is lived out, and thus its "truth" differs from the sort of objective truth one searches for in mathematics or the physical sciences.

So where do we stand? Clearly divided. Some defend *VS* as prophetic, much along the same lines of *Humanae Vitae*. [13] Others, myself included, are decidedly less enthusiastic about the encyclical precisely because of the confusion that the document seems to engender. Still others ground their resistance more broadly in terms of seriously questioning the notion of "intrinsic evil" and even any theory of the natural law. Borrowing a well-known line from the 1967 movie *Cool Hand Luke*, I believe "what we've got here is a failure to communicate." [14] Or, using a genre I became familiar with during my seven years in the Eternal City, what we have here is a *dibattito*. The cognate, of course, is "debate" and sometimes the term is translated as "discussion," but in reality it is neither. In the classic *dibattito*, speakers are lined up and take turns attacking from various angles the opponent. However, the opponent itself is not present, nor given an opportunity to speak on its own behalf. Instead, we witness a sort of shadow boxing: given the jabs and punches, we in some sense can intuit the general shape and position of the opponent, but never see the beast clearly in sharp relief.

I believe all sides on the intrinsic evil debate have been engaging in this sort of *dibattito* since at least the time of the more genuine debate over the morality of artificial birth control that occurred in the 1960s. [15] For *VS* the main shadow-boxing opponent is some sort of moral relativism, and the hoped-for knockout punch is wound around the metaphorical brass knuckles of a forced acknowledgment of "intrinsic evil." The "cornerman" is the "objective moral order" that coaches us with an array of moral norms, which are inflexibly absolute, from abortion to same-sex relations. The coach tells us that the only proper role of conscience is simply to identify the proper norm and apply it in a straightforward one-size-fits-all casuistry, often employing the so-called physicalist paradigm.[16]

Paradigm theory then may be the most helpful concept in understanding the current impasse regarding intrinsic evil as outlined in *VS*. It should be axiomatic that we acknowledge that only God can fully and completely grasp the objective moral order, just as it exists in both the abstract and the concrete. For the rest of us limited, finite creatures we must rely on models and paradigms both to explain and explore complex realities. Some, if not all, of our models will likely be incomplete at best, and misshapen at worst. A serious problem arises if we overlook this natural human limitation and conflate our particular, necessarily limited understanding of a complex concept such as intrinsic evil with the absolute fullness of that reality itself.

I believe this is what has happened with many of those who use *VS* to paint in too broad brushstrokes of largely black and white concrete situations that would be more accurately rendered in a greater color palate and with finer, more detailed—and perhaps even more tentative—brushstrokes.

BISHOP OLMSTED AND THE PHOENIX CASE OF PREGNANCY TERMINATION

In November 2009, a married mother of four children had her pregnancy terminated for medical reasons at St. Joseph's Hospital and Medical Center, the only such Catholic institution in the Diocese of Phoenix, Arizona. It was physically impossible to save the fetus, and if the placenta was not removed, the mother would die in very short order. The choice was stark: one death or two, and the medically (and morally) certain death would be the fetus. In other words, there was no choice of saving the mother over saving the fetus; the fetus was going to die regardless. This crucial point seems to have been insufficiently grasped by most individuals who subsequently criticized the decision.

So after carefully reviewing the medical facts of the case, and noting its grave emergency that prevented transfer of the woman to a non-Catholic hospital, the ethics board of the hospital, chaired by Sr. Margaret McBride, concluded that in this case the termination of the pregnancy constituted an "indirect" abortion and thus was allowed by the relevant sections of the U.S. Bishops *Ethical and Religious Directives for Catholic Health Care Services* (*ERDs*).[17]

The placenta, which was causing the life-threatening condition, was removed, terminating the pregnancy. The fetus died, but the mother survived. Some months later this case came to the attention of the local bishop, Thomas Olmsted, and this set off a series of events that included a statement by the bishop in May 2010 that Sr. McBride had incurred an "automatic" *latae sententiae* excommunication for her role in this decision, and subsequently the bishop stripped the hospital of its "Catholic" status on December 21, 2010, because its administrators refused to agree to his ultimatum that included an admission that the original decision amounted to a direct abortion—which, if true, would be a serious violation of the *Ethical and Religious Health Care Directives.*

Virtually no bishop in the country joined Bishop Olmsted's view that what the hospital had done was a morally illegitimate "direct" abortion, but neither did any hierarch directly criticize Olmsted. After the December decision, a number of groups, including the Catholic Health Association, issued statements backing St. Joseph Hospital's original position on this case. This support then led to a contrasting statement by the then president of the U.S. Catholic Conference of Bishops, Archbishop (now Cardinal) Timothy Dolan, which expressed support not for the actual "reading" of the case by Bishop Olmsted but rather for his jurisdiction and authority to take the actions he deemed appropriate. Bishop Olmsted himself said in his public statements that as bishop of the diocese it was he who determined what the natural law was—in Phoenix.

While this case has a wide range of canonical and ecclesial issues, foundational to the original decision is a contested reading over whether the surgical procedure to remove the life-threatening placenta was a direct or indirect abortion. If it were considered "direct" then it would constitute an intrinsic evil, which never could be condoned. If, on the other hand, it were considered "indirect," then the procedure could be allowed for sufficiently grave (i.e., "proportionate") reason, and would not violate the moral stricture against performing an intrinsic evil. This case, then, illustrates some of the practical difficulties surrounding the theory of intrinsic evil—difficulties, I would argue, that are hardly clarified by the presentation of intrinsic evil in *VS*.

Direct and indirect depend of course on the intention, but even more importantly on the circumstances in which the intention is formed and the moral object of the action is determined. Circumstances seem to be considerably underrepresented in this case, and this fact illustrates one of the critical dangers in relying too much on an overly abstract presentation of the moral act. This no doubt is due in large part to the common misperception that acts labeled "intrinsically evil" make no allowance whatsoever for *any* consideration of circumstances. But that is *not* what *VS* actually says. "Ulterior," from *VS*, 80, is the crucial missing modifier here. This basic point needs to be emphasized and elaborated, since many proponents of *VS* mistakenly hold that the encyclical posits a species of moral act that has no reference whatsoever to intention or circumstances. I believe that Bishop Olmsted may have been one such person who thought that any intentional termination of a pregnancy was ipso facto "direct" and therefore intrinsically evil.

However, as the established moral tradition holds, any genuine human moral act (*actus humanus*) must have all three of the *fontes moralitatis* of the object of the action, which is largely determined by the particular intention formed in light of the concrete circumstances. Any action utterly devoid of consideration of either the intention of the agent (*finis operantis*) and/or the concrete circumstances could not qualify as a moral act. At best, such an action devoid of consideration of the intention and/or circumstances would be what the tradition terms an *actus hominis*—an action performed by a human being, but without moral valence. Such an action would then lack a corresponding moral object.

What I have outlined here is simply the position of Thomas Aquinas (*Summa Theologiae*, I–II, q. 18).[18] Of course, referencing the Angelic Doctor does not necessarily seal the argument, but at least it should protect one from being termed heterodox or worse. There are different schools of interpretation of Thomas within the broader moral tradition, and one of the dangers of any magisterial intervention such as *VS*, or Leo XIII's *Aeterni Patris* is that only one school is considered by some to be legitimate, and that any real consideration of the genre of a *Quaestio disputata* is somehow disloyal, or just another example of Jesuit casuistry at its worst.

CONCLUSION: *VERITATIS SPLENDOR* AND INTRINSIC EVIL: CLASSIC, PERIOD PIECE, OR SHIBBOLETH?

Clearly, Pope John Paul II held that his Encyclical on Fundamental Moral Theology would become a classic edifice destined to stand for generations, and the presentation of intrinsic evil served as its cornerstone. I do believe there are some legitimate, positive examples of this usage that do transcend time and circumstances more readily, such as the prohibition of murder, torture, and genocide as being intrinsically evil. Using euphemisms such as "enhanced interrogation techniques" or "ethnic cleansing" neither justifies nor mitigates the intrinsic evil of such actions, and the fact that such proposals continue to be advanced by politicians and others shows that the strictures surrounding intrinsic evil still have not been sufficiently integrated into broader society.

While no credible moral theologian would justify these actions, simply labeling them "intrinsically evil" does not necessarily provide us with a convincing argument to carry the day, whether it be in Washington, DC; Afghanistan; Serbia; or Myanmar. Several of the other essays in this volume seem to argue that at best the notion of intrinsic evil as employed in Catholic theological ethics has seen its best days come and gone. These theologians would argue that the term functions something like a period piece, and depends on too many other ground concepts, such as the classicist and physicalist paradigms that are no longer credible in a postmodern world that finds the historicist and personalist paradigms more conducive to discernment in our increasingly morally complex world. Both the theoretical case of the Four Cardinals *Dubia* as well as the practical application used by Bishop Olmsted in the Phoenix Hospital Pregnancy Termination controversy could provide examples of how the notion of intrinsic evil outlined in *VS* exhibits such an array of significant difficulties that one could reasonably conclude that this concept no longer commands sufficient credibility to argue for its continued use.

However, regardless of what might be our professional recommendations and preferences about the continued use of intrinsic evil in Catholic ethics, I can confidently predict it will in fact continue to be employed in a cross-section of academic, ecclesial, political, and cultural fora. Therefore, in conclusion I return to propose as a viable third model for approaching the concept of intrinsic evil, namely that of the shibboleth (from the Hebrew שִׁבֹּלֶת in Judges 12) which I have adumbrated above. While Gilead used the word to separate friend from foe, I am suggesting that within the discipline of theological ethics we all still need to know the precise range of meanings and the grounding concepts of the moral act, the relation of the *finis operis* to the *finis operantis*, and the absolute necessity of consideration of circumstances in every *actus humanus*. This knowledge will help us not only to gain admittance into arenas of moral discourse and *dibattiti* from which we otherwise might be excluded, but also will be of aid to us as we endeavor to articulate the critical moral distinctions that would avoid either a repeat of the Phoenix controversy or even resolving some of the pitched battles over the interpretation, and application, of more recent papal magisterium such as *Amoris Laetitia* that we saw in the cardinalatial *Dubia*.

NOTES

1. William Levada (b. 1936) completed his 1971 doctoral dissertation *Infallible Church Magisterium and the Natural Law* under Francis Sullivan, S.J., at the Gregorian on the question of the competency of the Magisterium to pronounce infallibly on concrete material norms contained in the natural law, and concluded that even though no such pronouncement had been attempted, still it would be logically impossible to do so (78–79). Levada later went on to work as a *minutante* (staff member) at the Congregation for the Doctrine of the Faith under the prefecture of Joseph Ratzinger, who upon succeeding to the papacy appointed Levada as his successor to the CDF. Levada was a prominent member of the drafting commission for the 1992 *Catechism of the Catholic Church*.

2. "Debating Intrinsic Evil: Navigation between Shibboleth and Gauntlet," *Horizons* 41, no. 1 (2014): 116–29. I employ Robert Schreiter's notion of competence criteria of effectiveness and appropriateness in philosophical and/or theological 'intercultural' communication. At best, the expression "intrinsically evil only partially succeeds in fulfilling those criteria demonstrating, while it often is used as a gauntlet thrown down to sharpen sides in political policy debates." See also the response by Michael P. Jaycox, "Debating 'Intrinsic Evil,'" in the same issue at 142–65.

3. For a range of responses across the theological and ecumenical perspective see the essays in these volumes (listed alphabetically by editor): Michael E. Allsopp and John J. O'Keefe, eds. *Veritatis Splendor: American Responses* (Kansas City, MO: Sheed & Ward, 1995); J. A. DiNoia, O.P. and Romanus Cessario, O.P., *Veritatis Splendor and the Renewal of Moral Theology* (Princeton, NJ: Scepter Publishers; Huntington, IN: Our Sunday Visitor; Chicago: Midwest Theological Forum, 1999); Joseph A. Selling and Jan Jans, eds., *The Splendor of Accuracy: An Examination of the Assertions Made by Veritatis Splendor* (Grand Rapids, MI: William B. Eerdmans; Kampen, The Netherlands: Pharos Publishing Co., 1994); Miguel A. Velasco, *Los derechos de la verdad. Veritatis splendor: críticas y réplicas* (Madrid: Ediciones Palabra, 1994); John Wilkins, ed., *Understanding "Veritatis Splendor": The Encyclical Letter of Pope John Paul II and the Church's Moral Teaching* (London: SPCK, 1994); and Charles Yeats, *Veritatis Splendor—A Response* (Norwich: Canterbury Press, 1994). This last work gives twelve Anglican responses to *VS*, given in a series of addresses at Durham University.

4. Francis, "Amoris Laetitia," accessed April 25, 2018, http://w2.vatican.va/content/francesco/en/apost_exhortations/documents/papa-francesco_esortazione-ap_20160319_amoris-laetitia.html.

5. The *Dubia* Letter was signed by Their Eminences, Walter Brandmüller (German), Raymond L. Burke (American), Carlo Caffarra (Italian), and Joachim Meisner (German) and is widely available (http://www.ncregister.com/blog/edward-pentin/full-text-and-explanatory-notes-of-cardinals-questions-on-amoris-laetitia). They had asked explicitly for a "yes" or "no" answer to each of their *Dubia*. The four cardinals were either retired or semiretired from ecclesiastical office, and Meissner and Caffarra died in June and September of 2017 at the ages of eighty-three and seventy-nine, respectively. I discuss these *Dubia* in greater length in my article "*Responsum ad Dubia*: Harmonizing *Veritatis Splendor* and *Amoris Laetitia* through a Conscience-Informed Casuistry," *Journal of Catholic Social Thought* 15, no. 1 (2018): 211–22.

6. For one article which does treat this issue at greater length see my "*Responsum ad Dubia*," 211–22.

7. See my article "Conscience and *Veritatis Splendor* in the Church Today," *Studia Moralia* 55, no. 2 (2017): 271–95.

8. See especially chapter 5 of Klaus Demmer's *Deuten und handeln: Grundlagen und Grundfragen der Fundamentalmoral*, Studien zur theologischen Ethik, no. 15 (Freiburg: Verlag Herder, 1985).

9. See, for example, Jean Porter, "The Moral Act in *Veritatis Splendor* and in Aquinas's *Summa Theologiae*: A Comparative Analysis," in *Veritatis Splendor*, eds. Allsopp and O'Keefe, 278–95. Also helpful is Bernard Hoose's "Circumstances, Intentions and Intrinsically Evil Acts," in *The Splendor of Accuracy*, eds. Selling and Jans, 136–52.

10. On *intrinsece malum in se* (intrinsic evil) and *finis operis/finis operantis* see both the entries in Bretzke's *Consecrated Phrases* and his *A Handbook of Roman Catholic Moral Terms* (Washington, DC: Georgetown University Press, 2013).

11. Frankly, no credentialed moral theologian I know holds the supposed view that somehow "ulterior" in the sense of "additional" intentions and/or circumstances "transforms" the object of a morally bad deed into one that is either morally neutral or even good. However, the verbiage of *VS* would lead readers to believe that such heterodox opinions are widespread in the academic community and beyond.

12. I expand on these points in "Conscience and *Veritatis Splendor*," 271–95; and "In Good Conscience: What *Amoris Laetitia* can teach us about responsible decision making," *America*, April 8, 2016, http://americamagazine.org/issue/article/good-conscience; and in "The Sanctuary of Conscience: Where the Axes Intersect," chap. 4 of my *A Morally Complex World: Engaging Contemporary Moral Theology* (Collegeville, PA: The Liturgical Press, 2004), 109–43. Also very helpful is Linda Hogan's *Confronting the Truth: Conscience in the Catholic Tradition* (New York: Paulist Press, 2001), and the range of essays in Charles Curran, ed. *Conscience: Readings in Moral Theology*, vol. 14 (New York: Paulist Press, 2004).

13. For example, see Archbishop Charles Chaput, OFM, Cap., "*Veritatis Splendor* 2017," *First Things*, October, 2017, https://www.firstthings.com/article/2017/10/the-splendor-of-truth-in-2017.

14. If the phrase and its context is unfamiliar, see https://en.wikipedia.org/wiki/What_we%27ve_got_here_is_failure_to_communicate.

15. Tanker-sized wells of ink have been spilled on this topic, to bring us to our current stalemate impasse. For a helpful discussion over the Pontifical Birth Control Commission, see Robert B. Kaiser, *The Encyclical That Never Was: The Story of the Pontifical Commission on Population, Family and Birth, 1964–1966* (London: Sheed and Ward, 1985, 1987).

16. Still helpful in this regard is Brian V. Johnstone, C.Ss.R., "From Physicalism to Personalism," *Studia Moralia* 30 (1992): 71–96. I also discuss this in "Mapping a Moral Methodology," chap. 1 of my *A Morally Complex World,* 9–41.

17. The literature in this case is vast. For a helpful overview and links to some key medical and moral opinions see St. Joseph's Hospital and Medical Center, "St. Joseph's web-site," accessed March 27, 2018, https://www.dignityhealth.org/about-us/press-center/press-releases/diocese-of-phoenix.

18. For more on these critical terms and their distinctions, see the entries under *Finis* in my *Consecrated Phrases* and also the entries on "intrinsic evil," "intention," "circumstances," and so on, in my *Handbook of Roman Catholic Moral Terms* referenced earlier in note 10.

REFERENCES

Allsopp, Michael E., and John J. O'Keefe, eds. *Veritatis Splendor: American Responses.* Kansas City, MO: Sheed and Ward, 1995.

Brandmüller, Walter, Raymond L. Burke, Carlo Caffarra, and Joachim Meisner. "Seeking Clarity: A Plea to Untie the Knots in *Amoris Laetitia.*" Accessed April 27, 2018. http://www.ncregister.com/blog/edward-pentin/full-text-and-explanatory-notes-of-cardinals-questions-on-amoris-laetitia.

Bretzke, James T., S.J. "Conscience and *Veritatis Splendor* in the Church Today." *Studia Moralia* 55, no. 2 (2017): 271–95.

———. *Consecrated Phrases.* Washington, DC: Georgetown University Press, 2013.

———. "Debating Intrinsic Evil: Navigation between Shibboleth and Gauntlet." *Horizons* 41, no. 1 (2014): 116–29.

———. *A Handbook of Roman Catholic Moral Terms.* Washington, DC: Georgetown University Press, 2013.

———. "In Good Conscience: What *Amoris Laetitia* can teach us about responsible decision making." *America*, April 8, 2016. http://americamagazine.org/issue/article/good-conscience.

———. *A Morally Complex World: Engaging Contemporary Moral Theology.* Collegeville, PA: The Liturgical Press, 2004.

———. "*Responsum ad Dubia*: Harmonizing *Veritatis Splendor* and *Amoris Laetitia* through a Conscience-Informed Casuistry." *Journal of Catholic Social Thought* 15, no. 1 (2018): 211–22.

Chaput, Charles, OFM, Cap. "*Veritatis Splendor* 2017." *First Things*, October, 2017. https://www.firstthings.com/article/2017/10/the-splendor-of-truth-in-2017.

Curran, Charles, ed. *Conscience: Readings in Moral Theology*, vol. 14. New York: Paulist Press, 2004.

Demmer, Klaus. *Deuten und handeln: Grundlagen und Grundfragen der Fundamentalmoral.* Studien zur theologischen Ethik, no. 15. Freiburg: Verlag Herder, 1985.

DiNoia, J. A., O.P. and Romanus Cessario, O.P. *Veritatis Splendor and the Renewal of Moral Theology.* Princeton, NJ: Scepter Publishers; Huntington, IN: Our Sunday Visitor; Chicago: Midwest Theological Forum, 1999.

Francis. "Amoris Laetitia." Accessed April 25, 2018. http://w2.vatican.va/content/francesco/en/apost_exhortations/documents/papa-francesco_esortazione-ap_20160319_amoris-laetitia.html.

Hogan, Linda. *Confronting the Truth: Conscience in the Catholic Tradition.* New York: Paulist Press, 2001.

Jaycox, Michael P. "Debating 'Intrinsic Evil.'" *Horizons* 41, no. 1 (2014): 142–65.

Johnstone, Brian V., C.Ss.R. "From Physicalism to Personalism." *Studia Moralia* 30 (1992): 71–96.

Kaiser, Robert B. *The Encyclical That Never Was: The Story of the Pontifical Commission on Population, Family and Birth, 1964–1966.* London: Sheed and Ward, 1985, 1987.

Levada, William. "Infallible Church Magisterium and the Natural Law." PhD diss., Gregorian University, 1971.

Selling, Joseph A., and Jan Jans, eds. *The Splendor of Accuracy: An Examination of the Assertions Made by Veritatis Splendor.* Grand Rapids, MI: William B. Eerdmans; Kampen, The Netherlands: Pharos Publishing Co., 1994.

St. Joseph's Hospital and Medical Center. "St. Joseph's web-site." Accessed March 27, 2018. https://www.dignityhealth.org/about-us/press-center/press-releases/diocese-of-phoenix.

Velasco, Miguel A. *Los derechos de la verdad. Veritatis splendor: críticas y réplicas.* Madrid: Ediciones Palabra, 1994.

Wilkins, John, ed. *Understanding "Veritatis Splendor": The Encyclical Letter of Pope John Paul II and the Church's Moral Teaching.* London: SPCK, 1994.

Yeats, Charles. *Veritatis Splendor—A Response.* Norwich: Canterbury Press, 1994.

Chapter Six

What Are Intrinsically Evil Acts?

Sigrid Müller

James Bretzke, in his stimulating chapter on Intrinsic Evil in *Veritatis Splendor*, addresses the fact that the notion of "intrinsically evil acts" is being used metaphorically and politically, but without a clear concept of what intrinsic evil might be. If one were to ask the average person on the street what the expression means, a variety of meanings would be found, ranging from "no idea" to "really, really, really bad."[1] If the notion of intrinsic evil is so unclear, it does not seem meaningful to keep using it.

It might be necessary to explain here that different languages have different connotations with regard to the notion of "intrinsically evil acts." In my first language, which is German, "intrinsically evil acts" is a translation of *in sich schlechte Handlungen* which means "acts that are morally bad in themselves." The German wording does not have the metaphysical connotation of evil as "associated with the forces of the devil"[2] or the already mentioned dimension of "extremely wicked and immoral."[3] Nor does it denote the "morally neutral (descriptive) sense" of damage caused.[4] Rather, it signifies categories of acts that are already by their own name, judged to be morally wrong because it is known that they are destructive to personal life and basic human relationships.[5]

In Christian tradition, these categories of acts can be found in the negatively formulated commandments of the second table of the Decalogue (killing, stealing, committing adultery, etc.). This understanding of intrinsically evil acts as limited to a small number of commandments of the Decalogue was only recently given up, especially during the pontificate of Pope John Paul II. In *Veritatis Splendor,* 80, the notion entails a whole range of moral acts that had been used in *Gaudium et Spes* as examples of acts that prohibit the full flourishing of human beings, which are now categorized as intrinsically evil.[6] The extended number of intrinsically evil acts creates the problem that, if a large number of morally wrong acts can be said to be intrinsically evil, then the two notions become interchangeable, and the use of the category of intrinsically evil does not add substantial content to "morally wrong." Therefore the development in Church teaching presses the question that was raised above, namely whether Catholic moral theory should stop using the term "intrinsically evil"—not only because it is no longer understood, but also because it has become interchangeable with the judgment of being morally wrong.[7]

However, I would like to make an attempt, before giving up the use of the term right away, to clarify more concretely the conditions under which one could possibly still use the term in an ethically significant way. Therefore, I will concentrate on the concept itself, neglecting the question whether it is currently being used fruitfully in moral communication. In order to do so, I will put forth some ethical considerations that have been developed during the past couple of years among the German-speaking theological ethicists.[8] I will use these elements to approach the question of what the formal, epistemological, and moral characteristics of an intrinsically evil act need to be in order to make this concept valuable in light of contemporary theological-ethical theory.

On the way to reach such a description of intrinsically evil acts and their components, it will be necessary to engage in a few more specific issues. The first and shorter issue is how the objectivity of moral acts can be related to the statement made in James Bretzke's chapter to the effect that one can speak of an "absolute moral truth" that is founded in God's "objective moral order" which we fail to fully understand. This touches the epistemological question of how human beings recognize good and bad, theoretically and practically.

Secondly, I would like to reflect on the various relationships of the act and its object with circumstances and intention.[9] The questions raised here are: When can circumstances and intentions change the act's object and therefore its "species"—and when do they simply affect the accountability of the acting person, a dimension that refers to the difference between a mortal and venial sin? In the latter case, intentions and circumstances are only relevant for the evaluation of the "subjective" aspect of moral acts, while the act is taken to be already morally defined. It seems, however, possible to show that intentions and circumstances can also be relevant for defining the "objective" aspect of the act itself. I would like to show in this chapter that it is necessary to distinguish these two levels of looking at acts, because intentions and circumstances play different roles and have a different meaning at the two levels of reflection.

CAN WE DEFINE INTRINSICALLY EVIL ACTS?

As already mentioned, there are a variety of ways of understanding the expression 'intrinsic evil' in different discourses. It can be helpful to observe and distinguish the different ways in which this term is being applied and used for political purposes, that is, in order to stop further conversation on a topic. However, this effort does not excuse us from asking whether there is also a *moral* meaning of the expression. Does it make sense from an *ethical* point of view to speak about intrinsically evil acts; and if the expression makes sense, how would it be understood today?

Objective and Subjective Level: Intrinsically Evil Acts versus Personal Sin

In taking account of the objects, intentions, and circumstances which have classically been identified as the components of moral acts, it can be helpful to remember the difference between calling an act "intrinsically evil" and calling it a "mortal sin." "For a *sin* to be *mortal*, three conditions must together be met: 'Mortal sin is sin whose object is grave matter and which is also committed with full knowledge and deliberate consent.'"[10] Circumstances, in this understanding of the *fontes moralitatis*, do not influence the nature of an act, rather they decide about the gravity of a sin which reflects the relationship between the person and God.[11]

Sin, therefore, is a religious category that refers to an individual person, to the "subjective" level, with the exception of when the word "sin" is used in an analogous or metaphorical way, as in the expressions "structural sin" or "sins of our times." The elements of the classical *fontes moralitatis* can help to define, in cases of conscience and in the situation of confession, to what degree a person can be held accountable for what they did (not) do. But what can be said about the category of intrinsically evil acts? By abstracting from the agent, intrinsically evil acts are localized at the "objective," rather general level of defining and categorizing moral acts and not at the level of acting. It seems that the category of intrinsically evil acts is a moral category which does not address the personal accountability of an agent, but rather remains on a general and abstract "objective" level.[12] It is at this general level that *Veritatis Splendor* describes the characteristics of intrinsically evil acts: they are acts that are always forbidden, are categorically evil, and therefore are expressed in a negative form ("You shall not . . .").[13] In this description, the universality of the moral claim (always), its verbal expression (negative), and their content (evil) are linked together. In the reflections that follow I try to address these aspects separately.

This general judgment has been related to the theory of absolute moral truth.[14] The question, however, is raised as to how absolute moral truth and universal, categorical moral norms and personal moral judgment are related to each other. The encyclical says that calling a specific act "intrinsically evil" expresses the judgment that the concrete act can be categorized as belonging to a species of acts, which means that these acts have the same object[15] and that acts with this object can be universally recognized as being intrinsically evil. In this way, the claim is being made that universal, categorical moral norms exist.[16] At the same time, it is very interesting to note that the encyclical does express the idea that the attribution of a specific act to the species of "intrinsically evil" does not come about naturally, but by an act of recognition.[17] This leads us to reflect briefly about the epistemological presuppositions of the claim being made in the statement by James Bretzke that we can speak of an "absolute moral truth" that is founded in God's "objective moral order" that we fail to fully understand. Are failures in personal moral judgment caused by a failure to understand God's absolute moral truth?

HOW CAN WE UNDERSTAND ABSOLUTE MORAL TRUTH?

Klaus Demmer, in a remarkable article from 1987, analyzed the metaphysical presuppositions for understanding the relationship of acts and their moral species. In his essay, he judges the concept of intrinsically evil acts in Catholic moral teaching as sometimes helpful in determining certainty with respect to certain acts. But he also wants to make his readers aware of the fact that the concept is based on "essentialist and objectivist advance decisions."[18] By presupposing a moderate realism, he shows that the epistemological process, by which an object is recognized and classified, is embedded in history. Therefore, the clear distinction made a few years later by the encyclical *Veritatis Splendor* between a "moral judgment"—which claims to recognize that a certain reality is given—and an "arbitrary decision" taken with regard to a concrete situation, is misleading when it comes to understanding the way in which universal principles are perceived.[19] Reason, Demmer argues, judges and decides in one and the same act.[20]

As a consequence, it is clear that there are general moral principles that may not change in their wording and in the basic existential knowledge attached to them, but it is also clear that they can take on different practical meaning at a more concrete level when historical contexts change and bring about new contexts of interpretation and understanding that can broaden or narrow the "domain of definition" of a term.[21] Demmer claims that one should be aware of a certain analogy embedded in truth that allows distinguishing between the following three analogous senses of the notion of truth: (1) truth with regard to exterior facts (e.g., this man causes harm to a woman I love by beating her), (2) the anthropological truth which is a truth linked to the project of a person's life that brings about a pluralism of interpreting concrete situations (e.g., this is a woman I definitely want to save from mistreatment), and (3) a moral truth which is established by practical reason (e.g., if I deliberately kill the man who is mistreating the woman I love, this is murder).[22]

When Demmer develops his argument, he makes two statements relevant for our question. First, the recognition of moral principles that are linked to external reality, that is, facts and experiences (that some kind of things or acts cause harm) belongs rather to the field of "theoretical reason." When these are considered, all limitations that accompany the acquisition of theoretical knowledge apply, especially the limitation that our knowledge is embedded in a certain historical, hermeneutical setting. This is why human beings can formulate moral principles, as "you shall not kill." In their wording they refer to an experience that life is valuable and that purposeful putting an end to the life of someone causes harm so that the principle affirms this experience and general knowledge. Yet, their unfolding in moral norms and legal regulations makes it necessary to define the exact realm of the general principle. The more interpretation is needed, the greater is the influence of historical context. For instance, at the time when the Ten Commandments were formulated, the commandment did not include killing in war or killing persons belonging to other nations, nor did it refer to the death penalty, but it did include indirect killing (namely, willingly letting it happen).[23] By accepting the historical embeddedness of our epistemological acts, one also accepts that the concrete meaning of "unchangeable moral principles" can change even if their literal formulation, and the general existential knowledge of the values that these general principles protect, remain the same. There are a number of examples for such a historical development of interpretation in the teaching of the Catholic Church.[24]

Our understanding the meaning of principles can change not only when facts are interpreted differently, but also when facts are related differently to our anthropological views, and vice versa. Furthermore, when our moral attitude changes because of experiences that make us rearrange our implicit hierarchy of values, or when the range of moral values expands due to experience, our understanding of principles also evolves. As Demmer argues in his article, the physical, the anthropological, and the moral need to be distinguished from each other, but they are connected in analogous ways in which they create the hermeneutical background against which human beings understand the meaning of, acknowledge, and reaffirm moral principles. The principles therefore are seen as assuming the character of absolute moral truth that does not change. Yet their concrete understanding is dependent upon the interaction of various layers of theoretical knowledge (of facts and general principles) and practical reason (moral insight in the concrete situation) embedded in history. Our understanding, therefore, can broaden, narrow, include, or exclude new aspects.

The cautious formulation that moral principles are assuming the character of absolute moral truth refers firstly to the much discussed metaphysical question of whether absolute moral truth exists; and secondly to the episte-mological question: if it exists, how can human beings conceive of it. The metaphysical question has been discussed since Aristotle's critique of Plato, and both theories have made their way into the Christian tradition. In the Platonic Christian tradition, moral goodness corresponds to acting according to a given theoretical order that is established by an ordination to the highest good which is God. The Aristotelian line of argument would locate moral goodness in relation to the practical aim of human life which is (practical) perfection and the happiness that results from reaching it, distinct from the theoretical order of goodness in which human beings participate through their intellect. [25]

A third line of thought that influenced Christian tradition was Stoicism, which introduced the idea that human beings could observe the law of nature that was seen as divine so that the task of human beings was to bring their acting into harmony with this law. In spite of the differences in their accounts of theoretical and practical reasoning, it is clear that human practical acting is still understood to be dependent on human reasoning, while only general principles, as "good is profitable and worthy of choice and [. . .] all men assume righteousness to be beautiful," can be regarded as moral preconcepts given by nature to everybody. [26]

Let us, then, pursue the question of what the consequences would be if we affirm Bretzke's statement that we can maintain an absolute moral truth. According to Bretzke, absolute moral truth contains the knowledge about intrinsically evil acts, as part of God's moral order that human beings need to acknowledge but cannot recognize with certainty.

HOW CAN WE UNDERSTAND
GOD'S OBJECTIVE MORAL ORDER?

Absolute moral truth in the sense of being expressed by "general moral principles" that can be exemplified by the categorical, negatively formulated Commandments of the second table of the Decalogue can also be referred to in the practical order as "intermediate moral principles" or incomplete moral norms. [27] They are not as general as mere principles (e.g., do good, do justice, avoid evil, do what expresses love) but not as concrete as clear norms (pay taxes, do not beat your children, invite your parents to live with you when they are in need). Rather, they are general enough to appear unchangeable and yet open to a certain variation of meaning when the hermeneutic context changes. Does this justify the claim that general and intermediate principles are founded on God's "objective moral order" and explain the variability of the application of intermediate principles by the fact that human beings fail to fully understand that order?[28]

I would question whether it is very helpful to save the idea of an absolute moral order if it is understood as a metaphysical order established by God that is not approachable by human reasoning. It seems to me that this would confirm what *Veritatis Splendor* suggests in some of its formulations, namely that there is a kind of metaphysical moral order that human beings ought to recognize and obey. However, because people are not always willing or able to see that order, it is necessary that the Church bridges the gap to guarantee complete certainty for believers. While I understand the need for guidance and moral certainty, the claim that the gap between the divine order and a concrete situation can be filled by a general teaching of the Church can be questioned on various grounds. Following this line of thought, I will point to only one argument which is fundamental: claiming to bridge the gap in understanding with complete certainty would presuppose that the Church has a superhuman capacity of "seeing" God's order. This would presuppose direct revelation or verbal inspiration with regard to all moral questions. In contrast to this, on the practical level, all the other ways of establishing bridges of understanding fall under the hermeneutical and epistemological conditions described by Demmer. This means that they include the same historical conditionality and can exhibit the possibility of further changes.

Thus, once it is accepted that theoretical insight about (general) moral principles is at least to some degree conditioned by history, referring to God's objective moral order amounts to the same thing as referring to the moral order as described by human reason, to interpret the world and human beings in the light of the gospel. In other words, speaking of God's absolute moral order does not add to what is called a moral order established by natural law (understood in a non-naturalistic sense, which means under the condition of human recognition by reason at a given period of time) or simply a moral order established by moral reasoning in the context of Christian belief. Therefore, by referring to God's moral order, one does not receive further help to clarify doubts with respect to the moral order in the world. In other words, further judgments in the field of morality are needed that are made under the conditions of the limited human capacities to reflect, experience, and evaluate, in the light and context of faith.

As a result, we can conclude that even if we maintain a Platonic system of thought, and therefore claim that we can conceive of some order in the world, or if we talk about the law of nature in Stoic terms, we still need to draw on the interpretation of human reason to find out what the right order of acting might be. This means that there is no immediate influence of the concept of absolute truth on the outcome of concrete normative discussions in ethics that could avoid a series of interpretations and further practical judgments.

The requirement of interpretation had already been clearly identified in the medieval discussions on the relationship of theoretical and practical principles on the one hand, and ethical decision-making on the other. Duns Scotus, for instance, argued that the only principle deductible with scientific certainty from knowledge of God is that human beings should love Him. All further principles, according to Scotus, are not evident, but already refer to the level of human acquired knowledge.[29] This practical knowledge is regarded as *objective* (but not *absolute* because of its being dependent on human reasoning) when reason proposes it after a process of reflection. The human being is encouraged to approve of what reason tells him or her.

Having said this, it is clear that the only available practical knowledge is the knowledge provided by reason. The question whether this knowledge is objective knowledge (and not just subjective opinion or a result of moral construction) depends on the stand one takes in the discussion about moral realism in its different forms.[30] It also depends on presuppositions in philosophical anthropology as to whether human beings are driven by their instincts and passions alone or can use their reason objectively and therefore find themselves confronted with an objective moral truth, which is basic for every moral theory. These considerations allow us now to proceed and ask the question of how one can conceive of and define intrinsically evil acts with the help of moral reasoning.

INTENTION AND CIRCUMSTANCES AS COMPONENTS OF INTRINSICALLY EVIL ACTS

Against this backdrop of epistemological and hermeneutical reflections, I would like to accommodate the question of intrinsically evil acts in the general theory of morality that has been proposed by Peter Knauer and been followed up by Stephan Ernst.[31] Knauer developed the classical theory of the sources of morality and of the principle of double effect further, and Stephan Ernst adopted it for contemporary ethical questions. In his development of the theory, Ernst proposes that to declare an act to be morally right implies that the means applied are appropriate and not contraproductive with regard to the value that the act aims to realize. The means applied should help to pursue the value in a sustainable and impartial (therefore universal) way.[32] The intention and the circumstances that need to be observed in this case do not refer to personal motivation and feelings[33] or to the capacity of a specific human being to understand, which would be important for the evaluation of personal accountability. On the contrary, they refer to the objective situation, outcome, and consequences and confirm the universality of the claim that is being made. All these aspects form part of the act and are a necessary precondition for the determination of the "nature" or—in classical moral theological terms—the "object" of the act.

The term "intention" is usually used to refer to human persons who have specific aims in mind when they perform an act. An example for an act that can be carried out with different intentions taken from the discussion in the Middle Ages is giving money to a beggar. The same exterior act that in itself is a morally good act can turn to be bad when carried out because of a wrong intention, for example, to give a beggar money to gain glory.

At a general level however, "intentions" are not referring to the psychology of persons but to the aims of acts. They are an ingredient in the process of defining the object of an act. This difference between the aim pursued by a person and the aim of an act is reflected in Latin moral tradition in the distinction between *finis operis* (the aim of the act) and *finis operantis* (the aim of the agent). In the objective sense, the same physical act (giving money to someone) can, if respective intentions are included, become the core of acts of a different category and moral evaluation (help the poor, pay bribe money, pay salary). The two types of intentions can, but need not, fall together when a generally described act is put into concrete practice by a person.[34] Similarly, circumstances can be distinguished with respect to a personal and a general level. At a personal level, circumstances serve to understand whether a person can be fully held accountable for an act or not, for example, when someone did something wrong while he or she was under medication. On a general level, however, they refer to the cultural and historical situation in which the definition of a general act is formulated. For example, deforestation needed to be judged differently after its detrimental effects on the climate became known.

The complex and objective understanding of an act can also be applied when one tries to understand the nature of intrinsically evil acts. The species of intrinsically evil acts cannot be defined without reference to the general object of the act, and without regard to the general historical situation in which they are defined.[35] An example can illustrate the inherent complexity of what seems to be a simple, categorical, and universal moral command. The commandment not to kill, according to historical-critical exegesis, amounts to a commandment not to murder, which means to bring about the death of a member of the community with a mean intention, and leaving some other cases of "legitimate killing" out of consideration. Therefore, it is not surprising that the understanding of which acts fall under the commandment has changed over the centuries. It clearly allowed the killing of heretics and criminals during the Middle Ages and until very recently allowed the imposition of the death penalty under particular circumstances. When Pope Francis ordered to reject the death penalty in the *Catechism*, where it was previously portrayed as acceptable under certain conditions, he did so because today we presuppose that in the circumstances of our times, the death penalty is no longer an appropriate means to pursue the intention of saving the stability of a society. In addition, it affirms that the dignity of a human person also refers to one who is a criminal.[36] With regard to the dignity of human persons and the protection of human life, Pope Francis argues that some societies apply capital punishment without necessity and therefore without a justifying reason. The historical situation colors the acceptance of the death penalty in the *Catechism* or in state law with the shadow of revenge or even despotism instead of the light of justice.

Pope Francis's order to change the Catechism shows that an act that had not fallen under the verdict of the fifth commandment will be subsumed under it in the future. The moral character of the death penalty can change due to a change in social conditions and a new judgment about the way in which the value of safety in society can be pursued in a sustainable way. It also includes a new, positive interpretation of the criminal's dignity and basic right to life. A recent message by the Catholic news agency stated that the Sri Lankan Cardinal Malcolm Ranjith justified the decision of President Maithripala Sirisena to enact the death penalty against drug dealers who are already condemned to death and still organizing their criminal activities.[37] This took place after the first intervention by Pope Francis and demonstrates that circumstances do play a role when it comes to determining the object of an act, even where intrinsically evil acts are concerned, and that there is a need of moral reasoning even in these cases.[38] It is clear that the core issue (to protect the life of a human person) remains the same, but the immediate understanding of its application with respect to persons convicted of a serious crime is changing. In Europe, moral arguments against the death penalty can be traced back a couple of centuries, so a process of gradual expansion of this criticism, together with the development of the idea of human dignity, has resulted in the extension of the field of application of the universal principle not to kill.

By applying these considerations and developments, I would like to summarize, in a first step, that intrinsically evil acts obviously are a small group of moral acts that describe universal moral principles, formulated negatively at an intermediate level of generality and interdicting categorically. They refer to an existential knowledge about the value of human life and human relationships. According to moral reasoning, they cannot be pursued in a morally good way because the intention that determines the "object" is counter-productive against the background of the general circumstances within a universal moral perspective. The obvious question is, of course, What is the distinctive property that makes some morally wrong acts intrinsically evil acts?

HOW DO INTRINSICALLY EVIL ACTS
DIFFER FROM MORALLY WRONG ACTS?

The aforementioned definition of intrinsically evil acts does not establish a clear distinction between such acts and morally wrong acts. This is correct as long as morally wrong acts are regarded on a general level,[39] without reference to the concrete act which would entail the concrete circumstances of the agent. If we want to distinguish the group of morally wrong acts that we would call "intrinsically evil" from other morally wrong acts, we need to go a step further. First, we can recall that intrinsically evil acts are supposed to be so general that they can be used as categorical commandments and stand out as lighthouses for directing moral behavior. This means that they cannot be concrete norms, but need to stay at an intermediate level.

In an attempt to evaluate a concrete act, we usually try to establish a relationship between this concrete act and general principles (do good, avoid evil) as well as with the intermediate principles that are more specific (do not kill). In the process of evaluating the act in relation to intermediate principles we confirm either that the concrete act falls under the intermediate principle and that the intermediate principle encompasses the concrete act, or we detect that the intermediate principle does not apply in these sets of circumstances. This can be illustrated with the following example. As an intermediate principle that is foundational for order in a society because it protects intimate relationships and families, there is the commandment "do not commit adultery." While the Levirate marriage was an obligation in Old Testament times, we would interpret the act of taking my brother's widow as second wife as an act opposing this intermediate principle.

Another practical example from current discussions raises the question whether sexual acts in a second marriage after divorce fall under the commandment against adultery. The contemporary context of this question serves as an interesting example of how a general principle (the commandment) may no longer apply. In relation to this, we can refer to a consideration made by different popes and theologians in the context of the discussion about the admission of divorced and remarried Catholics to the Holy Eucharist. In the documents of the Church, there is an acknowledgment of the situation of persons living in a second marriage who have moral obligations because of children born into that relationship. It has been argued that this situation diminishes the gravity of the sin, because they cannot leave behind their second marriage without committing an equally grave sin.

Theologians have raised the question whether this situation not only diminishes the gravity of that sin, but also leads to a new understanding of the entire moral situation. Is it possible that once a marriage has definitely been broken and divorced, sexual acts in a second marriage need not be seen as falling under the category of adultery because the object of the act differs?[40]

While the Church documents' argument is based on the level of accountability for sin at a personal level, thus stating that the general norm applies to these situations, many theologians consider intention and circumstances at a general level that define the morality of the act itself. They therefore question whether the command "do not commit adultery" can be applied to the acts of a sexual relationship within a second marriage, as has Pope Francis.

ARE INTRINSICALLY EVIL ACTS FORMALLY OR REALLY BAD?

This brings us back to the question of the relationship between formality and content in intrinsically evil acts. As we have seen, the definition of "intrinsically evil acts" in *Veritatis Splendor* is associated with formal characteristics, negatively formulated and categorically wrong. It therefore already contains the negative moral judgment in its verbal expression (as in murder, adultery and theft), and such things are always forbidden. This is considered to be "moral knowledge" that persons are presumed to possess. But where does this presupposed moral knowledge come from?

I suggest that this moral knowledge comes from a judgment in the past that, at the time, was thought to be a means of protecting the worth and dignity of human beings, the necessary conditions for their flourishing, and the knowledge and experience of what damages that flourishing. However, if we consider intrinsically evil acts as a category that is only defined formally, we could provide other examples of acts that can be formulated containing a negative moral judgment which would imply that they are categorically forbidden. Suppose we suggest that it is intrinsically evil to kill an animal "just for fun." By adding the intention "just for fun," this definition would not exclude any justifying circumstances for killing animals, such as perceived threats from the animal or appropriately culling an overpopulated group of animals.

It could be suggested, and a significant number of responsible people agree, that killing "for fun" makes the act categorically evil and hence equivalent to unlawful killing, at least at the level of formality. But would we name it "intrinsically evil"? Perhaps ironically, in the current state of Western culture, which is supposedly dominated by Christian tradition and scientific approaches to nature, many would judge the killing of an animal for fun as marginal, at least as long as the life of human beings does not depend on the animal. Few people would speak about these kinds of acts as intrinsically evil even though they believe that they are categorically evil. From this example we can also conclude that acts referred to as intrinsically evil would not necessarily need to be of an extreme moral gravity if we regarded only the formal characteristics of intermediate principles and negative moral judgment, without referring to their content.

Obviously, the formal characteristics are not enough to describe what the category of an intrinsically evil act stands for. Rather we first and foremost refer to acts as intrinsically evil if they seriously damage the dignity of a human person or destroy the very fundaments of human life. For example, one can easily argue that sexual abuse is an example of an intrinsically evil act because it is obvious that it contradicts the dignity of a human person and the basics of human relationship.[41]

While this explanation stresses the dignity of the person that is acted upon, an alternative explanation has been proposed by Stephan Herzberg in this volume. When pointing to the interesting fact that Aristotle holds murder, adultery, and theft as categorical moral norms, Herzberg proposes a strong reading of this affirmation by saying that these are moral universals and the acts are bad in themselves because they damage the agent's soul through committing them. The consequence would be that they have to do with the nature of human beings and therefore are understandable by everybody. Thus, committing them would not only bring about damage to someone else but also to one's own understanding of oneself as a moral (and therefore human) person.

A DEFINITION OF INTRINSICALLY EVIL ACTS AS A WORKING TOOL FOR TODAY'S USE

In summary, we can formulate the following definition as a working tool for further reflection on this topic: Intrinsically evil acts are a group of moral acts that are formulated in a categorical way at the level of intermediate principles. According to their description, they cannot be pursued in a morally good way because the intention that determines the "object" is already judged as counterproductive against the background of the circumstances and the outcome perceived from a universal moral perspective. The group is defined, in addition to other morally wrong acts, by its content that is related to the destruction of the fundaments of human life and human relationship.

In this way, we would see intrinsically evil acts as a very small group of morally wrong acts that are to be avoided scrupulously because they concern the very fundaments of human life and social living. They would protect fundamental values such as human life itself which is a precondition for all other moral values. Their categorical use can be advocated because the defended basic values (life, human relationship) are universal in the sense that they are existentially known to human beings and are also philosophically defendable by reason. They can therefore be supposed to be acknowledgeable by everyone. Their strength—being sufficiently general, limited to the essentials, and referring to something already known—is also their weakness, since other, individual concrete acts and their circumstances cannot always be directly subsumed under the general principle.

The question remains: What would theological ethics lose if it did not use the term anymore? I believe it can be argued—as has been done in a couple of contributions to this book—that for educating human beings morally, at least at a certain age and personal maturity, teaching in the language of the Ten Commandments is not always adequate. What is needed is more positive moral authorship (and not simply the avoidance of error and guilt). Yet, there are other fields, often related to legal discussions in modern society, in which the language of defending the basic fundaments of all ethical discussions may benefit from such categorizations as "intrinsically evil." This can be very useful when established human rights are endangered and the fundaments of human life and flourishing find themselves subordinate to other interests. Of course, the countereffect can be provoked when the term is being used without acknowledging its "weak sides" and when the claims are made too quickly in cases when doubts are legitimate as to whether concrete acts fall under the general rule.[42]

NOTES

1. See the contribution of James Bretzke, "Intrinsic Evil in *Veritatis Splendor* and Two Contemporary Debates," in this volume.

2. See entry "Evil," in *Concise Oxford English Dictionary*, 12th ed., eds. Angus Stevenson and Maurice Waite (Oxford: Oxford University Press, 2011), 494–95.

3. Ibid.

4. Joseph Selling's appreciated intent to distinguish the moral words evil, bad, and wrong more clearly for the purpose of a more exact use of these, in which he proposes to use evil for the "morally neutral (descriptive)" meaning, would not be directly transferable into German (*Reframing Catholic Theological Ethics* [Oxford: Oxford University Press 2016], 173).

5. Mathew R. McWhorter, "Intrinsic Moral Evils in the Middle Ages: Augustine as a Source of the Theological Doctrine," *Studies in Christian Ethics* 29 (2016): 413, refers to the difference made by William of Auxerre between acts that are intrinsically evil morally (*malum in se*) and those acts that are in addition carried out with libidinous desire, which means with an intention to divert from God—these acts are called *malum secundum se* and cannot be dispensed of by God.

6. John Paul II, "Veritatis Splendor," accessed June 10, 2018, http://w2.vatican.va/content/john-paul-ii/en/encyclicals/documents/hf_jp-ii_enc_06081993_veritatis-splendor.html,   80 (with reference to *Gaudium et Spes*, 27): "Whatever is hostile to life itself, such as any kind of homicide, genocide, abortion, euthanasia and voluntary suicide; whatever violates the integrity of the human person, such as mutilation, physical and mental torture and attempts to coerce the spirit; whatever is offensive to human dignity, such as subhuman living conditions, arbitrary imprisonment, deportation, slavery, prostitution and trafficking in women and children; degrading conditions of work which treat laborers as mere instruments of profit, and not as free responsible persons: all these and the like are a disgrace, and so long as they infect human civilization they contaminate those who inflict them more than those who suffer injustice, and they are a negation of the honor due to the Creator."

7. I would like to express my gratitude to Nenad Polgar and Joseph A. Selling for their critical and very stimulating comments.

8. For the reception of the respective ideas developed by German moral theorists like Knauer and Fuchs in the American context of the discussion on moral absolutes see Mathew R. McWhorter, "Intrinsic Moral Evils," 409–23.

9. Peter Knauer, "Zur Lehre von den 'Fontes moralitatis' im Katechismus der Katholischen Kirche," *Theologie und Glaube* 95 (2005): 451–62, points at the difficulties related to determining the different sources and their relationship.

10. The Holy See, "Catechism of the Catholic Church," accessed June 11, 2018, http://www.vatican.va/archive/ENG0015/_INDEX.HTM#fonte, 1857. Cf. Paolo Carlotti, "L'intrinsece malum e la *Veritatis Splendor*," in *Divinarum rerum notitia. La teologia tra filosofia e storia. Studi in onore del Cardinale Walter Kasper*, eds. Antonio Russo and Gianfranco Coffele (Rome: Edizioni Studium, 2001), 141.

11. Stephan Ernst, "'Irreguläre Situationen' und persönliche Schuld in *Amoris laetitia*. Ein Bruch mit der Tradition?" in *Amoris laetitia—Wendepunkt für die Moraltheologie?*, eds. Stephan Goertz and Caroline Witting (Freiburg/Basel/Wien: Herder, 2016), 145. On page 149, Ernst refers to *VS*, 70 in order to show that the encyclical confirms this difference between the act and personal accountability.

12. In this sense, the encyclical *Veritatis Splendor* describes intrinsically evil acts as being categorized because of their object that is obviously seriously wrong: John Paul II, "Veritatis Splendor," 80: "[. . .] the Church teaches that 'there exist acts which *per se* and in themselves', independently of circumstances, are always *seriously wrong* by reason of their object." (Italics by author)

13. Ibid., 67: "But the negative moral precepts, those prohibiting certain concrete actions or kinds of behavior as intrinsically evil, do not allow for any legitimate exception. They do not leave room, in any morally acceptable way, for the 'creativity' of any contrary determination whatsoever."

14. See the contribution of James Bretzke in this volume.

15. John Paul II, "Veritatis Splendor," 79: "[. . .] *to qualify as morally evil according to its species*—its 'object'—*the deliberate choice of certain kinds of behavior or specific acts* [. . .]."

16. The encyclical uses the term absolute in many different contexts. It speaks of absolute truth with regard to God, and uses the phrase "absolute moral norms" especially when it contrasts deontological ethics with teleological ethics. Ibid., 75. For a detailed discussion see Werner Wolbert, "Die 'in sich schlechten' Handlungen und der Konsequentialismus," in *Moraltheologie im Abseits? Antwort auf die Enzyklika 'Veritatis Splendor,'* ed. Dietmar Mieth (Freiburg/Basel/Wien: Herder, 1994), 88–109.

17. John Paul II, "Veritatis Splendor," 67: "Once the moral species of an action prohibited by a universal rule is *concretely recognized*, the only morally good act is that of obeying the moral law and of refraining from the action which it forbids." (Italics by author)

18. Klaus Demmer, "Erwägungen zum 'intrinsece malum,'" *Gregorianum* 68, nos. 3–4 (1987): 614. See also p. 618 where he criticizes "hidden 'metaphysization' of moral truth and the use of juridical categories that distort the precision of moral standards."

19. The notion of principle is equivocal, since we can speak of moral values and virtues also as of moral principles, for example, justice, impartiality. For the present discussion, referring to moral principles means referring to the incomplete norms that are formulated in the Decalogue, which we can locate between pure principles and the formal principle of practical reason (do good, avoid evil) and concrete moral norms.

20. Here I interpret Demmer's phrase along the words used in VS. Demmer says literally: "The transition from Noumenon to Phainomenon does not pose the problem, but the immanent historicity of this process. The essence is created historically. Reason discovers and constitutes in one act." (English translation of the German text). Demmer, "Erwägungen," 615.

21. Ibid.

22. Ibid., 616.

23. Matthias Köckert, "Dekalog / Zehn Gebote (AT)," in *Das wissenschaftliche Bibellexikon im Internet (WiBiLex)*, accessed June 15, 2018, https://www.bibelwissenschaft.de/stichwort/10637/.

24. See, for example, Carlotti, "L'intrinsece malum," 155–58 with reference to the change in the Church's teaching about the deportation of Jews, torture of heretics, and slavery.

25. For an account of Aristotle's ethics with respect to intrinsically evil acts see the contribution of Stephan Herzberg in this volume. He points to the interesting fact that Aristotle holds murder, adultery and theft for universal moral norms, in spite of his teleological line of ethical thought.

26. Maryanne C. Horowitz, "The Stoic Synthesis of the Idea of Natural Law in Man: Four Themes," *Journal of the History of Ideas* 35, no. 1 (1974): 9, referring to Epictetus who was the only Stoic who saw these moral preconceptions as innate.

27. As an example, Aquinas, in his *Summa Theologiae*, I–II, q. 100 codefines moral commands contained in the Decalogue, such as to honor one's parents, not to kill or to steal, as deductible from human natural reason and therefore as part of the natural law. Other more detailed norms, such as how to honor the elderly, he argues, need some further instruction and cannot be directly deducted. Thomas Aquinas, "Summa Theologiae," accessed June 10, 2018, https://dhspriory.org/thomas/summa/index.html. For a detailed analysis of the tradition on intrinsically evil acts see Nenad Polgar, *The Origins, Meaning, and Relevance of the Concept of Intrinsic Evil* (forthcoming). See also Kevin G. Long, "The Nine Commandments: The Decalogue and the Natural Law," *The Aquinas Review* 3 (1996): 145.

28. In his contribution to this volume Bretzke argues "that only God can fully and completely grasp the objective moral order, just as it exists in both the abstract and the concrete." James T. Bretzke, "Intrinsic Evil in *Veritatis Splendor* and Two Contemporary Debates," this volume, 60.

29. Allan B. Wolter and Frank A. William, *Duns Scotus on the Will and Morality* (Washington, DC: The Catholic University of America Press, 1997), 276; Duns Scotus, *Ordinatio*, III, d. 37, q un.

30. For an account of realism see Kevin M. DeLapp, *Moral Realism* (London/New York: Bloomsbury, 2013).

31. Peter Knauer, *Handlungsnetze. Über das Grundprinzip der Ethik* (Frankfurt a.M.: Books on Demand GmbH., 2002) pursues a new interpretation of the classical theory of double effect. A summary of his theory on three pages is "Nichtreligiöse Ethikbegründung und christlicher Glaube," *Orientierung* 67 (2003): 124–26. His initial idea was published in English in 1967: Id., "The Hermeneutical Function of the Principle of Double Effect," *Natural Law Forum* 12 (1967): 132–62. Ernst has applied Knauer's line of argument in several journal articles, some of which will be quoted in later footnotes.

32. Stephan Ernst, "Pluralität und Verbindlichkeit sittlicher Werte," *Stimmen der Zeit* 8 (2017): 528.

33. Ibid., 527.

34. Demmer therefore concludes that the object normally decides about the morality of an act, but that there must be exceptions, especially when additional final causes are added. In this case, the intention of the agent is relevant for the moral judgment of the act. See Klaus Demmer, *Fundamentale Theologie des Ethischen* (Fribourg/Freiburg i.Br./Wien: Herder, 1999), 276.

35. The reference to the "general circumstances," which is nothing but the hermeneutical principle that we need to take historical contexts into account when we interpret reasoning, is not part of Knauer's and Ernst's ethical theory, but presents a prerequisite that I want to point out in order to explain the changes that can be observed. See p. 76 of this chapter.

36. Pope Francis's order to change the Catechism was announced by the *National Catholic Reporter* on August 2, 2018 in an article by Cindy Wooden, "Breaking: Pope revises catechism to say death penalty is 'inadmissible,'" accessed August 4, 2018, https://www.archbalt.org/pope-revises-catechism-to-say-death-penalty-is-inadmissible/. This decision was a consequence of what the Pope said in his "Address of His Holiness Pope Franciscus to Participants in the Meeting Promoted by the Pontifical Council for Promoting the New Evangelization," accessed July 20, 2018, http://w2.vatican.va/content/francesco/en/speeches/2017/october/documents/papa-francesco_20171011_convegno-nuova-evangelizzazione.html: "[. . .] In past centuries, when means of defense were scarce and society had yet to develop and mature as it has, recourse to the death penalty appeared to be the logical consequence of the correct application of justice. Sadly, even in the Papal States recourse was had to this extreme and inhumane remedy that ignored the primacy of mercy over justice. Let us take responsibility for the past

and recognize that the imposition of the death penalty was dictated by a mentality more legalistic than Christian. Concern for preserving power and material wealth led to an overestimation of the value of the law and prevented a deeper understanding of the Gospel. Nowadays, however, were we to remain neutral before the new demands of upholding personal dignity, we would be even more guilty. Here we are not in any way contradicting past teaching, for the defense of the dignity of human life from the first moment of conception to natural death has been taught by the Church consistently and authoritatively. Yet the harmonious development of doctrine demands that we cease to defend arguments that now appear clearly contrary to the new understanding of Christian truth. Indeed, as Saint Vincent of Lérins pointed out, "Some may say: Shall there be no progress of religion in Christ's Church? Certainly; all possible progress. For who is there, so envious of men, so full of hatred to God, who would seek to forbid it?" (Commonitorium, 23.1; PL 50). It is necessary, therefore, to reaffirm that no matter how serious the crime that has been committed, the death penalty is inadmissible because it is an attack on the inviolability and the dignity of the person." The address was held remembering the twenty-fifth anniversary of the publication of the *Catechism of the Catholic Church*, as the title of the German and Spanish versions of this text state.

37. "Sri Lanka: Kardinal Ranjith begrüßt Todesstrafe für Drogendealer," *Kathnet*, July 13, 2018, https://redaktion.kathpress.at/action/kpprod/download?&p=5981&c=2f92.

38. How difficult such a change is, becomes apparent when one reads Steven A. Long's account of Aquinas's argument for the death penalty and its application to today. Steven A. Long, *The Teleological Grammar of the Moral Act* (Naples, FL: Sapientia Press, 2007), esp. 61–62.

39. See Bretzke, "Intrinsic Evil," 57–58.

40. This argument obviously presupposes a change in the understanding of the sacramental bond that is no longer understood as a metaphysical bond that remains even when the concrete mutual relationship and love as *materia* of the sacramental bond have vanished. For the argument and further bibliography see Ernst, "'Irreguläre Situationen,'" 157–59. For the difficulty of cutting the Gordian knot of ethical, canonical, and dogmatic approaches with regard to this matter see Sigrid Müller, "Die Entflechtung des Gordischen Knotens. Zur Stärkung der Rolle der Moraltheologie durch Amoris laetitia," *Studia Teologiczno-Historyczne Śląsja Opolskiego* 37, no. 1 (2017): 79–103, doi: 10.25167/RTSO/37(2017)1/79-103.

41. Sigrid Müller, "Der Schutz von Minderjährigen vor sexuellem Missbrauch," *Münchener Theologische Zeitschrift* 62, no. 1 (2011): 22–32.

42. Peter Knauer, "Was bedeutet in sich schlecht?," in *Ethik der Lebensfelder, Festschrift für Philipp Schmitz SJ*, ed. by Paul Chummar Chittilappilli, CMI (Freiburg/Basel/Wien: Herder, 2010), 29–43. On p. 43 he warns that a deontological argument that does not pose the question whether a reason for approving of causing or tolerating damage is adequate would be problematic. This would come down to claiming that every killing is murder. Such an unqualified use of the term would cause immense confusion. Nicholas Lash has shown that this danger is present in some passages of *Veritatis Splendor* (Nicholas Lash, "Teaching in Crisis," in *Considering Veritatis Splendor*, ed. John Wilkins [Cleveland, OH: The Pilgrim Press, 1994], 27–34).

REFERENCES

Aquinas, Thomas. "Summa Theologiae." Accessed June 10, 2018. https://dhspriory.org/thomas/summa/index.html.

Carlotti, Paolo. "L'intrinsece malum e la *Veritatis Splendor*." In *Divinarum rerum notitia. La teologia tra filosofia e storia. Studi in onore del Cardinale Walter Kasper*, edited by Antonio Russo and Gianfranco Coffele, 144–69. Rome: Edizioni Studium, 2001.

DeLapp, Kevin M. *Moral Realism*. London/New York: Bloomsbury, 2013.

Demmer, Klaus. "Erwägungen zum 'intrinsece malum.'" *Gregorianum* 68, nos. 3–4 (1987): 613–37.

———. *Fundamentale Theologie des Ethischen*. Fribourg/Freiburg i.Br./Wien: Herder, 1999.

Ernst, Stephan. "'Irreguläre Situationen' und persönliche Schuld in *Amoris laetitia*. Ein Bruch mit der Tradition?" In *Amoris laetitia—Wendepunkt für die Moraltheologie?*, edited by Stephan Goertz and Caroline Witting, 136–59. Freiburg/Basel/Wien: Herder, 2016.

The Holy See. "Catechism of the Catholic Church." Accessed June 11, 2018. http://www.vatican.va/archive/ENG0015/_INDEX.HTM#fonte.

Horowitz, Maryanne C. "Pluralität und Verbindlichkeit sittlicher Werte." *Stimmen der Zeit* 8 (2017): 518–30.

———. "The Stoic Synthesis of the Idea of Natural Law in Man: Four Themes." *Journal of the History of Ideas* 35, no. 1 (1974): 3–16.

John Paul II. "Veritatis Splendor." Accessed June 10, 2018. http://w2.vatican.va/content/john-paul-ii/en/encyclicals/documents/hf_jp-ii_enc_06081993_veritatis-splendor.html.

Knauer, Peter. *Handlungsnetze. Über das Grundprinzip der Ethik.* Frankfurt a.M.: Books on Demand GmbH., 2002.

———. "The Hermeneutical Function of the Principle of Double Effect." *Natural Law Forum* 12 (1967): 132–62.

———. "Nichtreligiöse Ethikbegründung und christlicher Glaube." *Orientierung* 67 (2003): 124–26.

———. "Was bedeutet in sich schlecht?" In *Ethik der Lebensfelder, Festschrift für Philipp Schmitz SJ*, edited by Paul Chummar Chittilappilli, CMI, 29–43. Freiburg/Basel/Wien: Herder, 2010.

———. "Zur Lehre von den 'Fontes moralitatis' im Katechismus der Katholischen Kirche." *Theologie und Glaube* 95 (2005): 451–62.

Köckert, Matthias. "Dekalog / Zehn Gebote (AT)." In *Das wissenschaftliche Bibellexikon im Internet (WiBiLex)*. Accessed June 15, 2018. https://www.bibelwissenschaft.de/stichwort/10637/.

Lash, Nicholas. "Teaching in Crisis." In *Considering Veritatis Splendor*, edited by John Wilkins, 27–34. Cleveland, OH: The Pilgrim Press, 1994.

Long, Kevin G. "The Nine Commandments: The Decalogue and the Natural Law." *The Aquinas Review* 3 (1996): 137–52.

Long, Steven A. *The Teleological Grammar of the Moral Act.* Naples, FL: Sapientia Press, 2007.

McWhorter, Mathew R. "Intrinsic Moral Evils in the Middle Ages: Augustine as a Source of the Theological Doctrine." *Studies in Christian Ethics* 29 (2016): 409–23.

Müller, Sigrid. "Der Schutz von Minderjährigen vor sexuellem Missbrauch." *Münchener Theologische Zeitschrift* 62, no. 1 (2011): 22–32.

———. "Die Entflechtung des Gordischen Knotens. Zur Stärkung der Rolle der Moraltheologie durch Amoris laetitia." *Studia Teologiczno-Historyczne Śląsja Opolskiego* 37, no. 1 (2017): 79–103. doi: 10.25167/RTSO/37(2017)1/79-103.

Polgar, Nenad. *The Origins, Meaning, and Relevance of the Concept of Intrinsic Evil* (forthcoming).

Pope Francis. "Address of His Holiness Pope Franciscus to Participants in the Meeting Promoted by the Pontifical Council for Promoting the New Evangelization." Accessed July 20, 2018. http://w2.vatican.va/content/francesco/en/speeches/2017/october/documents/papa-francesco_20171011_convegno-nuova-evangelizazione.html.

Selling, Joseph. *Reframing Catholic Theological Ethics.* Oxford: Oxford University Press 2016.

"Sri Lanka: Kardinal Ranjith begrüßt Todesstrafe für Drogendealer." *Kathnet*, July 13, 2018. https://redaktion.kathpress.at/action/kpprod/download?andp=5981andc=2f92.

Stevenson, Angus, and Maurice Waite, eds. *Concise Oxford English Dictionary.* 12th ed. Oxford: Oxford University Press, 2011.

Wolbert, Werner. "Die 'in sich schlechten' Handlungen und der Konsequentialismus." In *Moraltheologie im Abseits? Antwort auf die Enzyklika 'Veritatis Splendor,'* edited by Dietmar Mieth, 88–109. Freiburg/Basel/Wien: Herder, 1994.

Wolter, Allan B., and Frank A. William. *Duns Scotus on the Will and Morality.* Washington, DC: The Catholic University of America Press, 1997.

Part IV

The Concept of Intrinsic Evil in Fundamental Theological Ethics

Chapter Seven

The Naming of Evil in Fundamental Theological Ethics

Joseph A. Selling

Moral theology is a discipline that is rather specific to Roman Catholic Christianity. Most non-Catholic Christians make use of various approaches to moral philosophy, but the Bible remains the primary source of moral preaching and decision-making. In the second half of the last century many moral theologians began adapting the designation of their discipline to be "theological ethics."[1] One of the reasons for this is the admission that much of the discipline is built upon principles that have little or nothing to do with revelation. Classic textbook moral theology, for instance, relied heavily on an interpretation of Thomas Aquinas who based a good deal of his ethical theory on Aristotle. The justification for this approach was the presumption that since God was the creator of heaven and earth, one could come to know God's will by "reading" the patterns that emerged from creation itself.[2]

The Catholic tradition has come to distinguish "fundamental" from "special" theological ethics. The latter refers to "special questions" such as social ethics, sexual ethics, environmental ethics, and so forth. The former studies the way in which one constructs an ethical way of thinking. How, for instance, does one go about making ethical evaluations; what is necessary to consider in order to create a sufficient basis for decision-making; or what are the criteria for determining good and evil? Fundamental theological ethics also explores how we use terminology (e.g., the difference between "good" and "right"), how we understand the decision-making process, and how we prioritize the various elements in that process (e.g., intention, activity, and consequences). This is generally referred to as an ethical method, the study of which is "methodology."

When Aquinas constructed his ethical method in the *Summa Theologiae* (ST), I–II, he began by describing the ultimate end of ethical living (qq. 1–5), which he called beatitude. He then presented the basic elements of functioning in an ethical way by describing the nature of voluntary acts and the circumstances that surround them; for in order to be moral, a human act must be voluntary (qq. 6–7). He followed this with an exposition of the primary instance of voluntary activity which is "internal" and includes volition, intention, and, after one's end is reached, enjoyment (qq. 8–12). Only after this did he turn his attention to external activity influenced by the interplay of reason and will through counsel, consent, choice, command, and performance (qq. 13–17). Finally, he described how we should evaluate human, voluntary activity, telling us that each of the elements has its place, but keeping in mind that it is the interior act of the will that first specifies the morality of the entire event (qq. 18–21).[3]

When moral theology became defined as a distinct theological discipline, after the Council of Trent, it was constructed to prepare priests to hear confessions. Although various forms of confessing one's sins to a priest existed before the council, there was a need to standardize the practice so that every priest followed the same procedure and understood what constitutes a sin. After a short, initial exchange with the penitent, the first thing that the priest hears in confession is the penitent's enumeration of the sins they believe they committed. In some cases, when the priest is not sure about the nature or the gravity of the sin, he might ask the penitent to describe some aspect(s) of what took place. This introduced the relevance of circumstances. Then, if the priest was still attempting to determine the level of engagement on the part of the penitent, he might inquire about the motive for doing or omitting whatever the penitent had confessed as a sin.

What Aquinas did was to describe *the process of ethical living and decision-making*. It starts with a person whose virtuous or vicious disposition motivates them to achieve an end that is respectively good or bad. It then goes through the steps of attempting to achieve that end in a concrete, external manner (through action or omission). We might schematize this by observing that he begins with the end, then surveys the various factors influencing concrete activity (circumstances), and lastly considers the kind of activity that might be performed to accomplish one's end.

end — circumstances — activity

What the moral theology constructed to help priests hear confessions did was to reverse this process. It began with a moral judgment about activities or omissions that are reported by the penitent. Recognizing that ethical activity is complex, the priest who may be attempting to ascertain a more detailed picture of what the penitent is reporting as sins may very well inquire about the circumstances of each commission of a sin. He may also eventually probe the reasons why the person pursued such a course of activity. We can schematize this by observing that this approach begins with the description and judgment of an activity, then surveys the various factors that may have influenced that activity (circumstances), and then optionally asks what may have motivated a person to act in such a manner.

activity — circumstances — end

Between the Council of Trent and Vatican II, the traditional method of analyzing and teaching morality stressed the main focus on human activity that was judged to be immoral, or sinful. It was believed that this could be done without any consideration of the persons performing those activities. Inquiry with respect to the circumstances of the activity or the penitent's motives (present in their intention), could increase or decrease the gravity of the sin or the level of the penitent's guilt. But they could not affect the initial judgment about the sinfulness of the activity itself.

For instance, stealing was understood always to be a sin, but it was a greater sin to steal from a poor person than it was to steal from a rich person. How much or how little was stolen also had a bearing on the accountability (guilt) of the sinner. The person's motive for stealing could mitigate some of that guilt, as when a person stole bread to feed their family, but the violation of the seventh commandment was still a sin. While this last example might appear to indicate that pre-conciliar moral theology was particularly rigid, at least part of this is traceable to the presumption that one could define evil, sinful activity with a single word or phrase, such as murder, stealing, or lying; and in the area of sexual ethics, masturbation, fornication, or homosexual acts. These "things" were considered so obviously sinful, that they were sometimes referred to as "intrinsically evil" because it was impossible to think of a human situation in which they could be performed without being "an objective sin."[4] This, however, is a point where confusion set in.

Linguistic and Ethical Confusion

While the declaration that some things are intrinsically evil may sound simple, (one of) the question(s) that exposes its convolution could be: does every activity that involves some kind of evil necessarily have to be immoral? In place of talking about murder, stealing, and lying, we could ask whether it is always immoral to kill someone, to take the property of another without their permission, or to say something that actually deceives another person? Before answering that question (which would probably take the form of, "It depends on . . ."), let's ask: what is the difference between murder and killing someone, between stealing and taking the property of another without their permission, and between lying and saying something that actually deceives another person? Materially speaking, there is no difference at all. We end up with a dead body, an item that has changed hands from its owner to someone not its owner, and a person who has been deceived. There has got to be something else hidden in the terminology of always immoral (intrinsic evil) that takes it beyond the level of physical, material activities or omissions.

That "something else" has to be either a circumstance or a specific intention, but not the material activity (killing [a person], taking [another's property], or deceiving [a person]) itself. All of these material acts clearly contain something that we refer to as evil: death, dispossession, and deception. Yet we read in *Veritatis Splendor*, 79,

> *One must therefore reject the thesis*, characteristic of teleological and proportionalist theories, *which holds that it is impossible to qualify as morally evil according to its species—its "object"—the deliberate choice of certain kinds of behavior or specific acts, apart from a consideration of the intention*[5] *for which the choice is made or the totality of the foreseeable consequences of that act for all persons concerned.* (emphasis in original)

It is clear that the author of *Veritatis Splendor*[6] was focusing on "kinds of behavior or specific acts." That was the primary concern, just like it was in the tradition of the moral theological textbooks. It describes the procedure of moral decision-making as if the choice of a particular behavior or act is precisely what that person wants: the person desires it and aims at its realization. But is this a valid meaning for making a "deliberate choice"? Common human experience reveals that we all make "deliberate choices" that we may neither want nor desire. We "deliberately choose" to ingest things that taste horrible because we hope that they will bring us some benefit. We make "deliberate choices" to omit ingesting things we might very much want and desire to eat because it seems like the best way to improve our health and fitness.

What has happened here is that the author has confused the meaning of intending and choosing. If we again look at the method suggested by Aquinas, the first act of the will is the interior act of intention. It is at this point that the person formulates a commitment to pursue an end or goal. Once one has established where they want (desire, wish) to arrive, they have a measure for determining which course of activity they might choose for doing so. One cannot make decisions about "means" before one knows precisely which ends those means are meant to achieve.

When the text quoted above refers to "the intention for which the choice is made," it makes no reference to an end or goal to be reached. "Intention" here might refer to experiencing pleasure, as in, '"I intend to eat that piece of cake because it tastes good." In fact, outside of a disciplined use of language, as should be found in theological ethics, "intention" can mean just about anything. The way that the word is used in the encyclical has no substantive meaning. This is somewhat confusing, for if the intention is not the focal point of consideration, by what standard would one evaluate any activity—means to an end—at all?

Referring to a "deliberate choice" is made to sound like an intentional commitment. However, to deliberate about something is merely to consider or think about it.[7] Relatively few ends can be reached in only one, exclusive manner. Most ends can be achieved in any number of ways, usually related to the person seeking that end, their life circumstances, their resources, their talents, the urgency, the consequences of one way versus another, and so forth. Deliberation is a matter of judgment, not commitment. Choice, by its very definition, implies considering a number of things. Saying that a choice is "deliberate" doesn't mean that it was intended or wanted but rather that the choice was something that the person examined and thought about before making a decision.

Dealing with Evil in Human Activity

When *Veritatis Splendor* was promulgated in 1993, I remember a colleague observing that apparently the Church had just taken a radical turn toward pacifism. For if the above statement applies to each and every "certain kind of behavior or specific act" that involves an evil, the Church would have to reverse its position on the issues of self-defense, just war, legitimate taxation, and the famous escape route referred to as "mental reservation."[8]

Of course this was not to be the case. Traditional moral theology had created "principles" to deal with the presence of evil in human activity, such as the "principle of totality" and the "principle of double effect" (PDE). The aim of these principles was to keep "evil" as far away from human intentionality as possible. It did this by pretending that any evil being dealt with was brought about only "indirectly," as an effect or consequence of doing something good. But precisely what does "indirect" mean? Does it apply to all the effects or consequences of human activity? One of the ways of understanding the PDE is sketched in figure 7.1 below.

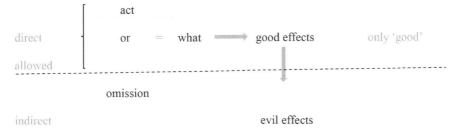

Figure 7.1.   The structure of traditional moral theological analysis.

Common sense would appear to suggest that all the "effects" of an act would be indirect, but the PDE existed for the very purpose of demonstrating that the acting person did not actually "bring about an evil." Peter Knauer suggested back in 1967 that identifying something as indirect has more to do with it being evil than it being an effect.[9]

The fatal flaw in the use of this principle is that it takes the act, "what is done or omitted," as the starting point of its argumentation. Consider an alternative approach drawn from Aquinas's understanding of the structure of the moral event presented in figure 7.2.

He begins with the importance of the intention-to-an-end (I–II, qq. 8–12). Persons are attracted to what they apprehend as good (which may be mistaken) and consider a commitment to achieve that end, a "state of affairs." The second step is an investigation (deliberation) about what kind of behaviors (acts + circumstances) might give them an opportunity to achieve that state of affairs (I–II, qq. 13–17). There may, in fact, be some evil elements in the contemplated behavior, but these are only "natural evils." If those evils work against the achievement of the end, or if they are so great that they overshadow[10] the good being aimed at, then clearly one may not ethically choose that (inappropriate) behavior.

A subtle but important difference between these two approaches is that in the model suggested by Aquinas one accepts the need to investigate both the circumstances of the person and the circumstances within which any act or omission might take place. The deliberate choice of an act may indeed be influenced by circumstances. For instance, while performing surgery may be "indicated" by the symptoms presented by a patient, the circumstances of the patient's age or general health may militate against this particular act and demand the consideration of alternative therapies.

Much less subtle is the fact that the intention of the person takes precedence in the order of evaluating human activity. That intention is not aimed at doing or omitting this or that act but rather is focused upon the goal that one is seeking to achieve. Intending the well-being of the patient may stimulate a surgeon to consider an entire set of alternatives, whereas intending the

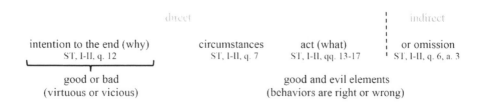

Figure 7.2.   An alternative approach based on Aquinas (ST, I–II, qq. 6–21).

prospective of making as much money as possible may encourage a surgeon to suggest procedures that may be harmful or not actually necessary.

The alternative approach allows that some form of evil may indeed be present (brought about) through the performance or omission of a possible procedure.[11] How one deals with that evil in the deliberate choice that one makes follows a similar consideration to what is key to invoking the principle of double effect, namely that there must be *a proportion between the good "done" and the evil "allowed."* What is intended is the achievement of a virtuous end, in this case, the well-being of the patient. What is (deliberately) chosen as act or omission is not wanted, not wished for, and indeed merely "allowed." The "good" accomplished through the procedure is the moral good, while one can only classify the performance of the procedure itself as a "useful good."[12]

Are There Behaviors That Should Always Be Forbidden?

The traditional approach of the moral handbooks sought to designate certain things as never morally acceptable by using the expression "intrinsically evil." Unfortunately, the use of this expression distorted the focus of moral analysis, for it concentrated largely on what we are calling "human behaviors" (with the mistaken assumption that it was making judgments about "acts-in-themselves"). In some instances, this *appears* to be correct, for some "acts" like injuring a person, hiding the truth, or causing pain do involve something evil. However, these are not really behaviors because more circumstances are necessary to place them in the real world. All the evils here are more accurately classified as natural (Aquinas),[13] physical (traditional), premoral (contemporary), or ontic (ethics of responsibility), which are not (yet) morally classifiable. For these behaviors may be justified in the cases of self-defense, using mental reservation to protect someone, or meting out punishment, respectively. That said, the perpetration of something evil should be avoided when it is inappropriate or disproportionate. A good example would be the use of excessive pain, injury, or stress to extract information from someone. The word "torture" is frequently used for this phenomenon, but it should be noted that the tipping point for this label is not the causation of pain, and so forth, but the inappropriate or disproportionate use of such "means."

I believe that it would be meaningful, perhaps even helpful, to state that some behaviors are wrong within given sets of circumstances and therefore should be forbidden. The description of the behavior, however, should be clearly stated if it is not already implicitly understood, as may be the case with certain words like murder, torture, rape, and so forth. Of course, this would presume the exercise of some intellectual and verbal discipline in stating one's case. The professional ethicist, or one who presumes to speak in a professional manner,[14] should have an awareness that their task is to *teach* others—that is, help others understand *precisely* why something should be avoided—and not to scare or threaten them.

Referring to wrong behaviors in such cases as "intrinsically" evil is both excessive and misleading. It is excessive because it presumes that simply by using this label the moral analysis has come to an end and further discussion is unnecessary. Experience demonstrates that what an observer of behavior may deem to be "wrong" may in fact be "right" when seen in light of circumstances about which the observer was unaware. Perhaps the causation of injury was not unjustified, the distortion of truth was not unwarranted, and the pain or discomfort inflicted as punishment was not disproportionate.

Referring to wrongful behaviors—even when the analysis is accurate—as intrinsically evil is misleading for several reasons. Using the phrase "intrinsically evil" does not contribute to our ability to have a coherent ethical conversation. Quite the contrary, it confuses much more than it clarifies. It short-circuits the need to engage moral discernment.[15] Defenders of its usage will claim that it streamlines the process of presenting moral advice and "gets right to the point." In reality, it belittles the intelligence of moral agents and discourages grappling with the complexity of moral decision-making. It can even dull one's moral sensitivity by leading one to believe that "mere evil" should not be as disturbing as "intrinsic evil"; thus something like "killing" is not so bad as long as one has a good reason, while using contraception is a major offence that will alienate one from God and bring about eternal damnation, regardless of whatever reason one had for using it.

Clarifying Our Vocabulary

When words like "intention" and "deliberation" appear to randomly exchange meaning, when an expression like "wrong behavior" leads one to jump to the conclusion of "bad intention," when the word "evil" is used almost exclusively to signify immorality, and when the adjective "intrinsic" adds nothing to one's understanding but functions simply as a kind of trump card for blanket condemnation, there is something drastically wrong with one's ethical vocabulary. The only way to alleviate that problem—not to mention the confusion it causes for nonethicists to comprehend what teachers or advisors in ethical matters are talking about—is to introduce more discipline into the way we use words and phrases.

Building upon the brief schema that I used to illustrate Aquinas's method for constructing his theological ethics, I suggest how we might understand and use the most important words for any fundamental moral discussion (see figure 7.3).[16] I am aware that at present there is little or no consensus about how we have been using these terms. However, that is precisely the problem being addressed. In the past, during the time of the moral handbooks, the method that was developed to aid the priest-confessor to understand what constituted a sin and to evaluate the moral accountability of the penitent used these terms in service to that practice. That approach never allowed for a critical examination of the terms themselves. The result was that the moral theological handbooks did not address ethical living but were only concerned with ethical failure.

If we, in particular the Roman Catholic Church, hope to instruct and inspire our fellow human beings to strive toward ethical living, we need a much more creative approach. At the very least, we need to use ethical vocabulary clearly and consistently. This will entail consistently using terms always to mean the same thing when we address ethical issues. Secondly, we need to examine our own goals when we approach ethical issues. Are we attempting to control people and their behavior, or are we trying to help people learn to develop informed ways of assessing ethical issues and evaluate their responsibility in those areas?

Finally, I would like to address an issue that surfaced during the discussions that took place in the course of the workshop for which these contributions have been prepared. When it comes to examining the role of intention in ethical decision-making, one or two participants suggested that persons usually have more than one intention playing a role in that process. That is undoubtedly the case. However, it is important to distinguish between immediate and longer-term, even ultimate, intentions that give direction to a person's life project. All of these should eventually harmonize in one's ethical

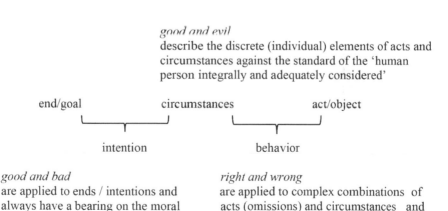

good and evil
describe the discrete (individual) elements of acts and circumstances against the standard of the 'human person integrally and adequately considered'

end/goal   circumstances   act/object

intention   behavior

good and bad
are applied to ends / intentions and always have a bearing on the moral evaluation of the entire moral event

right and wrong
are applied to complex combinations of acts (omissions) and circumstances and determined by the appropriateness of a behavior to achieve an intended end

Figure 7.3.   The designation of terms used in describing the moral event. This figure originally appeared in Joseph A. Selling, *Reframing Catholic Theological Ethics* (Oxford: Oxford University Press, 2016), 174. Used with permission of Oxford University Press.

living, but it is equally important to realize that when an ethical decision rises to the level of consciousness,[17] it needs to be addressed appropriately.

Of course we have many intentions. But they are alternatively aimed at immediate, short-term, longer-term, very long-term, and ultimate goals. What we can do and need to do is to be able to focus on current, present immediate goals and identify the precise "goal–intention" we are considering. At that point we should be able to consider whether that intention is virtuous or vicious, whether it represents an overall goal (e.g., to become a certain kind of person)[18] or merely an immediate one (e.g., seeking pleasure).

NOTES

1. The obvious question about why one would designate ethics to be "theological" would take us too far afield from the present focus of this chapter. One can find a development of that topic in my book, *Reframing Catholic Theological Ethics* (Oxford: Oxford University Press, 2016), 28–50, as well as on my website: https://theo.kuleuven.be/apps/christian-ethics/home. html.

2. One can see here the ultimate justification for "natural law." After the Reformation, non-Catholic theology took the position that human persons were corrupted by original sin and were subsequently unable to discover the will of God through their own efforts. Catholics, on the other hand, maintained the integrity of human nature which was "restored" through the Christ-event and subsequently capable of discerning good and evil. This belief was frequently linked to Rom 2:14–16.

3. A detailed analysis of this development can be found in my earlier publications, "Object, End and Moral Species in S.T. I–II, 1–21," *Ephemerides Theologicae Lovanienses* 84 (2008): 364–407, and "Looking toward the End: Revisiting Aquinas' Teleological Ethics," *The Heythrop Journal* 51 (2010): 388–400, both of which can be downloaded from my website at "Sources," https://theo.kuleuven.be/apps/christian-ethics/sources/sources.html).

4. Curiously, the word "objective" here can signify different things. The most obvious meaning points to what philosophers sometimes refer to as "naïve realism": what you sense (perceive), especially when others agree with your description of the same thing, represents what the thing actually is. In more contemporary terms, one frequently hears the phrase, "it is what it is." A second meaning lurks in the structure of traditional moral theology, especially when it was expressed in Latin. In many textbooks, the *actus moralis* is used to refer to the entire, complete activity, while the specific activity or omission that takes place is referred to as the object (*obiectus*) of the *actus moralis*. When the moral theological textbooks were translated into the vernacular, the word "act" became ambiguous because one did not know whether it stood for the physical activity/omission that was being done/omitted (*obiectus*), or for the "activity" as a whole (*actus moralis*), including the attendant circumstances and intention.

5. Another curious detail in this saga is that in the very next paragraph, *VS*, 80 we read, "With regard to intrinsically evil acts, and in reference to contraceptive practices whereby the conjugal act is *intentionally* rendered infertile [. . .]." (emphasis added). John Paul II, "Veritatis Splendor," accessed May 1, 2018, http://w2.vatican.va/content/john-paul-ii/en/encyclicals/documents/hf_jp-ii_enc_06081993_veritatis-splendor.html, 80. Does the description of something intrinsically evil involve intention or not?

6. The "technical language" of the second chapter of the encyclical suggests that Pope John Paul II was not the primary author of the text. Whoever wrote this was deeply involved in the conflict within moral theology regarding the primacy of intention and the need for proportionate thinking.

7. See Thomas Aquinas, "Summa Theologiae," accessed May 1, 2018, https://dhspriory. org/thomas/summa/index.html, I–II, q. 1, a. 1 & 3; q. 6, a. 2; q. 8, a. 3.

8. I am leaving aside here the observation that many of the things that we (and the Church) take for granted as legitimate also involve the causation of an evil. The most blatant example of this is punishment. To punish someone necessarily involves something that that person would experience as evil—a fine, imprisonment, restriction of rights, and so forth. If it did not include something that the person experiences as negative, how could it qualify as a "punishment"?

9. Peter Knauer, "The Hermeneutic Function of the Principle of Double Effect," *Natural Law Forum* 12 (1967): 132–62, and was reprinted in Charles E. Curran and Richard A. McCormick, eds., *Moral Norms and Catholic Tradition* (New York: Paulist Press, 1979), 1–39. This is a reworked version of a French original, "La Détermination du bien et du mal moral par le principe du double effet," *Nouvelle Revue Théologique* 87 (1965): 356–76.

10. Observing that an evil "overshadows" a good being aimed at leads to the judgment that whatever evil may be present in one's behavior is inappropriate, either because of "size" or of "kind." As in the case of the PDE, the decisions we make about whether an evil can be justified demands a sense of proportion.

11. With surgery this includes cutting the person, loss of blood, exposure to infection, causing pain, causing psychological stress (not only to the patient), leaving a scar, necessitating follow-up procedures, and usually financial loss.

12. See Thomas Aquinas, "Summa Theologiae," I–II, q. 8, a. 3, sc.: "Acts are diversified according to their objects. But the end is a different species of good from those things in service to the end, which are a useful good. Therefore the will is not moved to both by the same act." The question posed at Article 3 is "Whether the will is moved by the same act to the end and to those things in service to the end (*ea quae sunt ad finem*)?" Clearly, this has nothing to do with "utilitarianism." Aquinas uses the expression "useful good" because those things in service to the end—the "means"—are judged not simply by some inherent quality but on the basis of whether they are appropriate or proportionate.

13. See ibid., q. 1, a. 3, ad. 3.

14. One would like to think that those who are seen as "teachers" in the Church, namely bishops, would seek the advice of professional theological ethicists before they impose ideas on the faithful that lack sufficient explanation or justification.

15. This is particularly true in sexual ethics where blanket statements are made about particular behaviors without explaining, or perhaps even without being aware of, why these behaviors may be objectionable. Adultery, for instance, is considered always wrong because it consists in at least one of the two persons being married to another. But does not the wrongness of adultery consist in violating a promise that the married party made to their spouse, thus being a case of injustice rather than one of chastity? Using contraception was considered always wrong in the past because it was thought that the semen contained sufficient material to procreate a human being. When that theory was disproven, someone invented the theory that using contraception violates some "inseparable connection between the unitive meaning and the procreative meaning" of sexual intercourse, a theory that has no traditional precedent and only materialized in 1968.

16. This figure, as well as some of the text in this section of the essay are taken from my book, *Reframing Catholic Theological Ethics* (Oxford: Oxford University Press, 2016), chapter 7. This material is being (re)used with permission.

17. Most ethical decisions we make appear to be "spontaneous" because they fall within the contours of our overall understanding of who we are and where we are "going."

18. The "human person integrally and adequately considered" first appeared during the discussions about moral theology at Vatican II. It was adopted by Louis Janssens in setting out what he considered to be the key elements of that discipline in the "Pastoral Constitution on the Church in the Modern World," *Gaudium et Spes* (1965), in his article, "Artificial Insemination: Ethical Considerations," *Louvain Studies* 8 (1980): 3–29. I discuss the phrase extensively on my website.

REFERENCES

Aquinas, Thomas. "Summa Theologiae." Accessed May 1, 2018. https://dhspriory.org/thomas/summa/index.html.

Janssens, Louis. "Artificial Insemination: Ethical Considerations." *Louvain Studies* 8 (1980): 3–29.

John Paul II. "Veritatis Splendor." Accessed May 1, 2018. http://w2.vatican.va/content/john-paul-ii/en/encyclicals/documents/hf_jp-ii_enc_06081993_veritatis-splendor.html.

Knauer, Peter. "La Détermination du bien et du mal moral par le principe du double effet." *Nouvelle Revue Théologique* 87 (1965): 356–76.

———. "The Hermeneutic Function of the Principle of Double Effect," *Natural Law Forum* 12 (1967): 132–62. In *Moral Norms and Catholic Tradition*, edited by Charles E. Curran and Richard A. McCormick, 1–39. New York: Paulist Press, 1979.

Selling, Joseph A. "Looking toward the End: Revisiting Aquinas' Teleological Ethics." *The Heythrop Journal* 51 (2010): 388–400.

———. "Object, End and Moral Species in S.T. I–II, 1–21." *Ephemerides Theologicae Lovanienses* 84 (2008): 364–407.

———. *Reframing Catholic Theological Ethics*. Oxford: Oxford University Press, 2016.

Chapter Eight

Intrinsic Evil and the Sources of Morality

Werner Wolbert

The debate on intrinsic evil suffers, among other things, from the homonymy of the term often overlooked, especially by its defenders. I agree with J. Selling that it is "misleading for several reasons," that it "does not contribute to our ability to have a coherent ethical conversation," and that "it confuses much more than it clarifies."[1] My contribution will try to clarify some more of those confusions caused by the "richness" or ambiguity or homonymy of the relevant terms, especially those we find in the doctrine of the sources of morality (DSM).[2] In a former article Selling expresses doubts about the thesis: "that the principle factor in determining the morality of human activity was the choice of the object of a human act": he also adds, "I have been intrigued by the challenge that this presents to anyone who is persuaded by the idea that human activity can only be morally evaluated after all the relevant factors have been taken into account."[3]

ACTS, CIRCUMSTANCES, CONSEQUENCES

Selling distinguishes between an act-in-itself and the "moral event" or "some larger combination of elements such as a behavior (act + circumstances)" and criticizes the idea (called physicalism) "that a single, physical act or omission all on its own, without any addition of circumstances, can be morally determinative." Terms like single act, physical act, act-in-itself, however, seem to need some qualification without which we cannot precisely formulate the real point of the debate.

No "Act-in-Itself"

First, I doubt, that there is something like the "act-in-itself." This relates to the distinction between acts and circumstances as well as to that between acts and consequences. Eric D'Arcy states: "Circumstances may affect not only one's final moral evaluation of an act, but also one's characterization of it: in some circumstances X is P, in others it is Q."[4] D'Arcy gives the following example: with signing one's name, one may draw a check, enter a contract, give an autograph, issue a death warrant, or grant a reprieve. A second example: Macbeth stabbed Duncan, Macbeth killed the King, Macbeth succeeded to Duncan's throne.[5] By the way, none of these descriptions does already contain any ethical evaluation; what they illustrate is: *There is not necessarily one, and only one, correct description of a given act.*[6] There is also no "act-in-itself" independent from the description of the act. The description may vary "with the specialized interest of the inquirer or narrator."[7] It may also imply some intention; "abstaining from food" may be meant as dieting, slimming, hunger-striking or keeping a religious fast.[8] Special interests may also determine the terms which denote the acts and the consequences or circumstances:

> Gielgud might feel that the satisfaction derived from playing Othello for the first time was heightened by the circumstance of the performance's being at Stratford; but the Stratford Committee might feel that the fact of its being Gielgud's first appearance in the role was a circumstance that enhanced the production.[9]

D'Arcy draws two conclusions from these ambiguities: First, one cannot lay down two separate lists, one of words and phrases that count always as act-terms, the other of words and phrases that count only as circumstance-terms. Second, circumstances are, however, negatively definable in the sense that, once the act-description has been chosen, they are facts and considerations not included in the definition of the act-term employed.[10]

If what counts as circumstance is dependent on the words and phrases, circumstances cannot from the outset be regarded as irrelevant or secondary, nor as relevant or decisive, as again d'Arcy illustrates with the following example: "the act of sexual intercourse may, in different circumstances, constitute a case of adultery or of rape, or it may constitute an exercise of the rights of marriage; or again, the act of killing a man may, in different circumstances, constitute a case of murder, or of manslaughter, or of justifiable homicide."[11]

If the term used for the act does not entail any ethical evaluation, the circumstances may be relevant or decisive for the moral qualification of an action. This seems, at the first view, excluded by the traditional DSM and by the *Catechism of the Catholic Church* (*CCC*).

The Sources of Morality

The *CCC* states in no. 1754:

> The circumstances, including the consequences, are secondary elements of a moral act. They contribute to increasing or diminishing the moral goodness or evil of human acts (for example, the amount of a theft). They can also diminish or increase the agent's responsibility (such as acting out of a fear of death). Circumstances of themselves cannot change the moral quality of acts themselves; they can make neither good nor right an action that is in itself evil.

Would the authors of the *CCC* have to contradict D'Arcy's statement above? Probably not. They would have to stress that D'Arcy's "circumstances" are part of the moral act which is also called the "object" insofar as it is the object of the acting person's intention. Only an act whose moral quality (good, bad, indifferent) is already taken for granted (e.g., having sex with another man's wife is adultery) can be called an object. The physical act of sexual intercourse as such cannot be assessed as right or wrong apart from the circumstances; therefore it cannot be called the "object." D'Arcy and the *CCC* differ in their use of the term "circumstance." Furthermore, D'Arcy's "act" cannot be called an "object," or it has to be classified as an indifferent object permitting no moral evaluation. The *CCC*'s use of terms matches that of the manuals, for example, of Merkelbach.[12]

An act called "sexual intercourse" is, therefore, not yet constituted "*in esse suo morali.*" Though "circumstances," by definition, do not *constitute* the morality of the act, as also Aquinas states: "quod circumstantiae sunt extra actionem,"[13] they may, nevertheless, be morally relevant; they may *affect* the morality of the object (*CCC*, 1754: "acting out of fear of death"). Totally irrelevant factors, on the other hand, would not count as "circumstances" (e.g., stealing with the right or the left hand). It is, however, morally relevant whether I rob a bank alone or together with accomplices. Those circumstances are relevant, but are not constitutive of the act (object) which remains a case of bank robbery. Circumstances may also be relevant for the degree of moral goodness or badness of an act or for its imputability.[14]

So far the difference between the *CCC* and the "teleological and proportionalist theories," rejected by the Pope (*Veritatis Splendor* [*VS*], 79), is only terminological. A first real difference may be indicated when the *CCC* speaks of *secondary* (instead, as with Merkelbach, of *accidental*) elements, which creates another area of misunderstanding. This may be illustrated by a traditional standard example: A man steals a ladder in order to be able to enter the bedroom of a girl to have sex with her.[15] Assuming that the man is married, this act could count as theft or adultery. For the act being theft it is accidental (nonessential) that it serves for the goal of adultery (and vice versa).[16] But the goal of adultery is not "unessential," not unimportant or less important which the term "secondary" may falsely suggest (against the tradition of the DSM).[17] If, however, "circumstance" is categorized as an *accidens*, the first two phrases of *CCC*, 1754 could be understood as analytically true.[18]

Evaluative Words

If only factors not constitutive of the morality of an act are called "circumstances," the act (or "object") must be defined in a way that permits a definite moral evaluation. This can sometimes be done by using evaluative words (adultery, theft, murder),[19] by adding adjectives or adverbs as in *VS*, 80 ("*subhuman* living conditions, *arbitrary* imprisonment [. . .], *degrading* conditions of work"),[20] by excluding possibly opposing morally relevant factors (it is never right to kill a person only because I do not like her face), or by a deontological understanding.[21] In the first three ways one could invent innumerable acts wrong by their very object or (in this sense) intrinsically wrong. This is useless, however, because the question at stake is, normally, what action *counts* as murder, degrading conditions of work, and so forth.[22] Ambiguity of terminology[23] may also sometimes mean that the same term can be understood as evaluative or purely descriptive as the following objection against a proportionalist or teleological argumentation on mutilation illustrates:

> It has been argued that mutilation, the deliberate maiming or destruction of part of the body, may not be always wrong apart from circumstances and intention. It may be necessary, for example, to sacrifice a limb to save a life, as when a foot is caught in the railroad tracks. The argument is misplaced, however, because the correct description of the act to save a life would be amputation, which in some circumstances cannot be performed with surgical neatness. Thus, mutilation is always wrong, because it is not simply descriptive but includes a nefarious motive. Its relation to amputation or surgery parallels the relationship of murder and killing.[24]

Prümmer (who cannot be suspected to be a proportionalist), however, defines in the index of his manual: "Mutilatio sui semper est illicita, nisi adhibeatur ad vitam corporalem salvandam."[25] The difference between these two authors is purely linguistic; unlike Westberg, Prümmer uses the term "mutilation" in a non-normative sense. It is noteworthy, nevertheless, that, for Westberg, the nefarious or benevolent *motive* makes the difference; this would not fit the language of the DSM and its categorization of the end among the circumstances.

Principia Divisionis

The DSM lists the end among the circumstances; it is often called *circumstantia principalissima*.[26] Why is it nevertheless counted separately as the third source while the complete distinction between acts and circumstances seems to leave no room for a third source? It seems that two distinct *principia divisionis* are confused here. The first distinction is between act (object) and circumstances, the second between object and end. Acts and circumstances are distinguished according to the distinction between substance (or essence) and accident. Insofar as circumstances cannot change the moral quality of the act, they are of only accidental (nonessential) significance for the act whose substantial quality is in the object. In this sense it is accidental (though not unimportant) if I commit adultery with the wife of my best friend. It does not change the substance of adultery. When the end is called the *circumstantia principalissima*, this seems to indicate not a quantitative difference to the other circumstances, but a qualitative one. Therefore, the principle of the second distinction must be different from the first. The second distinction is between morality as something given, preset (*vorgegeben*) from morality as a demand or option (*aufgegeben*). That almsgiving is something good is true independent of my decision for or against it. The amount of money (a circumstance) given does not change the substance of the act of almsgiving, but it matters nevertheless; this circumstance and its significance is also something given, independent of my decision for that option. But it is up to me whether I practice it for the end of mercy (as it is indicated in the very term "almsgiving" from the Greek ἐλεημοσύνη, mercy) or for reasons of vanity (to win admiration; Mt 6: 1–8.). The second distinction is therefore between a *moralitas materialis* (morality as an option, a mere possibility) and a *moralitas formalis*. The moral goodness of almsgiving presents itself to me first as a mere option which becomes reality by my decision in favor of it and determines my own moral character.[27] The moral demand (e.g., that theft or adultery are wrong) is something given, not a matter of my choice or decision. But to fulfil the moral demand, to avoid the wrong and to decide in favor of the right is up to me. The end, therefore, is of higher importance for the moral act than the other circumstances on which I may have no influence.

VS, 78 states: "The morality of the human act depends primarily and fundamentally on the 'object' rationally chosen by the deliberate will." This is correct if morality is understood as *moralitas materialis*, the area of the morally right or wrong. By choosing the right and avoiding the wrong the person (or the will) becomes a good one. The distinction between object and end is about the relation between the moral right or wrong action to moral goodness or badness, to the morally good or bad conviction (*Gesinnung*) of the acting person. When the "choice for the object" is regarded as rational, the moral judgment on the action considered has already been settled. That, however, does not tell us anything about the criteria of that judgment, the criteria of right and wrong, about right- and wrong-making properties.[28] Aquinas is very clear on the difference between *moralitas materialis* and *formalis* when he states:

> [I]n exteriori actu potest considerari *duplex* bonitas, vel malitia: *una* secundum debitam materiam, et circumstantias; alia secundum ordinem ad finem. Et illa quidem, quae est secundum ordinem ad finem, tota dependet ex voluntate; illa autem, quae est ex debita materia, vel circumstantiis, dependet ex ratione: et ex hac dependet bonitas voluntatis, secundum quod in ipsam fertur.[29]

Pope John Paul II (and with him often traditional moral theologians) fails to distinguish between these two types of goodness and seems to insinuate that for "proportionalists" the second goodness may change the *malitia secundum debitam materiam* into something good or less bad. By distinguishing terminologically between the morally right and the morally good those misunderstandings could be avoided, especially the wrong impression that the question of the right- and wrong-making properties, the general problem of normative ethics, can be answered within the framework of the DSM, which the *CCC* insinuates by counting the consequences of an act among its circumstances.

Consequences

The distinction between act (action) and consequences is normally not made according to the distinction between substance and accident, and it is not a fixed one. D'Arcy states correctly:

> The term which denotes the act, in the description of a given incident, may often be elided into the term which denotes a consequence of the act: "doing X with the consequence Y" may often be re-described simply as "doing Y."[30]

Insofar as the consequences may already be part of the object,[31] they can only be of primary importance. In other cases we may not be able to give a simple name (doing X) to an action with all relevant consequences because of the lack of the respective linguistic resources.[32] Those consequences can never be of secondary significance.

The statement of the *CCC*, however, wants to reject a teleological normative approach and seems to overlook that traditionally only *some* acts are regarded as forbidden or wrong regardless of the consequences (and, in this sense, intrinsically evil or wrong), for example, lying, direct killing of the innocent, homosexual intercourse, and so forth. It is the deontologists' need to distinguish between act and consequences in order to stress that in some cases consequences do not matter. It is, however, misleading to say that the "act-in-itself" matters, and calling those acts intrinsically evil may support that misconception. What is relevant for a deontological ethical evaluation is a certain *property* of the act not related to its consequences for the well-being of the people concerned. In Catholic tradition those properties are the contradiction to nature (*contra naturam*) or lack of authority (*defectus iuris in agente*). A teleologist could avoid the language of consequences and speak of the "nature of the *whole action*" which has to be taken into account.[33]

EXCEPTIONS

Actions called intrinsically evil are generally regarded as not allowing exceptions[34] while teleologists seem to make exceptions possible.[35] The difference, however, is not about the possibility of exceptions, but about the reasons, the kind of arguments valid for justifying exceptions. The assertion that there are some norms not allowing exceptions may result from a prejudice we find, among others, in Kant's ethic. Kant presupposes that exceptions are (in general) made in favor of our inclination ("zum Vortheil unserer Neigung"); and these inclinations are (unthinkingly) understood in an egoistic sense.[36] Exceptions seem, therefore, in some way to contaminate moral purity, and the exclusion of exceptions may appear as a sign of moral seriousness or "radicalness." In fact, however, exceptions are often made in a general interest, while allowing them is often a demand of justice. There is also a linguistic aspect: the possibility or necessity of exceptions may depend on the complete or incomplete formulation of a norm. It makes no difference to say: "Direct killing of an innocent is always forbidden" or: "Killing of an innocent is always forbidden, except indirect killing and killing of a guilty."[37]

A teleologist could, for instance, formulate: torture is never allowed as a means of punishment. Whether there can ever be an "appropriate" use of torture to some good end[38] is a question of debate not to be solved by declaring torture intrinsically evil but by checking the arguments for and against its use. *VS*, 80 lists "physical and mental torture and attempts to coerce the spirit" among the intrinsically evil acts. I am not sure whether the pope would condemn the use of torture in order to get knowledge of a planned terrorist attack (because torture does not belong to the classical catalogue on intrinsically evil acts). It is a matter of debate whether the use of torture would be justified in that case from a teleological standpoint.

DIFFERENT PERSPECTIVES

According to Pope John Paul II, the key point of the debate in moral theology is a correct understanding of the DSM (*VS*, 74): "Precisely with regard to this problem there have emerged in the last few decades new or newly-revived theological and cultural trends which call for careful discernment on the part of the Church's Magisterium."

As the previous considerations should have shown, there may be some justified doubts whether the understanding of that doctrine in the *CCC* and in *VS* is the correct one. With regard to *VS*, it is not so much the Pope's presentation of that doctrine in *VS*, 78, but his conclusions about the problem of "intrinsic evil" that have to be questioned (79):

> *One must therefore reject the thesis,* characteristic of teleological and propor-
> tionalist theories, *which holds that it is impossible to qualify as morally evil
> according to its species*—its "object"—*the deliberate choice of certain kinds
> of behavior or specific acts, apart from a consideration of the intention for
> which the choice is made or the totality of the foreseeable consequences of that
> act for all persons concerned.* (emphasis in original)

Assuming that the two parts of this statement are not to be understood synon-ymously, the question arises what kind of theory is rejected in the first part. Is it something similar to a consequentialist theory rejected by the second part? I agree with Selling's comment on the role of intention and ends and some linguistic confusion in that debate. Selling mentions mutilation; the difference between him and the Pope would probably only be about the use of the term "mutilation." If both spoke instead of "surgery," the difference would probably disappear. When I speak of "almsgiving" the intention of alleviating misery is already implied in the term used. This observation illus-trates how opponents in the moral theological debate are often talking at cross purposes for which I try to give some reasons.

1. There is often a—reflected or unreflected—presumption that the solu-
    tion must come from a rereading of our moral theological tradition,
    especially of Aquinas. The doctrines mostly debated are DSM[39] and
    the principle of double effect. The debate on the correct understanding
    of Aquinas, however, is always in danger of mingling historical and
    systematic questions. It is nearly a commonplace to say that moral
    theology of the past served as instruction for confessors. What is most-
    ly overlooked is the different perspective resulting from that orienta-
    tion. The penitent's and the confessor's view on the penitent's behav-
    ior are retrospective. Since the choices and decisions have already
    been made, they have to assess the moral goodness of the act primarily
    (whether the penitent acted from a sincere conviction, whether there
    were mitigating or aggravating circumstances, whether he or she did
    the right thing perhaps with a bad intention or vice versa). The distinc-
    tion between object, circumstance, and end may be helpful for a care-
    ful judgment when confessor and penitent try to assess the morality

(moral goodness) of the act by checking its sources. The judgment is not about the moral rightness, except if the penitent asked the confessor whether his/her behavior was right or wrong. That question is normally regarded as settled when the penitent confesses that he/she lied or committed adultery or bank robbery. At that point, there will be no more uncertainty about the quality of the object and its "essential" meaning for the moral state of the penitent.

Unfortunately, critics of traditional moral theology (sometimes called "revisionist") tend to read the doctrine of the sources of morality as a treatise on normative ethics. But the normative question is how we determine the moral quality of the object (the rightness or wrongness of the action or behavior). John Paul II and conservative moral theologians[40] insinuate that for proportionalists a good intention or important circumstances may justify an act already judged as definitely wrong. Traditional moral theologians, however, know quite well that circumstances may change the object. In cases of extreme need the taking of foreign property may not count as theft. Insofar as the good intention of saving one's life and that of one's family may justify that kind of action which normally counts as theft; in that case the circumstances become elements of the new object. Why could not, similarly, the intention to save the life of the mother change the object of abortion? Those questions cannot be judged in the context of DSM, but by an inquiry on the problem of abortion and killing in general. Sometimes the argument is more about words and language, and even traditionalists sometimes seem not to understand the language of their tradition.

2. Selling's approach to the question of intrinsically evil acts starts from a consideration of the way ethical decisions are made which, for him, is misread by the DSM. But Selling's perspective is a prospective one, whereas from the retrospective perspective of the DSM the decisions have already been made and objects are classified as intrinsically evil. Distinguishing an essential "object" from accidental circumstances, however, makes little sense when I have still to decide what to do and to consider the ethical implications; that is, when I still need to ask, for instance, which circumstances are essential or/and which secondary.

3. Selling's description of moral decision-making seems to be dominated by a first-person perspective. But ethicists, at least, are used to judge from a third-person perspective and may be asked for ethical advice. The steps of the process of decision-making and its difficulties may count as mitigating circumstances for those who regard the decision made as wrong (e.g., in the case of an unsuccessful surgery), or they may contribute to a better understanding of the acting person's situa-

tion and its relevant factors. But they are neither a necessary nor sufficient criterion of the moral rightness or wrongness of the action.

4. This difficulty may be connected with another one: the relation of description and evaluation in Selling's approach. His description of moral decision-making seems to get some normative meaning from a kind of Knauerian normative theory he seems to hold and take for granted, more or less. The language of means that have to be proportionate to the end seems to fit into Selling's description.[41]

5. Selling states "that the intention of the person takes precedence in the order of evaluating human activity."[42] But there is often not only one intention. The acting person may have several intentions, several ends (e.g., in the case of abortion).[43] A physician may have the ends of curing patients, making money, and improving or maintaining his reputation. These ends may sometimes be in harmony (a difficult successful surgery is also useful for the surgeon's reputation), sometimes not (when an unnecessary surgery is made for economic reasons). The term "motivation" seems to presuppose a plurality of intentions and to denote the dominating intention often formulated with virtue- or vice-terms (ambition, vanity, avarice—mercy, helpfulness, honesty). The greedy motivation of a physician as such, however, does not make his decision a wrong one. The ambitious successful surgeon may do the right thing from a morally deficient motivation (even though not every kind of ambition is bad). And a good intention (e.g., alleviating pain or relieving from pain) does not as such justify the measure chosen in pursuing that end (e.g., mercy killing or theft). When it does, it changes the "object."

INTRINSIC WRONG

There will never be a fruitful debate on intrinsic evil without differentiating the various meanings of that term. A person not acquainted with Catholic moral theology would probably understand "intrinsic evil" as the opposite of "intrinsic good." The latter is roughly synonymous with "good for its own sake, as an end, as distinct from good as a means to something else."[44] Since "intrinsic evil" is about human acts in our context, we should prefer to speak of intrinsic *wrong*. During my dealing with problems of normative ethics, I have detected nine different meanings of "intrinsic wrong."

1. Wrong by its very nature, not by command of a lawgiver.[45]
2. Wrong by its object, not by its circumstances.
3. Wrong because of some property of the act (against nature or lack of entitlement (*defectus iuris in agente*); deontologically forbidden.

4. Wrong because against nature. Only the first deontologically relevant property makes the action intrinsically wrong.[46]
5. Wrong because of the evaluative term used (e.g., murder, usury, theft, adultery).
6. Wrong without exceptions.
7. Wrong because the evil consequences are implied in the description (e.g., poisoning).
8. Wrong because grave violation of human dignity.[47]
9. Mortal sin.

Because of its strong emotional force the term "intrinsic evil" seems to connote something grave, for example, a grave violation of human rights.[48] But even a relatively harmless lie is to be categorized as intrinsically wrong in the meanings (3) and (4) above. This demonstrates the need for distinctions as listed above, not least for pastoral reasons.

But there is also the problem of moral theologians confirming the position of *VS*, but pointing only to examples fitting to, for instance, meaning (8) and diverting the debate to issues undisputed and so taking their stand on the right side. The considerations offered above should have shown that the debate on intrinsically wrong acts concerns only the meanings (3) and (4).

CONCLUSION

The following conclusions should be drawn from the considerations offered in this chapter:

1. Whoever uses the language of intrinsic evil should declare precisely in what sense he or she uses the term.
2. Because of the homonymy of the term any moral theologian could affirm that there are intrinsically wrong (evil) acts.
3. The mere use of the term may, however, give the false impression of accordance with *VS* and may be sometimes intended in that way.
4. The term intrinsic evil connotes the idea of a grave evil (grave sin). But even a slight lie would be intrinsically evil from a deontological point of view. This could be fatal from a pastoral point of view. Another consequence could also be that it makes really great evils look less serious.
5. The best and most desirable solution would be to get rid of the term.

NOTES

1. Joseph A. Selling, "The Naming of Evil in Fundamental Theological Ethics," this volume, 160.

2. One of the best (or worst) examples of confusion of different meanings of "intrinsically evil" may be the book of Servais Pinckaers, *Ce qu'on ne peut jamais faire. La question des actes intrinséquement mauvais. Histoire et discussion* (Fribourg: Editions Universitaire; Paris: Editions du Cerf, 1986).

3. Joseph A. Selling, "Looking toward the End: Revisiting Aquinas' Teleological Ethics," *Heythrop Journal* 51 (2010): 388. Selling uses the language of *Veritatis Splendor* (*VS*) that speaks of the *choice* of the object though Aquinas says simply: "actio habet speciem ex objecto" ("an action is specified by its object"). Thomas Aquinas, "Summa Theologiae," accessed May 15, 2018, https://dhspriory.org/thomas/summa/index.html, I–II, q. 18, a. 2. The language of choice in *VS*, 79 ("deliberate choice") could be due to the influence of the New Natural Law Theory (John Finnis, Germain Grisez, Joseph Boyle).

4. Eric D'Arcy, *Human Acts* (Oxford: Oxford University Press, 1963), 1.

5. Ibid., 2.

6. Ibid., 10.

7. Ibid.

8. Ibid., 13.

9. Ibid., 59.

10. Ibid., 61.

11. Ibid. D'Arcy reminds one of the model of Bohr's atom: "*this* nucleus when surrounded or accommodated by *these* circumstances gives us *this* sort of atom; in the same way, *this* act when surrounded or accompanied by *these* circumstances gives us *this* sort of offence."

12. "Circumstantia moralis est accidens actus humani ipsum in esse suo morali iam constitutum moraliter afficiens" ("A moral circumstance is an accidental property of a human act that influences the act regardless of its being already morally constituted"). Benedictus H. Merkelbach, *Summa Theologiae Moralis*, vol. 1, 5th ed. (Paris: Desclée, 1946), no. 151. Cf. Bruno Schüller, "Die Quellen der Moralität," *Theologie und Philosophie* 59 (1984): 535–59; Werner Wolbert, *Gewissen und Verantwortung. Gesammelte Studien* (Freiburg i.Ue: Academic Press; Freiburg i.Br.: Herder, 2009), 227–46.

13. Thomas Aquinas, "Summa Theologiae," I–II, q. 18, a. 3, ad. 1 ("circumstances are outside the action").

14. In the second case, the circumstances are evaluated after the action, whereas normative reflections on right and wrong are done before; Johannes Gründel, *Die Lehre von den Umständen der menschlichen Handlung im Mittelalter* (Münster: Aschendorf, 1962), 2.

15. In Austrian and Bavarian popular language this is called with one word *fensterln* (derived from *Fenster*—window) and could be called a "single act" if one uses that German word.

16. For different concepts of "circumstance," for example, among the Dominican theologians, see Gründel, *Die Lehre*, 524, for Bonaventure see ibid., 651.

17. "Secondary" could, however, also be understood correctly. See Iosephus Gredt, *Elementa Philosophiae Aristoteolicae-Thomisticae*, vol. 2, 10th ed. (Barcinone: Herder, 1961), no. 923: "Secundaria moralitas est ex circumstantiis et ex fine" ("The secondary morality is from the circumstances and the end"), but comments (n. 923): "circumstantiae sunt extra substantiam actus moralis et quasi accidentia eius" ("circumstances are outside the substance of the moral act and like its accidents"). Cf. John R. Connery, "Catholic Ethics: Has the Norm for Rule-Making Changed," *Theological Studies* 42 (1981): 239. Connery uses the example given above in the following way to illustrate the difference between Aquinas and the "proportionalists": "While both admit a double malice in the act, the proportionalists relate it all to the end of the act; the stealing is wrong because of the absence of a proportionate reason." This sounds good "Knauerian," but is a misinterpretation of Knauer's ethical theory (which I do not share). Even Connery would probably not deny that taking the property of another person may be allowed in cases of necessity (to avoid dying of hunger or cold). But this would not be called "stealing." (It was called *fringsen* in Germany after World War II, because Cardinal Frings of Cologne had declared stealing coals from the allied forces as allowed.). Similarly Brian V. Johnstone,

"Intrinsically Evil Acts," *Studia Moralia* 42 (2005): 401: "But proportionalists were mistaken if they argued that ulterior intentions could transform the moral meaning of the act already constituted in the basic fundamental intention." Proportionalists may have sometimes used similar formulations that caused misunderstandings like that.

18. A quite different definition can be found in Jeremy Bentham, "An Introduction to the Principles of Morals and Legislation," in *The Collected Works of Jeremy Bentham: An Introduction to the Principles of Morals and Legislation*, eds. J. H. Burns and H. L. A. Hart (London/New York: Methuen, 1982), 89: "The circumstances are no objects of the intention. A man intends the act: and by intention he produces the act: but as to the circumstances, he does not intend *them*: he does not, inasmuch as they are circumstances of it, produce them."

19. These are the Aristotelian examples in his *Nicomachean Ethics* 1107a9ff (apart from examples of vices). This passage is not a proof for the traditional concept of intrinsic evil (in fact, most commentaries do not comment on that passage). Aristotle "is making a purely logical point which arises from the fact that certain words are used to name not ranges of action or passion but determinations within a range with the implication, as part of the meaning of the word, that they are excessive or defective, and therefore wrong." William F. R. Hardie, *Aristotle's Ethical Theory* (Oxford: Clarendon, 1968), 139. Two kinds of acts are called intrinsically evil by Aristotle: those which are wrong by definition (adultery) and those which are wrong by defect or excess. Francis Sparshott, *Taking Life Seriously. A Study of the Argument of the Nicomachean Ethics* (Toronto: University of Toronto Press, 1994), 108: The first kind of action that is ruled out is the kind that is wrong by definition. It is never right to commit adultery, because the word *adultery* means sexual intercourse of a kind that is defined as forbidden. It is an important fact about Aristotle's society, if not ours, that there is such a thing as adultery. The person who is contemplating sexual liaison and who realizes that it would be adulterous is prevented by that realization from debating the pros and cons of such an indulgence—the question "how much?" is ruled out as irrelevant. [. . .] The other kind of action that is ruled out is one that is excluded by the decision process itself. To speak schematically, as Aristotle does, if I have decided what the virtue of generosity requires of me in a certain situation, all other responses are defined as either excessive or defective. We may give them names: they are either stingy or spendthrift. But we have now divided our notional continuum into two contiguous continua; and on these two continua there are not "right amounts," because all degrees of stinginess and spendthriftiness are predetermined to be wrong. We could say, if we wished, that spendthriftiness and stinginess are wrong "by definition," just as adultery is; but Aristotle treats the two cases as differently, because adultery is made wrong by considerations of "justice"—in effect, contractual considerations, aspects of the social compact—and the term "adultery" is chosen to indicate that these conditions are violated; spendthriftiness and stinginess are wrong by excess and defect, and the terms are chosen to indicate that the relevant quantitative determination has already been made. There can't be a right amount of an excess or a defect.

20. Cf. Selling, "The Naming of Evil," 93: "excessive pain."

21. There is no problem to declare the following acts as intrinsically evil (wrong): Acting against one's conscience, acts of sacrilege, formal cooperation with injustice committed by other people, scandal, and induction to sin. See Eberhard Schockenhoff, *Grundlegung der Ethik. Ein theologischer Entwurf* (Freiburg i.Br.: Herder, 2007), 374. Those norms could be called reflexive (with Bruno Schüller, *Die Begründung sittlicher Urteile: Typen ethischer Argumentation in der Moraltheologie*, 3rd ed. [Düsseldorf: Patmos, 1987], 76) because those phrases express the relation of morality to itself: It is morally good to decide in favor of the morally good (and so to follow one's conscience). It is morally bad (intrinsically evil) to approve or to entice to morally bad behavior. There is no problem with such a kind of intrinsically evil. When Schockenhoff speaks of "external consequences" (*äußere Handlungsfolgen*), however, he presents these analytical phrases as arguments for a deontological position. Besides: whether consequences are internal or external, depends on the term used for the act. If I "poison" somebody, the following death will count as internal consequence; if I "give cyanide" it may count as external.

22. This is overlooked by *Veritatis Splendor*. Jean Porter, "The Moral Act in *Veritatis Splendor* and in Aquinas' *Summa Theologiae*: A Comparative Analysis," in *Veritatis Splendor: American Responses*, eds. Michael Allsopp and John J. O' Keefe (Kansas City, MO: Sheed and

Ward, 1995), 281: "The difficulty is this: Veritatis Splendor reflects a widely shared assumption that Aquinas' criteria for the evaluation of an action can be applied to specific acts prior to and independently of the process of determining the moral evaluation of a specific action" and 284: "The determination of an object of an act presupposes that we have described the act correctly from a moral point of view."

23. Selling, "The Naming of Evil," 90–91.

24. Daniel Westberg, "Good and Evil in Human Acts (Ia IIae, qq. 18–21)," in *The Ethics of Aquinas*, ed. Stephen J. Pope (Washington, DC: Georgetown University Press, 2002), 95. It is noteworthy that the nefarious or benevolent *motive* makes the difference which would be excluded within the DSM and its terminology. Cf. Selling, "The Naming of Evil," 90–91.

25. Dominicus M. Prümmer, *Manuale Theologiae Moralis*, vol. 3 (Freiburg: Herder, 1923), 651: ("Mutilation is always illicit unless it is performed in order to save corporal life.") This is a kind of summary of the respective paragraph in II n. 116 where this phrase is not to be found.

26. Thomas Aquinas, "Summa Theologiae," I–II, q. 7, a. 4.

27. Josephus de Finance, *Ethica generalis*, 3rd ed. (Romae: Aedes Universitatis Gregorianae, 1966), 253 (no. 238): "Agere propter debitum finem est ita agere ut actus cum omnibus suis circumstantiis sumptus, cohaereat cum proposito generali agendi secundum rationem" ("In order to act for the end, one is obliged to choose means in such a way that the act with all its circumstances is in accordance with the general intention to act according to reason").

28. Joseph Schwane, *Allgemeine Moraltheologie* (Freiburg: Herder, 1885), 48, heads the chapter on the sources of morality: "Über die Quellen der Moralität und ihren bestimmenden Einfluß auf das Genus, die Spezies und den Grad der Moralität" ("On the sources of morality and their specifying influence on the genus, species and degree of morality"; quoted from Schüller, "Die Quellen," 551).

29. Thomas Aquinas, "Summa Theologiae," I–II, q. 20, a. 2, resp ("[W]e may consider a twofold goodness or malice in the external action: one in respect of due matter and circumstances; the other in respect of the order to the end. And that which is in respect of the order to the end, depends entirely on the will: while that which is in respect of due matter or circumstances, depends on the reason: and on this goodness depends the goodness of the will, in so far as the will tends towards it.") See also Antonio Ballerini, *Opus Theologicum Morale in Busenbaum Medullam*, vol. 1 (Prati: Giacchetti, 1898) no. 82: Distinguenda est autem potissimum bonitatis *materialis* et *formalis*. Prior est convenientia actus cum regula, non habita ratione agentis et idcirco actus materialiter spectatur: ita v.gr. ablatio rei alienae, periurium. etc. Altera est convenientia actus cum regula, prout actus procedit a libera voluntate et praevia cognitione eiusdem regulae. Tunc enim solum haberi potest formalis bonitas et malitia actus, cum hic scienter et libere ponitur; hoc enim est proprium actus humani. ("Above all, one has to distinguish between material and formal goodness. The first is the concordance with the rule independent of the judgment of the agent, e.g., taking another person's property, perjury, etc. The other one is the concordance of the act with a rule, insofar as the act proceeds from a free will and previous knowledge of the same rule. Therefore it is sufficient to have the formal goodness and badness of the act because it is done knowingly and freely; this is the property of the human act.")

30. D'Arcy, *Acts*, 15.

31. In German, one could distinguish *handlungsbeschreibende* and *nicht-handlungsbeschreibenden Folgen*; Michael Lehmann, "Gesinnung und Erfolg. Zur normativ-ethischen Diskussion in der deutschsprachigen Ethik um die Wende zum 20. Jahrhundert," (PhD diss., University of Münster, 1990), 166.

32. German popular language offers this in the case of *fensterln* and *fringsen*; see footnotes 15 and 17.

33. Walter T. Stace, *The Concept of Morals* (Gloucester, MA: Peter Smith, 1975) 119; similarly Louis Janssens, "Norm and Priority in a Love Ethics," *Louvain Studies* 9 (1977): 231.

34. Generally, but not always. Cf. Joannes P. Gury, *Compendium Theologiae Moralis* (Ratisbonae: Joseph Manz, 1853), no. 23.2. Gury distinguishes: intrinsece mala sunt triplicis classis: 1° Quaedam talia sunt *absolute*, et independenter ab omni circumstantia; quia ex sese necessariam involvunt repugnantiam cum recto ordine, ut est odium Dei, blasphemia, etc. – 2° Alia sunt *intrinsece* mala, non praecise in se, sed ratione adjuncti aut conditionis alicuius quae

pendet a dominativa potestate Dei, aut hominis; talia sunt ablatio rei alienae, laesio corporis vel famae, et similia quae aliquando licita evadunt. – 3° Alia tandem mala sunt tantum ratione periculi quod ordinarie adjunctum habent ut aspectus objecti turpis, lectio pravi libri, etc. Haec, data rationabili causa, licita fiunt." ("[T]here are three classes of intrinsic evils: 1 Some are intrinsically evil in an absolute sense and independent of every circumstance; they involve in itself a contradiction to the right order, e.g., hate of God, blasphemy, etc. – 2 Others are intrinsically evil, not precisely *in se*, but because of some additional condition depending on the commanding power of God or of man, as taking another's property, causing bodily harm or ruining another's reputation and similar things which are sometimes allowed. – 3 Others are evil because of some danger normally connected with them as looking at a bad object, reading of a bad book, etc. [. . .]. These things are allowed given a rational reason.")

35. That was B. Schüller's idea in his first article on that subject ("Zur Problematik allgemein verbindlicher ethischer Grundsätze," *Theologie und Philosophie* 45 [1970]: 1–23; trans.: "What Ethical Principles Are Universally Valid," *Theology Digest* 19 [1971]: 23–28). Later, after having read, for example, R. Hare's *Freedom and Reason*, he understood that universalizability is an essential property of every normative ethical judgment. Unfortunately, that article is one of the few translated into English and often serves to present Schüller's position. For a correct report on the European debate see Bernard Hoose, *Proportionalism: The American Debate and its European Roots* (Washington, DC: Georgetown University Press, 1987).

36. Immanuel Kant, *Grundlegung zur Metaphysik der Sitten* (Köln: Anaconda Verlag, 2016), 424: Wenn wir nun auf uns selbst bei jeder Übertretung einer Pflicht Acht haben, so finden wir, daß wir wirklich nicht wollen, es solle unsere Maxime ein allgemeines Gesetz werden, denn das ist uns unmöglich, sondern das Gegentheil derselben soll vielmehr allgemein ein Gesetz bleiben; nur nehmen wir uns die Freiheit, für uns oder (auch nur für diesesmal) zum Vortheil unserer Neigung davon eine Ausnahme zu machen. ("Now if we attend to ourselves in every transgression of a duty, then we find that we do not actually will that our maxim should become a universal law, for that is impossible for us, but rather will that its opposite should remain a law generally; yet we take the liberty of making an exception for ourselves, or [even only for this once] for the advantage of our inclination.")

Sometimes colleagues from other theological disciplines feel obliged to show moral theologians the right path. Karl-Heinz Menke (professor for Dogmatics in Bonn) argues that in the case of exceptionless norms one should not argue according to the principle of self-determination, because this would make the truth "zum Spielball meiner Interessen und meines Nutzens" ("a toy of my interests and my benefit"). Karl-Heinz Menke, *Macht die Wahrheit frei oder die Freiheit wahr?* (Regensburg: Pustet, 2017), 99; quoted from Stephan Goertz, "Wider die Entweltlichung," *Herder Korrespondenz* 71, no. 12 (2017): 14. Kant's concerns may be legitimate as a warning or caveat against self-deception, but not as a valid argument in ethical controversies.

37. For Gury, *Compendium*, no. 23.2, those traditional prohibitions allow for exceptions because of a *defectus iuris in agente*; see footnote 34.

38. I would, at least, have strong doubts about that.

39. Todd Salzmann, *Deontology and Teleology: An Investigation of the Normative Debate in Roman Catholic Moral Theology* (Leuven: Leuven University Press, 1995), 267–503; Gerhard Stanke, *Die Lehre von den "Quellen der Moralität": Darstellung und Diskussion der neuscholastischen Aussagen und neuerer Ansätze* (Regensburg: Pustet, 1984); Richard Bruch, "Grundsätzliches zur Thomas-Interpretation," in his *Moralia Varia. Lehrgeschichtliche Untersuchungen zu moraltheologischen Fragen* (Düsseldorf: Patmos, 1981), 102–4. Bruch observes that Aquinas suffered the same fate as the Bible of which the reformed theologian Petrus Werenfels (+1703) remarked in a famous distich (103): "Hic liber est, in quo quaerit sua dogmata quisque; invenit et pariter dogmata quisque sua" ("This is the book into which everyone looks for his [her] dogmas and he [she] will find them").

40. Connery, "Catholic Ethics."

41. For Knauer's approach, its development and critical remarks see A. Weiß's contribution in this volume.

42. Selling, "The Naming of Evil," 92.

43. In this case, the "intention for which the choice is made" does count for Germain Grisez, contrary to *VS*, 79; *The Way of the Lord Jesus II: Living a Christian Life* (Quincy, IL: Franciscan Press, 1993), 500: "Sometimes intentional abortion does not involve intentional killing." In cases of health problems for the mother and of rape "the proposal adopted is, not to kill the unborn baby, but to have him or her removed from the womb, with death as a foreseen and accepted side effect. An abortion carrying out such a choice would not be an intentional killing." Even though this "still involves wrongfully accepting the baby's death" (ibid. 501), intention determines the object in that case.

44. Charles L. Stevenson, *Ethics and Language*, 2nd ed. (New Haven, CT: Yale University Press, 1946), 174; Werner Wolbert, "Good and Evil," in *The Oxford Encyclopedia of the Bible and Ethics*, vol. 1, ed. Robert L. Brawley (New York: Oxford University Press, 2014), 343–49.

45. Plato's dialogue *Euthyphron*. An example for something possibly extrinsically wrong would be fasting; Alphons of Liguori, *Theologia Moralis*, vol. 2 (Mechliniae: Verhoeven, 1845), a 4 § 2XXXVI: "Si extrinsece tantum, et vi legis positivae est rationi conforme, uti ieiunium, tunc potest esse aliquando bonum, aliquando vero malum ex circumstantial" ("If fasting is only extrinsic, and in conformity with reason by virtue of positive law, then it can be sometimes good, but sometimes bad due to the circumstances").

46. Concerning the second deontological argument see Gury, *Compendium*, no. 22. For the first one, see Werner Wolbert, "Die Weisheit der Natur. Natürliche und künstliche Empfängnisverhütung," in *Humanae Vitae—Die anstößige Enzyklika: Eine kritische Würdigung*, eds., Konrad Hilpert and Sigrid Müller (Freiburg i. Br.: Herder, 2018), 61–73.

47. The list of intrinsically evil acts in *VS*, 80 is taken from *Gaudium et Spes*, 27; that paragraph is titled: "*De reverentia erga personam humanam*" and does not use the term "intrinsic evil." John Paul II, "Veritatis Splendor," accessed May 25, 2018, http://w2.vatican.va/content/john-paul-ii/en/encyclicals/documents/hf_jp-ii_enc_06081993_veritatis-splendor.html, 80; Second Vatican Council, "Gaudium et Spes," accessed May 25, 2018, http://www.vatican.va/archive/hist_councils/ii_vatican_council/documents/vat-ii_const_19651207_gaudium-et-spes_en.html, 27.

48. According to John Paul II, "Veritatis Splendor," 80, "they radically contradict the good of the person made in his image."

REFERENCES

Aquinas, Thomas. "Summa Theologiae." Accessed May 15, 2018. https://dhspriory.org/thomas/summa/index.html.

Ballerini, Antonio. *Opus Theologicum Morale in Busenbaum Medullam*, vol. 1. Prati: Giacchetti, 1898.

Bentham, Jeremy. "An Introduction to the Principles of Morals and Legislation." In *The Collected Works of Jeremy Bentham: An Introduction to the Principles of Morals and Legislation*, edited by J. H. Burns and H. L. A. Hart. London/New York: Methuen, 1982.

Bruch, Richard. *Moralia Varia. Lehrgeschichtliche Untersuchungen zu moraltheologischen Fragen*. Düsseldorf: Patmos, 1981.

Connery, John R. "Catholic Ethics: Has the Norm for Rule-Making Changed." *Theological Studies* 42 (1981): 232–50.

D'Arcy, Eric. *Human Acts*. Oxford: Oxford University Press, 1963.

De Finance, Josephus. *Ethica generalis*. 3rd ed. Romae: Aedes Universitatis Gregorianae, 1966.

De Ligorio, Alphonsus. *Theologia Moralis*. Mechliniae: Verhoeven, 1845.

Goertz, Stephan. "Wider die Entweltlichung." *Herder Korrespondenz* 71, no. 12 (2017): 13–16.

Gredt, Iosephus. *Elementa Philosophiae Aristoteolicae-Thomisticae*, vol. 2. 10th ed. Barcinone: Herder, 1961.

Grisez, Germain. *The Way of the Lord Jesus II: Living a Christian Life*. Quincy, IL: Franciscan Press, 1993.

Gründel, Johannes. *Die Lehre von den Umständen der menschlichen Handlung im Mittelalter.* Münster: Aschendorf, 1962.

Gury, Joannes P. *Compendium Theologiae Moralis.* Ratisbonae: Joseph Manz, 1853.

Hardie, William F. R. *Aristotle's Ethical Theory.* Oxford: Clarendon, 1968.

Hoose, Bernard. *Proportionalism: The American Debate and Its European Roots.* Washington, DC: Georgetown University Press, 1987.

Janssens, Louis. "Norm and Priority in a Love Ethics." *Louvain Studies* 9 (1977): 207–38.

John Paul II. "Veritatis Splendor." Accessed May 25, 2018. http://w2.vatican.va/content/john-paul-ii/en/encyclicals/documents/hf_jp-ii_enc_06081993_veritatis-splendor.html.

Johnstone, Brian V. "Intrinsically Evil Acts." *Studia Moralia* 42 (2005): 379–406.

Kant, Immanuel. *Grundlegung zur Metaphysik der Sitten.* Köln: Anaconda Verlag, 2016.

Lehmann, Michael. "Gesinnung und Erfolg. Zur normativ-ethischen Diskussion in der deutschsprachigen Ethik um die Wende zum 20. Jahrhundert." PhD diss., University of Münster, 1990.

Menke, Karl-Heinz. *Macht die Wahrheit frei oder die Freiheit wahr?* Regensburg: Pustet, 2017.

Merkelbach, Benedictus H. *Summa Theologiae Moralis,* vol 1. 5th ed. Paris: Desclée, 1946.

Pinckaers, Servais. *Ce qu'on ne peut jamais faire. La question des actes intrinséquement mauvais. Histoire et discussion.* Fribourg: Editions Universitaire; Paris: Editions du Cerf, 1986.

Porter, Jean. "The Moral Act in *Veritatis Splendor* and in Aquinas' *Summa Theologiae*: A Comparative Analysis." In *Veritatis Splendor: American Responses,* edited by Michael Allsopp and John J. O' Keefe, 278–95. Kansas City, MO: Sheed and Ward, 1995.

Prümmer, Dominicus M. *Manuale Theologiae Moralis,* vol. 3, Freiburg: Herder, 1923.

Salzman, Todd. *Deontology and Teleology: An Investigation of the Normative Debate in Roman Catholic Moral Theology.* Leuven: Leuven University Press, 1995.

Schockenhoff, Eberhard. *Grundlegung der Ethik. Ein theologischer Entwurf.* Freiburg i.Br.: Herder, 2007.

Schüller, Bruno. *Die Begründung sittlicher Urteile: Typen ethischer Argumentation in der Moraltheologie.* 3rd ed. Düsseldorf: Patmos, 1987.

———. "Die Quellen der Moralität." *Theologie und Philosophie* 59 (1984): 535–59.

———. "Zur Problematik allgemein verbindlicher ethischer Grundsätze." *Theologie und Philosophie* 45, no. 1 (1970): 1–23. (English: "What Ethical Principles Are Universally Valid." *Theology Digest* 19 [1971]: 23–28).

Second Vatican Council. "Gaudium et Spes." Accessed May 25, 2018. http://www.vatican.va/archive/hist_councils/ii_vatican_council/documents/vat-ii_const_19651207_gaudium-et-spes_en.html.

Selling, Joseph A. "Looking toward the End: Revisiting Aquinas' Teleological Ethics." *Heythrop Journal* 51 (2010): 388–400.

———. *Reframing Catholic Theological Ethics.* Oxford: Oxford University Press, 2016.

Sparshott, Francis. *Taking Life Seriously. A Study of the Argument of the Nicomachean Ethics.* Toronto: University of Toronto Press, 1994.

Stace, Walter T. *The Concept of Morals.* Gloucester, MA: Peter Smith, 1975.

Stanke, Gerhard. *Die Lehre von den "Quellen der Moralität": Darstellung und Diskussion der neuscholastischen Aussagen und neuerer Ansätze.* Regensburg: Pustet, 1984.

Stevenson, Charles L. *Ethics and Language.* 2nd ed. New Haven, CT: Yale University Press, 1946.

Westberg, Daniel. "Good and Evil in Human Acts (Ia IIae, qq. 18–21)." In *The Ethics of Aquinas,* edited by Stephen J. Pope, 90–102. Washington, DC: Georgetown University Press, 2002.

Wolbert, Werner. "Die Weisheit der Natur. Natürliche und künstliche Empfängnisverhütung." In *Humanae Vitae—Die anstößige Enzyklika: Eine kritische Würdigung,* edited by Konrad Hilpert and Sigrid Müller, 61–73. Freiburg i. Br.: Herder, 2018.

———. *Gewissen und Verantwortung. Gesammelte Studien.* Freiburg i.Ue: Academic Press; Freiburg i.Br.: Herder, 2009.

————. "Good and Evil." In *The Oxford Encyclopedia of the Bible and Ethics*, vol. 1., edited by Robert L. Brawley, 343–49. New York: Oxford University Press, 2014.

Part V

The Future of the Concept
of Intrinsic Evil

Chapter Nine

Intrinsic Evil in Different Ethical Perspectives

Andreas M. Weiß

A number of relevant aspects of *intrinsece malum* are discussed in this book. A classical meaning of "intrinsically evil act" is the thesis that a certain description of an act without any addition of circumstances can be morally determinative.[1] Calling a certain act intrinsically evil in this sense expresses the conviction that the prohibition is adequately justified and further ethical debate is unnecessary.[2] Whether this thesis is accepted or rejected is substantially tied up with the context in which the term is used and with the type of ethical theory to which one subscribes. The common denominator of intrinsically evil acts is the evaluative term evil, which expresses a moral value judgment about human actions. Used in different contexts, the term intrinsic expresses additional assumptions relevant for the perspective.

In the debate about ethical theories, the concept of intrinsically evil acts was and still is used to prevent critical discussion about moral norms and to attack the credibility of teleological ethical theories. As other authors have shown in this volume, some discussions and misunderstandings in the debate on deontological and teleological ethical theories might result from a confusion of meanings of the term and its application in different perspectives. According to Bruno Schüller sometimes metaethics, normative ethics, and the doctrine of the sources of morality are confused when the term intrinsically evil act is used in the debate about deontological norms and proportionalism.[3] The doctrine of the sources of morality, normative ethics, and metaethics are different kinds of inquiry that we find within theological ethics. I will suggest that the terms intrinsic evil or intrinsically evil act have different meanings in these different perspectives.

Without claiming completeness, we can recognize at least four perspectives from which one might consider the term intrinsically evil acts: (1) normative ethics, (2) the doctrine of the sources of morality, (3) metaethics, and (4) parenetic speech. In what follows I will try to explain these contexts, specific questions that are addressed by labeling an act as intrinsically evil, and some misunderstandings that might result if the different questions are not discerned sufficiently.

NORMATIVE ETHICS

As already mentioned, the notion of an intrinsically evil act might be understood as closing or avoiding any debate on a particular issue. It seems to reject the search for further information and any consideration whether the act could be morally evaluated differently in specific cases:

> But the negative moral precepts, those prohibiting certain concrete actions or kinds of behavior as intrinsically evil, do not allow for any legitimate exception. They do not leave room, in any morally acceptable way, for the "creativity" of any contrary determination whatsoever. Once the moral species of an action prohibited by a universal rule is concretely recognized, the only morally good act is that of obeying the moral law and of refraining from the action which it forbids. (*VS*, 67)

The reason why many criticize this use of this notion is that they presume that the task of ethics is to provide a valid justification for a moral judgment based upon reason and not to stop discussion simply by giving directives and demanding obedience. Therefore, the term seems to reject the central task of normative ethics. W. K. Frankena defines normative ethics as the search for acceptable judgments of moral obligation, of moral value, and of nonmoral value.[4]

Concerning moral obligation, normative ethics does not simply tell us what we should do, but also wants "to guide us in our capacity as agents trying to decide what we should do in this case and in that."[5] Therefore, the central question of normative ethics is about "the basic principles, criteria, or standards by which we are to determine what we morally ought to do, what is morally right or wrong, and what our moral rights are."[6]

Even if calling a certain act intrinsically evil expresses the conviction that a prohibition is evaluated adequately and sufficiently and further ethical debate is unnecessary, the task of normative ethics remains to give a valid justification and to be mindful of relevant factors that could have been overlooked or could have changed. This general perspective of normative ethics seems to be a good reason not to use the term intrinsically evil act within normative ethical debates. It does not add anything to the term morally evil or morally wrong and seems to demand what normative ethics cannot do: to stop further critical thinking.

Two main types of ethical theory and of ethical norms are usually distinguished as teleological and deontological theories respectively.[7] The determining difference between deontological and teleological theories is the position about right- and wrong-making properties. Teleological theories are presented in different ways, including differences in the representation of the structure of a "moral act."[8] One difference is between an agent-relative and an agent-neutral perspective.[9] Schüller explains a teleological approach in an agent-neutral perspective. Referring to C. D. Broad, he defines a teleological theory as a position about the rightness or wrongness of actions distinct from the moral value of the acting person. He regards all the foreseeable consequences as criteria for the rightness or wrongness of the act:

> Deontological theories hold that there are ethical propositions of the form "such and such a kind of action would always be right (wrong) in such and such circumstances, no matter what its consequences might be [. . .]." Teleological theories hold that the rightness or wrongness of an action is always determined by its tendency to produce certain consequences which are intrinsically good or bad. [10]

According to Joseph A. Selling teleological approaches attempt to judge human activity as a whole, beginning with a consideration of the end that the person is attempting to achieve.[11] This position is critical against the talk of intrinsically evil acts because intention is neglected. It is also critical toward an agent-neutral perspective: "[. . .] without a sense of the ends or goals we are attempting to achieve, normative ethics remains legalistic."[12] Another example is Peter Knauer who also emphasizes this agent-relative perspective of intention in his reinterpretation of the principle of double effect.[13] His argument against deontological norms is: "The purely physical series of events is irrelevant to the moral qualification of good or bad."[14] In spite of differences in the reconstruction of the moral act, teleological theories oppose deontological norms because they are based on a limited description of the act and are judged without consideration of further properties.

A special problem arises if the notion intrinsically evil act is combined with deontological norms and used as an argument to reject critical debates about the correctness of such norms, their justification, and the underlying ethical theory.[15] Some authors and also the encyclical *Veritatis Splendor* have answered the critique of deontological norms by insisting on the notion of intrinsically evil acts. It seems to be easier to justify the judgment intrinsically evil act within a deontological theory, according to which a limited description of the act is sufficient.[16] If, for example, an act is described as "against nature" or as "direct killing of an innocent human being," further properties are no longer relevant.[17]

Within a teleological or proportionalist approach, moral evaluation requires a full description of the act including all the foreseen consequences, and, in an agent-relative perspective, the intention. This is more difficult for a norm of some generality. By using the term intrinsically evil combined with deontological norms, the wrong impression is given that deontological norms give a higher certainty than teleological ones. The term seems to designate a moral prohibition as binding in all cases without exception. Therefore, further critical thinking is suspected to hold that "these precepts should be considered as operative norms which are always relative and open to exceptions" (*VS*, 75). But teleological theories do not reject norms without exception. The controversy is about which cases are certain and which are uncertain,[18] not about norms without exceptions in general. There are good reasons to regard exceptions as a matter of complete or incomplete formulation of norms and not as characteristic of certain ethical theories.[19] From a teleological perspective, deontological norms include an incomplete description of the act: "This sort of action is always morally right (or wrong) regardless of its consequences."[20] Applied to a deontological norm, the meaning of the term intrinsically evil is "that it would always be wrong to choose this particular action or omission, no matter what the circumstances or intention of the person"[21] or "morally prohibited although desirable in respect of the consequences."[22]

THE DOCTRINE OF THE SOURCES OF MORALITY

As others have explained before, the notion of an intrinsically evil act has its primary place in the doctrine of the sources of morality.[23] This doctrine gave an answer to the moral question: what act is good or bad? Without going into details, the central theses are: There are three sources of morality: object, circumstances, and end. The object could be good, evil, or indifferent. Some actions are defined as intrinsically good or evil. This means that these acts are good or evil because of one source, the object. In this case the moral quality cannot be changed by the other sources. An intrinsically evil act cannot become a good one by circumstances or by the intended end. Werner Wolbert shows how this is analytically true, as soon as the terms are understood correctly.[24] If acts are evaluated as intrinsically evil within the logic of the sources of morality, further circumstances cannot change their moral quality. By definition, circumstances are not constitutive of the object.

The formal analogy between the sources of morality and deontological norms, both of which exclude the consideration of further circumstances or intention, leads to debatable positions with regard to ethical theories. A questionable assumption is that teleological ethics denies that acts are intrinsically evil as stipulated in the doctrine of the sources of morality. In *Veritatis*

Splendor the discussion about ethical theory is combined with the doctrine of the sources of morality:

> *One must therefore reject the thesis*, characteristic of teleological and propor-
> tionalist theories, *which holds that it is impossible to qualify as morally evil*
> *according to its species—its "object"—the deliberate choice of certain kinds*
> *of behavior or specific acts, apart from a consideration of the intention for*
> *which the choice is made or the totality of the foreseeable consequences of that*
> *act for all persons concerned. (VS, 79)*[25]

In a proportionalist view, as has been shown in the passage about normative ethics, consideration of intention or the foreseeable consequences is always necessary to establish a valid moral judgment about an act. Within the doctrine of the sources of morality consequences are part of the circumstances that per definition cannot change an intrinsically evil act (object) into a good one. These would be contradicting theses if they answered the same question.

But the doctrine of the sources of morality is not a specific position in normative ethical theory. The doctrine of the sources of morality and normative ethics deal with judgments on the moral quality of acts on a different level of critical thinking. Arguing with the sources of morality already presupposes specific normative principles and applies them to certain acts. It presupposes what normative ethics tries to answer: what is the morally correct definition of the act or object?[26] Schüller described the specific difference as follows: "All this makes it clear that the treatise, 'On the Sources of Morality', deals not with normative ethics but with a formal taxonomic model that can help us to describe actions in order to judge them morally against the standard of already given normative principles that are considered valid."[27] According to Selling it is best understood as "a technique for determining moral accountability" and "a tool developed for the purpose of hearing confessions."[28]

Within the doctrine of the sources of morality the notion intrinsically evil act has the technical meaning that an act is morally evil because of the object and independent of circumstances and intentions. What is included in the object and how the presupposed evaluation of an act as evil is justified, cannot be answered within the sources of morality. This is the task of normative ethics that does not simply apply moral norms, but tries to justify those norms on a critical level, including reflections about the right- or wrong-making properties of actions.

If this analysis is correct and the justification of norms is not the goal of the doctrine of the sources of morality, there seems to be no necessary conflict with teleological ethical theories. Teleological critique against certain presupposed deontological norms is not necessarily against the doctrine of the sources of morality. Vice versa, the doctrine of the sources of morality is not a good argument to support deontological norms against teleological approaches.

METAETHICS

Sometimes as critique of proportionalism a questionable thesis about meta-ethics is added: a teleological theory seems to deny "the existence of any intrinsically bad actions"[29] in the metaethical meaning of universally binding moral norms without any exception, the so called "moral absolutes." In her famous article about modern moral philosophy Elizabeth Anscombe emphatically rejects the consideration of consequences in the discussion about certain moral norms: "But if someone really thinks, in advance, that it is open to question whether such an action as procuring the judicial execution of the innocent should be quite excluded from consideration—I do not want to argue with him; he shows a corrupt mind."[30] *Veritatis Splendor* accuses teleological theories in general of denying absolute moral prohibitions:

> The teleological ethical theories (proportionalism, consequentialism), while acknowledging that moral values are indicated by reason and by Revelation, maintain that it is never possible to formulate an absolute prohibition of particular kinds of behavior which would be in conflict, in every circumstance and in every culture, with those values. (*VS*, 75)

Condemnation of certain acts as intrinsically evil is described as a central aspect of moral obligation: "As is evident, in the question of the morality of human acts, and in particular the question of whether there exist intrinsically evil acts, we find ourselves faced with the question of man himself, of his truth and of the moral consequences flowing from that truth" (*VS*, 83). Anyone who tries to question this kind of moral judgment in certain cases or in principle, is suspected of relativizing moral obligation in general, of "undermining the whole notion of morality."[31] However such arguments seem to confuse normative-ethical debates about the justification of certain norms and epistemological questions about truth and the human capability to recognize objective, binding moral obligation. This is evident in *VS*, 115: "Each of us can see the seriousness of what is involved, not only for individuals but also for the whole of society, with the *reaffirmation of the universality and immutability of the moral commandments*, particularly those which prohibit always and without exception intrinsically evil acts" (emphasis in original).

Frankena describes metaethics as follows: "There is also 'analytical,' 'critical,' or 'meta-ethical' thinking. [. . .] It does not consist of empirical or historical inquiries and theories, nor does it involve making or defending any normative or value judgments. It does not try to answer either particular or general questions about what is good, right, or obligatory. It asks and tries to answer logical, epistemological, or semantical questions [. . .]."[32] Schüller explains the epistemological meaning of the term *actus intrinsecus bonus/malus*: the term signifies moral norms as based on natural law in contrast to norms based on positive law, on a specific decision or imposed by authority:

> A directive is based on natural law insofar as it says of conduct: this is commanded because it's good, forbidden because it's bad: φύσει δίκαιον, φύσει ἄδικον. As such it must be distinguished from a directive based on positive law. Conduct that because of its intrinsic qualities is of necessity morally good and commanded, or morally bad and forbidden, is what tradition calls an *actus intrinsecus bonus* or an *actus intrinsecus malus*.[33]

"Natural law" in a metaethical sense expresses a cognitivist position: Each act that is evaluated as morally evil in normative ethics is intrinsically evil in this sense of the term: It is not evil because of the decision of somebody, but because of qualities that can be recognized by reason. In this metaethical perspective the term intrinsically evil act can be understood as designating a moral prohibition as objectively or universally (= for all people)[34] binding based on intrinsic qualities of the act.

If someone takes a cognitivist position as granted, the evaluation of an act as morally evil is always understood as intrinsically evil in the metaethical sense. Within normative ethics the term intrinsic does not add an additional qualification to the normative judgment. It just expresses the universal validity of every correct moral norm.[35] Proportionalists criticize deontological norms presented as absolute prohibitions and based on the argument *contra naturam*. But they do not reject natural law in the metaethical sense of the term:

> For some reason it strikes certain theologians as clear that such natural law directives and deontological norms are one and the same. This would mean that teleological ethics denies the existence of any intrinsically bad actions. In reality it is far from making any such denial, but it differs from the deontological approach in its view of the internal properties of an action that necessarily lend it its particular moral character.[36]

The identification of natural law directives in the metaethical sense with specific deontological norms (*contra naturam* as argument in normative ethics) is the approach that proportionalists would reject, because this identification inhibits critical debate about these norms.

The three perspectives sketched above might show how some of the arguments result from a confusion of terms based on the wrong "impression that actions judged from a deontological standpoint, actions defined as bad just on account of their object and intrinsically bad actions are one and the

same."[37] The logic of the *fontes moralitatis* and the idea of universally binding moral norms both seem to support deontological norms. But the principles presupposed by the sources of morality do not have to be equivalent to
deontological norms, nor is the metaethical question of exceptions (binding
in all cases) or universality (binding for all people) a difference between the
disputed ethical theories.[38] The debate about teleological theories is a debate
about specific positions in ethical theory, in the method of justifying norms.
A teleological theory is not about the doctrine of the sources of morality, not
about the theoretical or practical possibility to formulate certain norms without exceptions, and it is not a specific epistemological position. Most of these
discussions are misplaced within normative ethics. The debate is about right-
and wrong-making properties, about good and bad arguments for justification of moral norms and about consideration of all relevant circumstances in
describing and evaluating human acts.

PARENETIC SPEECH AND
MORAL ENCOURAGEMENT

Intrinsic evil in general is not only used as a moral term. There is another
context where a strong interest in clear and simple statements, even in the
form of slogans, is typical. James Bretzke speaks of "shibboleths."[39] Sometimes moral norms are expressed with a practical intention of performative
speech or a public moral appeal to people not even to think about doing such
actions. Schüller used the distinction of parenetic speech (he called it "moral
exhortation") and normative ethics to analyze texts of Biblical ethics, where
the question about rightness or wrongness is already answered.[40] The intended end of parenetic speech is not to convince by argument but rather to
motivate and encourage one to act or not to act in specific way. It aims not
toward the education of conscience but the support of a strong will that
ensures acting in accordance with specific moral norms. "Exhortation is to be
evaluated not primarily in terms of its truth-value but in terms of its effect-
value, that is, according to whether it is effective or ineffective, whether it
succeeds or fails."[41] Using intrinsically evil with this motivational goal is
another perspective outside the debate of deontological and teleological theories.

   In this perspective the term could express a strong moral appeal, a public
declaration, to unmistakably support some historically achieved moral consensus.[42] From a practical perspective this may have some advantages. Especially in a more legalistic conception of morality, the primary focus is com-
pliance with moral obligations and prohibitions, conformity and reliability of
moral behavior. A list of acts denoted as intrinsically evil may be perceived
as a strong and attractive statement. Uncompromisingly rejecting such acts

may be welcomed as clear guidance and orientation. It reduces complexity, sets strict limits, and enables identification. Sometimes this is more stimulating and encouraging than the complex field of moral reasoning.[43]

The term intrinsically evil act should be used in this context only if the moral evaluation of an act is considered finished and the work of normative ethics has come to an end. The moral act should be completely considered, the norm convincingly justified, and the normative sentence precisely formulated. If this is achieved and if there is a high degree of consensus—for example, about the condemnation of torture or the prohibition of chemical weapons—the talk of intrinsically evil acts could have some motivational effect. A notable restriction is to use the term only for moral prohibitions of high relevance for the welfare of the whole society.[44] Eberhard Schockenhoff, for instance, rejects the term in sexual ethics, where he assumes basic goods with "free zones of responsible choice" and limits it to the prohibition of killing and torture, because in those cases "it guarantees the necessary space protecting free and responsible development of one's personality."[45]

Although the term is synonymous with morally evil or morally wrong in the context of normative ethics, it could express an explicit consensus about a prohibition and a strong dissociation of certain behavior. It includes some emotional accent, and this is sometimes more motivating then pure reason. To avoid the confusing debates on *intrinsece malum*, one could use alternative terms like "damage to human dignity" or "crime against humanity." But these terms are also in danger of being misused as limits to critical thinking. There will always be some tension between the common interest in clear normative statements in society and in religious communities on the one side, and the task of normative ethics as a struggle for critical analysis of moral norms on the other. Critical debates can sometimes be provocative for people searching for moral orientation and certainty.

But a list of acts rejected as intrinsically evil is not helpful if consensus is lacking and severe moral controversies are present. As history has shown, the rejection of critical thinking by using the term intrinsically evil is not really effective. In the long run it does not help, if deontological arguments do not find common acceptance as in the discussions about artificial birth-control, remarried couples, or abortion in special cases. Proclaiming intrinsic evil instead of giving good arguments could be counterproductive, as the debate about abortion in Ireland has shown.

SHOULD WE STOP USING THE TERM "INTRINSICALLY EVIL"?

Speaking of intrinsically evil acts in the perspective of normative ethics and of ethical theory does not add something additional to the terms morally bad or morally wrong, but it does cause confusion about terms and raise more questions. Awareness of the plurality of meanings and the clear distinctions that are made in different moral theories could help to avoid some misunderstandings and enable a discussion of the real differences between teleological and deontological theories. It might also help in the necessary critical analysis of some controversial norms. If one is pessimistic about the chance for terminological clarity, a strategy of avoidance could be seen as a solution. Joseph Selling pleads for the elimination of the term within what he calls "personal ethics."[46] As an alternative, he proposes terms of virtue-ethics: "inappropriate or disproportionate for living virtuously."[47] As the term intrinsically evil is not necessary within normative ethics, this seems to be a good remedy.

But is it realistic to eliminate a term from moral language? There is no one who could enforce such a solution. If only some theologians do not use the term anymore, the avoidance of a certain terminology could once again be misunderstood, as Schüller noted, because "many people suspect that someone avoiding a specific word is dodging the thing which this word customarily stands for."[48] Maybe we could also learn from Knauer who did not avoid ambiguities, but used them to express his new theory. He maintained the traditional terminology in his reinterpretation of the principle of double effect. He continued to speak of intrinsically evil acts, but in a way that is compatible with a teleological theory.[49] He reduced the term to the general and unspecific meaning of "simply evil": "This is a thesis which has special significance for contemporary ethics. It says that 'morally evil' and 'intrinsically evil' are synonymous expressions."[50]

NOTES

1. Joseph A. Selling, *Reframing Catholic Theological Ethics* (Oxford: Oxford University Press, 2016), 20: "This entire moral position could be encapsulated in a single, short, easy to remember, and in a curious kind of way, catchy expression. Certain human actions must, by their very nature, be seen as morally unacceptable and may therefore never be performed. Neither good intentions nor any circumstances whatsoever may justify the performance of these acts because they have been found to be evil-in-themselves or 'intrinsically evil.'"

2. John Paul II, "Veritatis Splendor," (VS), accessed May 18, 2018, http://w2.vatican.va/content/john-paul-ii/en/encyclicals/documents/hf_jp-ii_enc_06081993_veritatis-splendor.html, 67.

3. Bruno Schüller, *Wholly Human: Essays on the Theory and Language of Morality* (Dublin: Gill and MacMillan; Washington, DC: Georgetown University Press, 1986), 192.

4. William K. Frankena, *Ethics* (Englewood Cliffs, NJ: Prentice-Hall, 1963), 10.

5. Ibid., 11.

6. Ibid., 47.

7. Ibid., 13–16; Schüller, *Wholly Human*, 171–72.

8. Eric D'Arcy, *Human Acts* (Oxford: Oxford University Press, 1963), 10–39; Christopher Kaczor, *Proportionalism and the Natural Law Tradition* (Washington, DC: The Catholic University of America Press, 2002), 45–90.

9. Selling, *Reframing*, 169–86, distinguishes a "normative approach" and a "goal-oriented approach."

10. Schüller, *Wholly Human*, 171.

11. Selling, *Reframing*, 10–12.

12. Ibid., 12.

13. Knauer defined every evil done with a proportionate reason as indirectly willed according to the principle of double effect: "If the chosen value is sought in its entirety in a commensurate way, the evil falls outside what is directly willed. In other cases when the reason of the act is not commensurate, the evils which arise are themselves directly willed even if they are not in the least desired in themselves" ("The Hermeneutic Function of the Principle of Double Effect," in *Readings in Moral Theology No. 1: Moral Norms and Catholic Tradition*, eds. Charles E. Curran and Richard A. McCormick [New York, NY/Ramsey, NJ/Toronto: Paulist Press, 1979], 16); see also "Fundamentalethik: Teleologische als deontologische Normenbegründung," *Theologie und Philosophie* 55 (1980): 339.

14. Knauer, "The Hermeneutic Function," 20. Later Knauer seems to have moved from this agent-interpretation of acts to an event-interpretation. By asking about the values that "should be aspired to" the perspective is changed to an agent-neutral perspective ("Was bedeutet 'in sich schlecht?'" in *Ethik der Lebensfelder: Festschrift für Philipp Schmitz*, ed. Paul Chummar Chittilappilly [Freiburg im Breisgau/Wien: Herder, 2010], 39).

15. Peter Knauer, "A Good End Does Not Justify an Evil Means—Even in a Teleological Ethics," in *Personalist Morals. Essays in Honor of Professor Louis Janssens*, ed. Joseph A. Selling (Leuven: Leuven University Press, 1988), 78: "Hence, the deontological foundation of norms, if understood as contrary to the teleological, is probably in reality only an unnecessary and regrettable renunciation of detailed argumentation. Under the appearance of special loyalty to ethical duty, these deontologians are missing an opportunity to establish their claims in a way that would be convincing for others as well, namely by argumentation. In place of this, they wrongly claim the a priori evidence of their statements."

16. Henry Sidgwick, *The Methods of Ethics*, 7th ed. (Indianapolis, IN; Cambridge: Heckett Publishing Company, 1907), chap. 7. He called this deontological claim of evidence without need for further argumentation "intuitionism."

17. Schüller, *Wholly Human*, 179.

18. John Paul II, "Veritatis Splendor," 76: "These theories cannot claim to be grounded in the Catholic moral tradition. Although the latter did witness the development of a casuistry which tried to assess the best ways to achieve the good in certain concrete situations, it is nonetheless true that this casuistry concerned only cases in which the law was uncertain, and thus the absolute validity of negative moral precepts, which oblige without exception, was not called into question."

19. Werner Wolbert, "Intrinsic Evil and the Sources of Morality," this volume, 105: "The possibility or necessity of exceptions may depend on the complete or incomplete formulation of a norm." See also Id., "Wege und Umwege einer ethischen Normierungstheorie," in *Grundlagen und Probleme der heutigen Moraltheologie*, ed. Wilhelm Ernst (Leipzig: St. Benno-Verlag, 1989), 76–79; Andreas M. Weiß, *Sittlicher Wert und nichtsittliche Werte: Zur Relevanz der Unterscheidung in der moraltheologischen Diskussion um deontologische Normen* (Freiburg i. Ue.: Universitätsverlag; Freiburg i. Br.: Herder, 1996), 64–68.

20. Schüller, *Wholly Human*, 171–72.

21. Selling, *Reframing*, 179, fn. 12.

22. Werner Wolbert, "Der Proportionalismus und die in sich schlechten Handlungen," *Studia Moralia* 45 (2007): 384: "sittlich verboten, obwohl von den Folgen her wünschenswert."

23. Werner Wolbert, "Die 'in sich schlechten' Handlungen und der Konsequentialismus," in *Moraltheologie im Abseits? Antwort auf die Enzyklika 'Veritatis Splendor'*, ed. Dietmar Mieth (Freiburg: Herder, 1994), 90–94; Joseph A. Selling, "Veritatis Splendor and the Sources of Morality," *Louvain Studies* 19 (1994): 3–17; Schüller, *Wholly Human*, 191; Wolbert, "Der Proportionalismus," 393.

24. Wolbert, "Der Proportionalismus," 393.

25. Wolbert, "Die 'in sich schlechten' Handlungen," 89–90; Selling, "Veritatis Splendor," 6.

26. Wolbert, "Die 'in sich schlechten' Handlungen," 103; Cf. Kaczor, *Proportionalism*, 95.
27. Schüller, *Wholly Human*, 191; Cf. Kaczor, *Proportionalism*, 91–118.
28. Selling, "Veritatis Splendor," 16f; *Reframing*, 23–24.
29. Schüller, *Wholly Human*, 192.
30. Gertrude E. M. Anscombe, "Modern Moral Philosophy," *Philosophy* 33, no. 124 (1958): 17.
31. See the report of Gerhard Höver's critique of the term "intrinsically evil": Edward Pentin, "Pontifical Academy for Life Member: Term 'Intrinsically Evil' Too Restricting," *National Catholic Register*, January 29, 2018, http://www.ncregister.com/blog/edward-pentin/pontifical-academy-for-life-member-term-intrinsically-evil-too-restricting.
32. Frankena, *Ethics*, 4.
33. Schüller, *Wholly Human*, 192; Wolbert, "Der Proportionalismus," 377–78.
34. Wolbert, "Der Proportionalismus," 393.
35. Schüller, *Wholly Human*, 193: "[. . .] the immutability that tradition claims for the natural law is only a logical trivial consequence drawn from the notion of the natural law."
36. Ibid., 192.
37. Ibid.
38. Wolbert, "Der Proportionalismus," 379.
39. James T. Bretzke, "Intrinsic Evil in *Veritatis Splendor* and Two Contemporary Debates," this volume, 63.
40. Schüller, *Wholly Human*, 16–32.
41. Schüller, *Wholly Human*, 25.
42. *VS*, 80–81 is a problematic passage, because it takes the text from *GS* 27 that has a strong appellative character as argument in the debate about *intrinsece malum* and ethical theories. Wolbert, "Die 'in sich schlechten' Handlungen," 89–91.
43. An example is the idea of Pope Francis completely and unconditionally to condemn the death penalty. Many people welcome such a claim, although in principle the question seems to be answered in a correct way in the *Catechism of the Catholic Church*. The Holy See, "Catechism of the Catholic Church," accessed May 26, 2018, http://w2.vatican.va/content/francesco/en/speeches/2017/october/documents/papa-francesco_20171011_convegnfundamentalethiko-nuova-evangelizzazione.pdf, 2267.
44. Stephan Herzberg, "Aristotle on Intrinsically Bad Actions," this volume, 8.
45. Eberhard Schockenhoff, *Grundlegung der Ethik: Ein theologischer Entwurf*, 2nd ed. (Freiburg/Basel/Wien: Herder, 2014), 567. Cf. John Paul II, "Veritatis Splendor," 90, claiming that norms prohibiting intrinsically evil acts aim at the protection of human dignity. Which ethical norm does not?
46. Selling, *Reframing*, 200.
47. Ibid.
48. Schüller, *Wholly Human*, 193.
49. Peter Knauer, "Das rechtverstandene Prinzip von der Doppelwirkung als Grundnorm jeder Gewissensentscheidung," *Theologie und Glaube* 57 (1967): 107–33.
50. Knauer, "The Hermeneutic Function," 7. This sentence was added in the English version and was not part of the earlier French and German articles from 1967.

REFERENCES

Anscombe, Gertrude E. M. "Modern Moral Philosophy." *Philosophy* 33, no. 124 (1958): 1–19.
D'Arcy, Eric. *Human Acts*. Oxford: Oxford University Press, 1963.
Frankena, William K. *Ethics*. Englewood Cliffs, NJ: Prentice-Hall, 1963.
John Paul II. "Veritatis Splendor." http://w2.vatican.va/content/john-paul-ii/en/encyclicals/documents/hf_jp-ii_enc_06081993_veritatis-splendor.html (Accessed May 18, 2018).
Kaczor, Christopher. *Proportionalism and the Natural Law Tradition*. Washington, DC: The Catholic University of America Press, 2002.
Knauer, Peter. "Das rechtverstandene Prinzip von der Doppelwirkung als Grundnorm jeder Gewissensentscheidung." *Theologie und Glaube* 57 (1967): 107–33.

————. "Fundamentalethik: Teleologische als deontologische Normenbegründung." *Theologie und Philosophie* 55 (1980): 321–60.

————. "A Good End Does Not Justify an Evil Means—Even in a Teleological Ethics." In *Personalist Morals. Essays in Honor of Professor Louis Janssens*, edited by Joseph A. Selling, 71–85. Leuven: Leuven University Press, 1988.

————. "The Hermeneutic Function of the Principle of Double Effect." In *Readings in Moral Theology No. 1: Moral Norms and Catholic Tradition*, edited by Charles E. Curran and Richard A. McCormick, 1–39. New York, NY/Ramsey, NJ/Toronto: Paulist Press 1979 (*Natural Law Forum* 12 [1967]: 132–62).

————. "Was bedeutet 'in sich schlecht?'" In *Ethik der Lebensfelder: Festschrift für Philipp Schmitz*, edited by Paul Chummar Chittilappilly, 29-43. Freiburg im Breisgau/Wien: Herder 2010.

Schockenhoff, Eberhard. *Grundlegung der Ethik: Ein theologischer Entwurf.* 2nd ed. Freiburg/Basel/Wien: Herder, 2014.

Schüller, Bruno. *Wholly Human: Essays on the Theory and Language of Morality.* Dublin: Gill and MacMillan; Washington, DC: Georgetown University Press, 1986.

Selling, Joseph A. *Reframing Catholic Theological Ethics.* Oxford: Oxford University Press, 2016.

————. "Veritatis Splendor and the Sources of Morality." *Louvain Studies* 19 (1994): 3–17.

Sidgwick, Henry. *The Methods of Ethics.* 7th ed. Indianapolis, IN; Cambridge: Heckett Publishing Company, 1907.

Weiß, Andreas M. *Sittlicher Wert und nichtsittliche Werte: Zur Relevanz der Unterscheidung in der moraltheologischen Diskussion um deontologische Normen.* Freiburg i. Ue.: Universitätsverlag; Freiburg i. Br.: Herder, 1996.

Wolbert, Werner. "Der Proportionalismus und die in sich schlechten Handlungen." *Studia Moralia* 45 (2007): 377–99.

————. "Die 'in sich schlechten' Handlungen und der Konsequentialismus." In *Moraltheologie im Abseits? Antwort auf die Enzyklika "Veritatis Splendor,"* edited by Dietmar Mieth, 88–109. Freiburg: Herder 1994.

————. "Wege und Umwege einer ethischen Normierungstheorie." In *Grundlagen und Probleme der heutigen Moraltheologie,* edited by Wilhelm Ernst, 75–93. Leipzig: St. Benno-Verlag 1989.

Chapter Ten

Pope Francis's Heresy?

Edward C. Vacek, S.J.

Reactions to Pope Francis's position on divorce and remarriage have at times been apoplectic. In his criticism of *Amoris Laetitia*, Christian Brugger writes that "We are a million miles from *Veritatis Splendor.*"[1] Brugger sharply favors Pope John Paul II's view on intrinsic evil (IE) over against Pope Francis's view. In retort, a few writers claim that anyone who disagrees with the papacy are themselves heretics.[2] Having myself been attacked previously on IE, I happily find myself in company with my fellow Jesuit, Pope Francis. I welcome the opportunity once again to examine this contentious topic.[3]

Fred Martinez joins the catastrophizing critics. "The unscholarly Pope Francis has promoted the heresy of the denial of intrinsically evil acts."[4] Martinez explains that the pope's teaching "appears to deny the truths of the Decalogue." Like many who appeal to the Decalogue, Martinez himself seems oblivious to the fact that, due to Jesus's incarnation and resurrection, the Catholic Church has for almost two millennia ignored at least two of the ten commandments: images and Sabbath. Martinez claims that this papal heresy "destroys all Catholic moral doctrine." Even worse, he writes, the pope's view leads to the "Collapse of Catholic and Western Civilization"[5]— no small accomplishment for a few paragraphs in a papal letter.

Scholarly outbursts also occurred. Theologian Josef Seifert asserted that the pope's position "has the capacity to destroy all Catholic moral teaching."[6] Well-known philosophers such as Germain Grisez and John Finnis argue somewhat more coyly that if the pope means what his advocates take him to mean, then the pope is a heretic.[7] Several bishops and at least one cardinal likewise have denounced the pope's position. In response, advocates of Francis's position might accuse these critics of the Gnosticism and Pelagianism that the pope rejected in his apostolic exhortation *Gaudete et Exsultate.*[8] The neo-Gnostics are certain that they know the true meaning of Catholic teaching, while the neo-Pelagians hold that people can and must do the humanly impossible, if only those people would just try harder.[9]

INTRINSIC EVIL

It is worth noting that Pope John Paul II, like most others in this absolutist school of thought, simply asserts the teaching on IE without much explanation or proof that there are any acts that are IE. Indeed a few authors seem ignorant of the meaning of IE. For example, Bishop Morlino considers private property along with marriage to be areas where any aberrance is IE.[10] Apparently, when the state exercises a right of eminent domain or permits divorce, he thinks these infringements are IE. By contrast, Aquinas argued that, although one should respect private property, one should not return a sword to its drunken owner who is threatening to do harm.[11] Some in the tradition have argued that killing in personal self-defense is IE, while others have claimed that making false claims even to save a life is IE. But few hold those positions today.

To be sure, there are other meanings of the term "intrinsic evil" than the technical term discussed in this chapter. In a medical sense, debilitating diseases such as congenital blindness are IE. Further, one might argue that some acts are IE "by definition"—for example, if a lie is understood to be an unjustifiable telling of a falsehood, then a lie cannot be justified. Such norms are one kind of "formal norm," to be distinguished from material norms, which hold for the most part.[12] Also all moralists can say that any moral evil is IE, but this judgment is made at the end of a process when all relevant considerations have already been included. It applies to the conclusion. In its technical use, IE is a moral claim about a particular object that is made exclusive of considerations of context, alternatives, and intentions.

Those who use the category of IE are often not very careful in what they include in the category. For example, John Paul II cited a list from Vatican II that includes "any kind of homicide," which, unlike murder, is clearly not part of the IE tradition. The list includes subhuman working conditions and demeaning wages, surely both evils, but evils that can be chosen when they are the only way to feed one's family, such as in a famine. The list refers to "deportation," which a nation often rightly uses to exclude spies. In other contexts, speaking about marital matters, John Paul II considered the use of contraception to be an IE, and he tried a novel way to justify this claim, requiring nothing less than "total" self-giving in all acts of marital sexual intercourse. Good married people know that, amid the many obligations of life, total self-giving is rare and its absence is not a matter of damning sin.[13] Total love does not spring full bloom with the exchange of vows. Debates on fundamental option have at least the merit of acknowledging that we humans rarely if ever totally give ourselves.

The technical meaning of IE as found in *Veritatis Splendor* is a behavior that is evil in itself quite apart from circumstances, intentions, or consequences.[14] It is this technical meaning that scholars increasingly reject. This concept of IE requires that we exclude consideration of all reality except the deed itself. We are to focus only on the immediate deed apart from broader intentions and context, an abstraction that would leave most human deeds unintelligible. To hold that an act is IE claims that we can know in advance that there can be no possible contexts, historical eras, different worlds, divine revelations, and so forth, in which there could be exceptions. Because of the near infinite possibilities of real and imaginary cases, it seems impossible to assert that some particular action is an IE—with one exception: the one act that is *semper et pro semper* evil is to hate God.

There is much inconsistency in the list of acts that are IE.[15] Put simply, there seem to be no noncircular criteria for *what* counts as an IE, *how* we would know a particular kind of act is IE, and *why* it is an IE. To take an example, the Church generally teaches that taking another's property or killing another is wrong, but it does not claim these are IE since there are occasions like war when they can both be justified. If we look at second marriages, we recognize that some come about through the death of a spouse, so the problem is not just a sexually active second or third marriage. Rather it would seem that the problem is divorce itself. Needless to say, people ought not break their promises. But once promises have been broken, it is ordinarily appropriate to make amends and move forward. People in consecrated life take vows that are "perpetual," but the Church allows them to be dissolved. Marriage and ownership, which once would have been sins against their vows of chastity and poverty, now become arenas of grace. According to John Paul II, an IE is an activity that cannot be "ordered to the good and to the ultimate end, which is God."[16] The obvious question is why in a second marriage both lovemaking and shared reception of the Eucharist cannot be so ordered. The reason given is not that the sin of divorce cannot be forgiven. Rather the reason is that divorce is impossible.

Contrary to what one might then expect, the Church urges persons who are living in what appear to be second marriages to take an active role in the Eucharist service, in prayer, and in works of justice. The Catholic Church allows divorce-in-reality to happen under the rubric of separations. While temporary separations can be part of married life, deliberately lifelong separations are not. We might recall that most if not all other religions have not had the insight that divorce and remarriage is impossible or that sexual activity therein is IE. Perhaps this is so because there is no insight to be had. Indeed, most human beings do not agree with the strict Catholic view which holds that second marriages are not marriages at all. Pope Francis recommends that theologians seriously consider these alternative views.[17] His approach recognizes that the people of God inside and outside the Catholic Church may have some wisdom and, thereby, might contribute to the Church's teaching.

Finally, the current Church teaching on IE occasionally puts the Church at odds with itself. For example, an older teaching argued it was required to let a pregnant woman die, along with her fetus, rather than directly remove the fetus when, for example, the presence of the fetus was causing her heart to fail. The Church's "affirmation of life" is undermined by its theory. Similarly, according to more recent Vatican teaching, when an embryo has been frozen, the official teaching has held that there is literally nothing we can morally do. It is said that to implant the embryo in a willing, adopting mother is IE. As John Paul II claimed, there is "no morally licit solution." Better the embryo die than reproductive technology take place to give it life. The doctrine of IE casts doubt on the Church's pro-life stance.[18] Similarly, the claim that those married who no longer live together are still married reduces the meaning of marriage to the existence of a document in a parish vault. It undercuts the Church's theology of marriage. In sum, as David Cloutier observes, the term "intrinsic evil is no longer a technical term used to analyze moral action, but an intimidating buzzword used to elevate certain issues to prominence."[19]

IRREGULAR SITUATIONS

The chief offending, supposedly heretical papal passages are from *Amoris Laetitia*. We should develop; the pope writes in 301,

> an adequate understanding of the possibility and need of special discernment in certain "irregular" situations [. . .]. Hence it can no longer simply be said that all those in any "irregular" situation are living in a state of mortal sin and are deprived of sanctifying grace. More is involved here than mere ignorance of the rule. A subject may know full well the rule, yet have great difficulty in understanding "its inherent values," or be in a concrete situation which does not allow him or her to act differently and decide otherwise without further sin.

A few comments are in order. The pope writes of "special discernment," indicating that the usual deductive approach of the moral manuals need not be followed. The pope speaks of "irregular situations." The human world has been in irregular situations since the sin of Adam. The pope wrote, "it can no longer be said"—a very daring claim because he sets aside the very position that many moralists, Vatican officials, and ordinary Catholics still assert. The pope acknowledges but then makes clear that he is not primarily concerned with one of the basic reasons why persons in an irregular situation may not be sinning, namely, they are unaware of the moral rule they are offending. This is an important pastoral consideration, but there is nothing new in that as far as Church teaching goes.

The pope, however, raises two other quite different possibilities. The first is on the subject's side, namely, persons may intellectually "know" but not comprehend the moral significance of what they are doing. Moral theologians, such as Richard Gula and a host of others, point out that conceptual knowledge is different from evaluative knowledge.[20] Evaluative knowledge, as I have elsewhere been at pains to demonstrate, refers to the knowledge we gain through our affections.[21] The second possibility is that there are concrete situations in which it is impossible to follow the standard moral rule without bringing about other or new evils. This kind of comparison has been at the basis of the school that deals with proportionalism, within which my own writing lies.[22]

The pope considers cases such as when a woman is in a second marriage with children. He asserts it would be wrong for her to simply abandon her second husband and their children just so that she could return to her first spouse, who himself might also be married with new children. The solution of a theologically induced dilemma ought not be to recommend serious new human evils. Also the solution should not be to just do nothing, say, by walking away from both marriages, as if separation would be a way to be faithful to either marriage. Permanent separation, though allowed by the Church, is the end of a marriage in its human meaning. A house we once owned, but has been washed away by the ocean, is no longer a house, even if we might still have the original deed. Paradoxically, for each of the twice married to have sexual relationships with their previous spouse could, according to official teaching, be morally upright, whereas legally it would be adultery.

John Paul II gave excellent pastoral advice when he encouraged the remarried to "attend the Sacrifice of the Mass, to persevere in prayer, to contribute to works of charity and to community efforts in favor of justice."[23] But his strict theology should instead have announced that, if they were still sexually active, none of this brings grace and that, as enemies (mortal sinners) who hate God, their acts could even be considered to be an affront to God. Fortunately, few people actually draw further conclusions that follow from this law-based theology: for example, if they were to get an annulment from their first marriage, then the sexual acts that produced children in the first marriage would have been "objectively sinful" because they were not "marital sexual acts" and the sexual acts of the second marriage could now, after proper processes, be retrofitted to be objectively acts of marital goodness. Fortunately, in a gracious gesture, Canon Law c. 1137 declares that children of what was, because of an annulment, not a real marriage are nevertheless "legitimate." When theology becomes this distant from reality, it is time to reassess.

DISCERNMENT

Later, in *Amoris Laetitia*, 303, Pope Francis remarkably reframes the moral situation in terms of discernment rather than simply deduction:

> conscience can [. . .] also recognize with sincerity and honesty what for now is the most generous response which can be given to God, and come to see with a certain moral security that it is what God himself is asking amid the concrete complexity of one's limits, while yet not fully the objective ideal. [. . .] This discernment is dynamic; it must remain ever open to new stages of growth and to new decisions which can enable the ideal to be more fully realized.

This paragraph again challenges the common view. Although none of us can ever be sure that we are in a state of grace, still we may have "a certain moral security" that we are acting out of a good heart.[24] To be sure, self-deception is common.[25] Nevertheless a couple's sincere decision likely is a response to God. Further, Francis praises this discerned response not as minimalistic but as generous to God. Remarkably, the pope adds that it is God who is asking a person to continue in this irregular situation. This is a bold claim, since it asserts that the reception of Eucharist in the irregular situation may not only be justified before but also even demanded by God. If so, those who would refuse the Eucharist to the divorced and remarried might well be opposing the will of God. Finally, the text urges virtuous marital growth, rather than strong willed stasis. The tendency of traditional thinking has been either/or. Francis speaks of good enough and better. What for Francis is a never-achievable "ideal" was for John Paul II the minimum necessary.

It should be noted that Francis describes this process as discernment. In the Ignatian tradition which he shares, religious discernment is usually not directed to doing the best or the ideal. Discerners are to be personally indifferent to wealth/poverty or even to great Christian accomplishments. Rather, they are to discover what God wants them in particular to do. Francis's discussion asks people in second marriages to discern what is appropriate in their present situation, while being open to new challenges from God.

Unlike John Paul II who distinguished an acceptable "law of gradualism" from an unacceptable "gradualism of the law," Pope Francis argues for suitable alternatives to a morally unworkable law. The good that is now impossible in the first marriage may well be achieved within the second marriage. He proposes that the challenge some people face is not how gradually to get out of the second marriage and return to the first marriage. Nor is their challenge how to gradually reduce involvement in the second marriage, beginning with avoiding love-making sexual activity. Rather, the context of their second marriage can and should include sexual activity as an expression of and contributor to their marriage. Married love should grow.

MERCY AND CONSCIENCE

One way of exploring the differences between Pope Francis and his objectors is to consider his emphasis on mercy. In the present discussion, it is not a matter of mercy versus truth, as if Francis is in a look-the-other-way, forgiving mood while his detractors insist on facing moral truth. Rather, his emphasis on mercy focuses on what is sometimes called the pastoral realm, the realm of people's messy lives. It can and should be noted that this approach is not pastoral because it is mushy. Rather, it is pastoral since it focuses on the particularities of the lives of unique persons. His move parallels that of the moral methodology of proportionalism which John Paul II rejected.

In the above papal text, Francis refers to conscience. The oft-praised heuristic from Timothy O'Connell on conscience #1, #2, and #3 is helpful here.[26] #1: Moral theologians devote considerable intellectual effort to understanding the very meaning of being moral. They might debate, for example, whether the ultimate maxim should be "Do good and avoid evil" or "Do good and overcome evil." The latter, more Marxist view, has gained some adherents. #2: Most people, however, are concerned with the various subareas of morality and the norms appropriate to those areas. For example, love in marriage should be fruitful, and reneging on promises is bad. #3: The disputed areas of this chapter, however, refer to personal and social practical decisions. This third exercise of conscience deals with resolving particular situations that may be riddled with the conflicts of actual living. For example, for conscience #2, taking another person's property is wrong; but for conscience #3, since my children are starving to death, I may have a positive obligation to grab some fruit from an idle orchard.

Mercy in such exercises of conscience #3 is not a willingness to forgive or overlook the sin. That is a different kind of mercy. A second, different kind of mercy is offering the compassion needed when a person just does not have the strength to do what ought to be done. Here the merciful person accompanies the weak, with the hope that their strength will grow, and then they will be able to do the proper act. Third, for Francis the exercise of mercy enters into the mess of people's lives, and it enables them to make the best of a bad or irregular situation when the alternative is worse. God's mercy in Christ also took this third form. When Christ mercifully entered into a sinful world, he did not return humanity to a prelapsarian paradise. Rather his redemption enables humans to live graced lives in an irregular world. His mercy enters into the brokenness of people's lives, and it enables them to work out what is a morally appropriate decision in that kind of world. The insights generated by this kind of mercy, Pope Francis suggests, may decide that it is morally appropriate to work at actually improving one's second marriage. That would be totally inappropriate if that marriage were sinful. Instead, Francis indicates, abandoning or limiting the second marriage may itself be sinful, against God's loving will. Bloom where you are replanted.

Those who insist on IE reject mercy in this third sense. They can stand outside, casting the stones provided for them by their theory. The approach that John Paul II took with respect to married couples who use artificial birth control was sternly consistent. He concluded that they degrade one another and falsify their love, no matter how much love they feel and how dedicated they are to one another.[27] More strikingly, John Paul II even argued: "It is not possible to practice natural methods as a 'licit' variation on the decision to be closed to life, which would be substantially the same as that which inspires the decision to use contraceptives."[28] That position was consistent with his usual position, but it skipped over the actual needs of many married persons who turned to NFP for precisely that reason. In the same way, he would conclude, those who are in second marriages are not really in second marriages, since, one deduces, there simply can be no second marriages while the first spouse is alive.

Following this pattern, some theologians are secure that the moral norms arrived at in Conscience #2 suffice, and so they conclude that love-making in second marriages is just hateful adultery. The couple's lives might look in almost every respect like a good marriage, but, one should conclude, theirs is not a marriage. They ought to abandon their current family, especially if it is an ongoing source of damning temptation. To the contrary, Pope Francis observes, abandoning their second marriage would itself likely be sinful. Indeed, in what is one of his strongest claims, Francis writes that it may well be God's will that they not only stay with their current family but that they also grow stronger in that commitment.

NEW CONTEXT

Context changes the meaning of sexual activity. Sex inside marriage is morally different from premarital sex and again from preceremonial sex. So also in a second marriage, after the first marriage has *de facto* ended, sex is not well described as adultery. Indeed Church teaching has over the centuries changed the meaning of sex within marriage. Before Vatican II loveless but procreative sex or even sex to satisfy lust was, according to Canon Law, normatively right. After Vatican II and the new demands of contemporary marriage, loveless, lustful sex in marriage became morally suspect. Over the last hundred years human lives on average have extended from approximately thirty to seventy years. The possibilities of a long-term harmful coexistence grew. This new context is crucially and deliberately absent in the thinking of those who argue for the absolute indissolubility of marriage. As a pastoral consequence, recourse to annulments had to increase. Creative canonists modified the criterion of annulments such that, for example, it could sometimes be shown that a ten-year marriage with two children never really existed because of some defect.

Context matters, though in limited ways. It is usually a matter of indifference whether, for example, one votes in the morning or in the afternoon. On the other hand, acts that are declared to be IE are by definition independent of context and intention. For example, if abortion is IE, abortion to save the life of the mother can never be justified. Better two deaths than one IE. Of course, moralists strove to be more merciful, and so they creatively distinguished between an indirect and a direct abortion. Better one cutting off of an impregnated fallopian tube than the death of a pregnant woman. Useful though the principle of double effect is, it led to convoluted thinking in order to meet its first criterion, namely, that the act-in-itself was not IE. In innumerable cases, context and intention change the meaning of the act-in-itself.[29] Thus there may be unforeseen contexts in which a particular material deed might have a different meaning.

Francis suggests that we should seriously consider what is proportioned to the "concrete possibilities of man." That is essential both in making moral norms and making particular judgments. He recognizes ideals as goals that, realistically, may be beyond attainment. Discernment may then suggest the possibility or even the necessity of an alternative. He indirectly rejects the more stringent position of John Paul II, who wrote: "It would be a very serious error [. . .] to conclude that the Church's teaching is essentially only an 'ideal' which must then be adapted, proportioned, graduated to the so-called concrete possibilities of man."[30] What John Paul II says must not be done is what Francis does. That which is not concretely possible is not required. Speaking from pastoral experience, Francis recognizes that moral possibility is not the same as abstract possibility. He speaks of marriage as an evolving love union of persons rather than of an institution whose existence is independent of the actual lives of those within it. In official teaching, the institution firmly exists even when it does not fulfill or actually contravenes the very purposes for which it was established. The pastor in Francis recognizes that the best can be the enemy of the good. That is, the ideal can actually undermine the here-and-now-really-possible good.

SCRIPTURAL CONCERNS

Over recent decades, there has been legitimate criticism, explicitly in Vatican II, that Catholic ethicists fail to connect their thinking with their Christian sources, especially the scriptures. There are reasons for that omission, of course, chiefly the desire to do natural law ethics which can be shared with non-Christians. Still it is remarkable that within its own ranks and in the Church's official teaching, there has been so little reference to major scriptural conundrums that challenge IE.

Many of the practical issues dealt with by IE concern sex and killing. A quick glance shows that violations against so-called IE are practiced and presumably justified in our scriptures. Those include the God-mandated direct killing of the innocent; not to mention the stealing of property or the initiation of nondefensive wars (Joshua 6:20–26; Deuteronomy 20:16–17; 1 Chronicles 20:1–2; 2 Samuel 11:1). They seem to include rites that induce abortion, "make your womb discharge," in cases of marital infidelity (Numbers 5:27). Although many conservative Catholic ethicists are opposed to homosexual actions, to my knowledge, none, including Vatican officials, currently insist on following the clear biblical injunction to kill people who are homosexually active (Leviticus 20:13).

More centrally, the circumstances of Jesus's birth and death are not very favorable to teaching on IE. If we wanted to, we could easily redescribe his conception as a divinely inspired instance of artificial (that is, nonnatural) reproduction. But few would say that Mary agreed to mortal sin with her "Fiat." The tradition happily claims that the Holy Spirit, not Joseph her own husband, overshadowed her, and that she got pregnant before they were fully married. Another perplexing oddity is that later tradition, in order to preserve her virginity, redescribed the bible's reference to her six or more children (Matthew 12:46; 13:55; Mark 6:3; John 2:12; 7:3, 5, 10; Acts 1:14; 1 Corinthians 9:5; Galatians 1:19). Even if, as the Catholic tradition has claimed without biblical confirmation, the children were Joseph's from an earlier marriage, the bible suggests that Mary and Joseph each had to deal with what Pope Francis describes as an "irregular" situation. We may want to think of these stories as theological accounts rather than as history. Still, they cast doubt on the claim that "irregular" marriages are IE.

Concerning issues of death, similar oddities occur that should be faced by those who argue against practices they describe as IE. According to the scriptures, when Jesus sensed that, as part of his mission, he would be killed, he deliberately went toward, not away from, Jerusalem. His action created the conditions of avoidable grave injustice on the part of many. He knowingly, though indirectly, cooperated with what could be called the world's greatest sin. Yet the church teaches that his action saved the human race. Again, historically, Jesus may have had no such ideas in his mind. He may have been an unwitting victim of his own generosity. But the theological tradition holds that his was an act of supreme love in which no one took his life from him but rather he laid it down on his own authority in response to God (John 10:18). No one judges Jesus for cooperating, even indirectly, in IE. Nor does anyone criticize God for demanding an act that, according to the theology of IE, can never be permitted under any circumstances. To reply that such acts are not wrong when it is God who invites them is to open the possibility that the typically named IE are not wrong if, through discernment, a person learns that God invites people in their particular circumstances to do what otherwise is an IE. In fact, the latter is near what Pope Francis suggests.

The Sabbath law was said to be from God, and Jesus dared to revise the law. Humans were not made for the Sabbath, but the Sabbath was made for humans (Mark 2:27). Marriage is made for humans. If the Sabbath law did not serve human life, it could be set aside, as Jesus was recorded to do seven times in the scriptures. Thus when scholars refer to Jesus's statement on those who commit divorce and remarry, there should be hesitancy to understand that he thought that such remarriage was an IE that can never be permitted. The bible seems clear that he said "Don't divorce!" It is not clear that he meant to say that divorce is impossible. Already in the early Church exceptions were made. Matthew cites Jesus's words on divorce, and then adds "except for adultery (*porneia*)" (Matt 5:32). Paul allows divorce for the sake of "peace" (1 Corinthians 7:12–15). The Church has done so ever after. According to the Pauline and Petrine privileges, approximately 70 percent of the world's marriages can be divorced with remarriage possible.

AFFECTIVE CONVERSION

It is perhaps obvious that there are different mind-sets at work in this debate. I have suggested that at least part of the difference involves different understandings of conscience. Is the transition from this or that moral norm (Conscience #2) to this or that particular situation (Conscience #3) simply a deduction? Thomas Aquinas spoke of descending to particulars, where the judgment about what to do is not simply a deduction but rather is an exercise of prudence or wisdom. The norm says that it is wrong to lie, yet wisdom urges us to tell the Nazi soldier that there are no Jews living in our attic. To be sure, sophisticated moralists have found ingenious ways to explain such exceptions, for example, mental reservation or lack of a right to the truth. In other situations, they have created justifications such as the difference between intending and permitting, or between direct and indirect. I do not intend here to cast aspersions on such efforts. Rather I propose that at least sometimes these convolutions of thought become too far removed from reality.

In divorce situations, emotions that once gave strength to the absoluteness of the conviction that marriage should last forever now give way to emotions that acknowledge the wrongness of staying in a bad marriage. In each case, emotions reveal values that are at stake. This occurs not because emotions are "fickle," but because they unveil the ethical significance of a new situation. A person says, "There is real irregularity here, and that feels bad because it is bad. The old promises are no longer practically possible and now there are other, more important goods at stake." Such irregularities are pre-moral evils. Life is full of them. One should avoid or resist such evils as much as is practically possible. That requires working to overcome them. But when the fig tree no longer produces fruit, it seems appropriate to move on rather than starve. Discerning persons may rightly feel that God is inviting them to engage in a new love-relationship. God may be inviting them to pursue a life that is both possible and on the whole good.

I point here to affective conversions. We can usefully distinguish several kinds of conversion: intellectual, moral, and religious, as well as sensitive, aesthetic, and practical. Conversion is a process that involves a significant change in which one leaves behind or even repudiates characteristic features of one's previous perspective or practice.[31] Affective conversion refers to a change in one's *ordo amoris*.[32] As we have seen above, the affective rejection of IE on the issue of divorce and remarriage is seen by its critics as a descent into madness. Rather, those who set aside the abstract claims of IE theory see themselves as rising to wisdom. They experience the affective process of mercy. Their sense of mercy enables them to appreciate the messiness and possibilities of human life in a new, more appreciative way. This affective conversion appears in the difference between classical and historical consciousness.[33] Classical thinking is well exemplified in mathematics: what was true is true now and will be true. The historical mind-set is much more affectively attuned to particulars. The meaning of marriage, while possessing some stability, has changed over time and cultures. Such variation continues, as is evident in the changes of the Church's teaching on marriage over the past one hundred years, shifting from a baby-making contract to a love-making covenant.[34] Of course, not all differences are improvements or even appropriate. Any variation must embody marital values and be revised so as to enable people better to love God and one another.

The present pope, with his multiple experiences among so many ordinary people, seems to have undergone a conversion. He found inadequate the standard teaching that denies the Eucharist to people who otherwise seem to be living good lives in second marriages. His sense of mercy overcame the idea that these people were still violating their first marriage; rather they were lovingly involved in their current marriages and families. Francis develops a pastoral practice that assures sexually active, remarried people that not only should they attend Mass but it is possible that they can worthily participate in communing with God.

My own position should be obvious. I think Pope Francis has a better understanding of human life, at least on the issues discussed. The absolutist mindset that served John Paul II so well in fighting communism did not serve him well in understanding the tough places in marital life. Early in his Jesuit life, Jorge Bergoglio is said to have inhabited that strict world, and he enforced it on others. But then he changed. His work in the *barrios* prepared him to see and appraise the world differently. He was converted to a God who entered human history born of an unwed mother in a homeless shelter and who later died bloody on a cross for, among other acts, not strictly insisting on the law. This Jesus did not refuse the Eucharist to those who would shortly betray him but who then would take up a new ministry after the resurrection. Jesus did not cling to his divinity but humbled himself to share in the messiness of human life. Life often does not work like it is supposed to; nevertheless love can still be practiced and contribute in a proleptic way to the Kingdom of God.

NOTES

1. Christian E. Brugger, "Five Serious Problems with Chapter 8 of *Amoris Laetitia*," *The Catholic World Report*, April 22, 2016, https://www.catholicworldreport.com/2016/04/22/five-serious-problems-with-chapter-8 of amoris-laetitia. Somewhat snidely, he adds, finally "the *German bishops get all they want*."

2. Stephen Walford, "'Filial Correction' of Pope Marked by Glaring Hypocrisy, Risible Accusations," *National Catholic Reporter*, September 28, 2017, https://www.ncronline.org/news/opinion/filial-correction-pope-marked-glaring-hypocrisy-risible-accusations.

3. Edward Vacek, S.J., "Proportionalism: One View of the Debate," *Theological Studies* 46, no. 2 (1985): 287–314.

4. Fred Martinez, "Pope Francis, Intrinsically Evil Acts, Schonborn/Haring and the Collapse of Catholic & Western Civilization," *Catholic Monitor*, September 29, 2017, http://catholicmonitor.blogspot.com/2017/09/was-pope-francis-mislead-by-schoenborn.html.

5. Fred Martinez, "Pope Francis, Intrinsically Evil Acts, Haring and the Collapse of Catholic & Western Civilization," August 3, 2017, http://www.freerepublic.com/focus/f-religion/3574086/posts.

6. Pete Baklinski, "Fired Catholic Philosopher: Pope Francis' Teaching Could 'Lead Many Souls . . . to Hell,'" September 6, 2017, https://www.lifesitenews.com/news/fired-philosopher-i-questioned-pope-francis-because-his-teaching-could-lead.

7. John Finnis and Germain Grisez, "The Misuse of *Amoris Laetitia* to Support Errors against the Catholic Faith," December 9, 2016, https://www.catholicculture.org/culture/library/view.cfm?id=11463&repos=1&subrepos=0&searchid=1827954.

8. Francis, "Gaudete et Exsultate," accessed May 12, 2018, http://w2.vatican.va/content/francesco/en/apost_exhortations/documents/papa-francesco_esortazione-ap_20180319_gaudete-et-exsultate.html, 36–42, 48–49.

9. Pope Francis, "Amoris Laetitia," accessed May 12, 2018, https://w2.vatican.va/content/dam/francesco/pdf/apost_exhortations/documents/papa-francesco_esortazione-ap_20160319_amoris-laetitia_en.pdf.

10. Robert C. Morlino, "Subsidiarity, Solidarity, and the Lay Mission," August 16, 2012, http://www.madisoncatholicherald.org/bishopscolumns/3366-bishop-column.html.

11. David Cloutier, "'Intrinsic Evil' and Public Policy," *Commonweal*, October 31, 2012, https://www.commonwealmagazine.org/%E2%80%98intrinsic-evil%E2%80%99-public-policy.

12. Richard Gula, S.S., *Reason Informed by Faith* (New York: Paulist Press, 1989), 286–99.

13. Christina Traina, "Papal Ideals, Marital Realities: One View from the Ground," in *Sexual Diversity and Catholicism*, eds. Patricia Beattie Jung and Joseph Coray (Collegeville, MN: Liturgical Press, 2001), 269–88.

14. John Paul II, "Veritatis Splendor," accessed May 12, 2018, http://w2.vatican.va/content/john-paul-ii/en/encyclicals/documents/hf_jp-ii_enc_06081993_veritatis-splendor.html, 79–80.

15. Jana Bennett, "Voting against Intrinsically Evil Acts: A Working List?," August 27, 2012, https://catholicmoraltheology.com/voting-against-intrinsically-evil-acts-a-working-list/.

16. John Paul II, "Veritatis Splendor," 79.

17. John Crossin, OSFS, "Responding to Difficult Situations in Orthodox/Catholic Marriages," accessed May 12, 2018, http://www.usccb.org/beliefs-and-teachings/ecumenical-and-interreligious/ecumenical/orthodox_teaching_remarriage.cfm.

18. Congregation for the Doctrine of the Faith, "Instruction Dignitas Personae on Certain Bioethical Questions," accessed May 12, 2018, http://www.vatican.va/roman_curia/congregations/cfaith/documents/rc_con_cfaith_doc_20081208_dignitas-personae_en.html, 19; also see Congregation for the Doctrine of the Faith, "Regarding the Instruction Dignitas Personae," accessed May 12, 2018, http://www.vatican.va/roman_curia/congregations/cfaith/documents/rc_con_cfaith_doc_20081212_sintesi-dignitas-personae_en.html, part 2. Fortunately, other, often conservative contemporary moralists are trying to get around this obstacle created by holding that such reproductive technology is IE.

19. Cloutier, "'Intrinsic Evil' and Public Policy."

20. Gula, *Reason Informed by Faith*, 85–87.

21. Edward Vacek, S.J., "Passions and Principles," *Milltown Studies* 52 (2003): 67–94; "Orthodoxy Requires Orthopathy: Emotions in Theology," *Horizons* 40 (2013): 218–41.

22. Vacek, "Proportionalism," 287–314.

23. John Paul II, "Familiaris Consortio," accessed May 12, 2018, http://w2.vatican.va/content/john-paul-ii/en/apost_exhortations/documents/hf_jp-ii_exh_19811122_familiaris-consortio.html, 84.

24. Gula, *Reason Informed by Faith*, 88.

25. Edward Vacek, S.J., "Do 'Good People' Need Confession? Self-Deception and the Sacrament of Honesty," *America* 186, no. 6 (February 25, 2002): 11–15.

26. Timothy O'Connell, *Principles for a Catholic Morality*, rev. ed. (New York: Harper & Row, 1990), 110–14.

27. John Paul II, "Familiaris Consortio," 32.

28. John Paul II, "Natural Family Planning," *Origins*, 20, no. 31 (January 10, 1991): 5.

29. Cathleen M. Kaveny, "Intrinsic Evil and Political Responsibility?" *America*, October 27, 2008, https://www.americamagazine.org/issue/673/article/intrinsic-evil-and-political-responsibility.

30. John Paul II, "Veritatis Splendor," 103.

31. Todd Salzman and Michael Lawler, *Sexual Ethics: A Theological Introduction* (Washington, DC: Georgetown University Press, 2012), xv.

32. "Personal Growth and the *'Ordo Amoris,'*" *Listening* 21, no. 3 (1986): 197–209. This whole issue of *Listening* deals with conversion.

33. Salzman and Lawler, *Sexual Ethics*, xvi.

34. Edward Vacek, S.J. "Catholic Marriage Morality in Twentieth Century: From a Baby-Making Contract to a Love-Making Covenant," (manuscript).

REFERENCES

Baklinski, Pete. "Fired Catholic Philosopher: Pope Francis' Teaching Could 'Lead Many Souls . . . to Hell.'" September 6, 2017. https://www.lifesitenews.com/news/fired-philosopher-i-questioned-pope-francis-because-his-teaching-could-lead.

Bennett, Jana. "Voting against Intrinsically Evil Acts: A Working List?" August 27, 2012. https://catholicmoraltheology.com/voting-against-intrinsically-evil-acts-a-working-list/.

Brugger, Christian E. "Five Serious Problems with Chapter 8 of *Amoris Laetitia*." *The Catholic World Report*, April 22, 2016. https://www.catholicworldreport.com/2016/04/22/five-serious-problems-with-chapter-8-of-amoris-laetitia.

Cloutier, David. "'Intrinsic Evil' and Public Policy." *Commonweal*, October 31, 2012. https://www.commonwealmagazine.org/%E2%80%98intrinsic-evil%E2%80%99-public-policy.

Congregation for the Doctrine of the Faith. "Instruction Dignitas Personae on Certain Bioethical Questions." Accessed May 12, 2018. http://www.vatican.va/roman_curia/congregations/cfaith/documents/rc_con_cfaith_doc_20081208_dignitas-personae_en.html.

———. "Regarding the Instruction Dignitas Personae." Accessed May 12, 2018. http://www.vatican.va/roman_curia/congregations/cfaith/documents/rc_con_cfaith_doc_20081212_sintesi-dignitas-personae_en.html.

Crossin, John, OSFS. "Responding to Difficult Situations in Orthodox/Catholic Marriages." Accessed May 12, 2018. http://www.usccb.org/beliefs-and-teachings/ecumenical-and-interreligious/ecumenical/orthodox_teaching_remarriage.cfm.

Finnis, John and Germain Grisez. "The Misuse of *Amoris Laetitia* to Support Errors against the Catholic Faith." December 9, 2016. https://www.catholicculture.org/culture/library/view.cfm?recnum=11463.

Francis. "Amoris Laetitia." Accessed May 12, 2018. https://w2.vatican.va/content/dam/francesco/pdf/apost_exhortations/documents/papa-francesco_esortazione-ap_20160319_amoris-laetitia_en.pdf.

———. "Gaudete et Exsultate." Accessed May 12, 2018. http://w2.vatican.va/content/francesco/en/apost_exhortations/documents/papa-francesco_esortazione-ap_20180319_gaudete-et-exsultate.html.

Gula, Richard, S.S. *Reason Informed by Faith*. New York: Paulist Press, 1989.

John Paul II. "Familiaris Consortio." Accessed May 12, 2018. http://w2.vatican.va/content/john-paul-ii/en/apost_exhortations/documents/hf_jp-ii_exh_19811122_familiaris-consortio.html.

———. "Natural Family Planning." *Origins*, 20, no. 31 (January 10, 1991): 283–84.

———. "Veritatis Splendor." Accessed May 12, 2018. http://w2.vatican.va/content/john-paul-ii/en/encyclicals/documents/hf_jp-ii_enc_06081993_veritatis-splendor.html.

Kaveny, Cathleen M. "Intrinsic Evil and Political Responsibility?" *America*, October 27, 2008. https://www.americamagazine.org/issue/673/article/intrinsic-evil-and-political-responsibility.

Martinez, Fred. "Pope Francis, Intrinsically Evil Acts, Haring and the Collapse of Catholic & Western Civilization." August 3, 2017. http://www.freerepublic.com/focus/f-religion/3574086/posts.

Morlino, Robert C. "Pope Francis, Intrinsically Evil Acts, Schonborn/Haring and the Collapse of Catholic & Western Civilization." *Catholic Monitor*, September 29, 2017. http://catholicmonitor.blogspot.com/2017/09/was-pope-francis-mislead-by-schoenborn.html.

———. "Subsidiarity, Solidarity, and the Lay Mission." August 16, 2012. http://www.madisoncatholicherald.org/bishopscolumns/3366-bishop-column.html.

O'Connell, Timothy. *Principles for a Catholic Morality*. Rev. ed. New York: Harper & Row, 1990.

Salzman, Todd, and Michael Lawler. *Sexual Ethics: A Theological Introduction*. Washington, DC: Georgetown University Press, 2012.

Traina, Christina. "Papal Ideals, Marital Realities: One View from the Ground." In *Sexual Diversity and Catholicism*, edited by Patricia Beattie Jung and Joseph Coray, 269–88. Collegeville, MN: Liturgical Press, 2001.

Vacek, Edward, S.J. "Catholic Marriage Morality in Twentieth Century: From a Baby-Making Contract to a Love-Making Covenant." Manuscript.

———. "Do 'Good People' Need Confession? Self-Deception and the Sacrament of Honesty." *America* 186, no. 6 (February 25, 2002): 11–15.

———. "Orthodoxy Requires Orthopathy: Emotions in Theology." *Horizons* 40 (2013): 218–41.

————. "Passions and Principles." *Milltown Studies* 52 (2003): 67–94.

————. "Proportionalism: One View of the Debate." *Theological Studies* 46, no. 2 (1985): 287–314.

Various Authors. "Personal Growth and the *'Ordo Amoris.'" Listening* 21, no. 3 (1986): 197–209.

Walford, Stephen. "'Filial cCorrection' of Pope Marked by Glaring Hypocrisy, Risible Accusations." *National Catholic Reporter*, September 28, 2017. https://www.ncronline.org/news/opinion/filial-correction-pope-marked-glaring-hypocrisy-risible-accusations.

What Is Intrinsic Evil?

Nenad Polgar and Joseph A. Selling

In the minds of many, if not most people, ethics or morality is a relatively simple, straightforward enterprise. There are good and bad attitudes, there are right and wrong behaviors. The majority of these attitudes and behaviors are identified by laws or norms that tell us what we should and should not do. These laws and norms come from different sources. We have all heard of the Ten Commandments, and most of us accept the fact that because these are rather succinct, scholars, teachers, and the leaders of our communities have elaborated more specific norms from them. Thus, while the eighth commandment forbids "giving false witness against one's neighbor," from ancient times it has been pointed out that any form of willful deception in our communication is offensive not just to individuals but indeed for the entire community which understands that honest communication is a crucial element for the integrity of social living.

In the Catholic Christian tradition, the justification for deriving specific norms from basic or fundamental commandments or principles[1] is the belief that the universe was created by God who must have had a plan about how things should be and should work. In response to the obvious question about how mere human beings might come to know what that plan might be, the Catholic tradition holds that by creating human beings with an intellect, often (too) simply referred to as the "use of reason," righteous persons should be able to figure this out by observing the world around them and taking account of their shared, accumulated experience. Because this was associated with a (too) simple presumption about the "natural world," the norms that were derived from this observation and experience are frequently referred to as "natural laws."

This all appears very well and good, except for the fact that in our day and age we have come to realize that what we call "nature" is anything but straightforward. Add to this the understanding that "experience" is not a universally shared phenomenon, but rather something strongly influenced by history and culture, and we become aware of a proliferation and diversity of ethical or moral norms that are not always congruent. Sorting out which norms are relevant and applicable, which are primary or even crucial, and which merely signal convention or preference is not always an easy task.

Furthermore, we should take into account that most Western cultures that enjoy freedom of inquiry and communication have developed a sensitivity to the fact that our increasingly complex lives demand specialized and sometimes highly technical attention to be given to the ethical dimensions of our ways of living. The "worlds" of economics, medicine, environmental sustainability, and communication itself, to name just a few areas of ethical challenge, have each developed a form of specialized ethics that seeks to provide guidelines and norms of good practice and decision-making in those fields. There are ethical committees and codes that investigate and evaluate sometimes complex and nuanced situations that will have an impact not only on the agents functioning in these fields but also on the general and particular publics who are affected by those practices and decisions.

Given the proliferation and complexity of ethical experience and the norms meant to guide us in so many different fields, one can appreciate that the very formulation of those norms must be done and presented carefully, with sufficient clarity and a significant level of transparency. It must recognize that it is very difficult for one to focus one's efforts on applying a norm that makes little or no sense, at least if not especially, for one's personal life situation. The days of the church simply dictating obligations and prohibitions are long gone, and anyone who ignores that is destined to lose credibility.

In light of all this, how is it possible for people to think that offering ethical advice, or even articulating a moral obligation or prohibition, can be reduced to a four- or five-word statement? Granted there are phrases and even single words, such as child abuse, terrorism, or murder, that carry their own moral connotation. Everyone knows that these things are unacceptable, that they are synonymous with serious evil and should never be considered as behavioral options.

There are other words that, at first sight, appear to signal something morally objectionable that should never be done, such as stealing, homicide, lying, and adultery. While one might readily agree with this, it would be hard to believe someone who classified each and every one of these as a major offense that merited severe punishment. Stealing a bar of soap from a hotel room or lying about your age are hardly grounds for social (or eternal) banishment; homicide can be accidental; and even adultery could, in an extreme case, be assessed as a case of mistaken identity.

All of these things, even in their merely descriptive usage, infer the notion that there is something about them that is not good. There is an evil attached to the perception of these activities that usually does and should make us uneasy. But we think that we could agree that this does not, ipso facto, warrant the label of "intrinsic evil." For the phrase implies not only qualitative (what are we talking about) but also quantitative (this is something very serious) dimensions of what is being singled out. The more extreme examples of perpetrating evil, such as torture and child abuse, do not need to be called intrinsically evil, while some of the things that are labeled as such are considered by thoughtful persons to be relatively unimportant, such as being less than truthful about trivial matters or using some forms of contraception.

So why is the phrase still used in the teaching of the church? Many people think that the phrase signifies something so horrifically evil that even contemplating it would itself be sinful. Others consider it to be the conclusion of a logical proposition that could only be arrived at by moral philosophers. Then there is the observation that the expression is little more than a trump card used to condemn certain forms of activity and prevent any conversation that might question the validity of that position.

THE WORKSHOP

This question suggested a starting point for the workshop held in Vienna at the end of January 2018. Each of the participants at the workshop approached the topic from their own particular perspective, one which reveals the core elements of their own research. We arranged their contributions in what we thought was a developmental schema and will just highlight the salient points that they brought to the discussion.

Investigating the longer history of our Western and Catholic tradition, we have seen that the idea that there are certain kinds of behavior which one should never perform was recognized early on and formed part of Aristotle's ethics. Even at that stage, however, there was also a recognition that describing such things entailed an implicit, and frequently explicit, account of intentions and circumstances necessary to determine such conclusions (Herzberg). In the Catholic theological tradition, although the term "intrinsic evil" did not appear until the fourteenth century, there was an earlier tradition that acknowledged that certain human activities should never be done. Although some would like to see this as a kind of precursor to the concept of intrinsic evil, it was specifically different from the latter idea because it maintained that a consideration of intention and circumstances was still relevant to making such a judgment (Polgar).

It did not escape the attention of the participants of the workshop that the majority of—at least those more contentious—claims of intrinsic evil are to be found in an entire range of issues within the field of sexual ethics. The position shared by most of the participants was that the invocation of intrinsic evil in this area has proven something of an obstacle to clear thinking. Its use was characterized as "eclectic, selective, and theologically unhelpful." Although it might still have some use when turned toward questions of racism or structural evil, it appears to be a concept that has outlived its relevance (Pope). That said, deconstructing the use of intrinsic evil in sexual ethics invites the researcher to broaden our understanding of sexual ethics. Not infrequently, what may have been understood as an offense against chastity is in fact an offense against justice, as in forcing a sexual relationship upon a person without their consent. Reconstructing a specifically theological understanding of human sexuality reveals that conclusions reached in the past were largely built upon presumptions rather than demonstrable facts. A hermeneutic study of natural law thinking in *Humanae Vitae* clearly reveals its weakness and the need for a more personalist approach. None of this, of course, means that there is no longer any normative way to govern sexual behavior. An exemplary sketch of this can be found in the work of Margaret Farley[2] (Prüller-Jagenteufel).

Beyond sexual ethics one might characterize the use of intrinsic evil as a kind of *shibboleth* of Catholic identity, something that makes the People of God stand out, such as a long-standing tradition of dealing with objective moral evil. Curiously, while Pope John Paul II insisted upon the use of the term across the whole of moral theology in *Veritatis Splendor*, Pope Francis is currently being criticized by four cardinals who find fault with his failure to uphold the language of intrinsic evil in his response to the Synod on the Family, *Amoris Laetitia*. While there is a great deal to be said about how the hierarchy is dealing with the concept, one might prefer to expand the understanding of *intrinsece malum in se* to signify the church's teaching on absolute moral truth (Bretzke). A similar approach that accepts the concept of intrinsic evil as representative of an objective moral order, attempts to balance its overextension in the pastoral field by drawing attention to the role of intentionality and circumstances that have an impact on the role of personal accountability. While accepting the notion of objective and even absolute principles, following Klaus Demmer one needs to remember that our knowledge of those principles is embedded in the epistemological acts that take place in a specific historical context that can only be understood with an adequate hermeneutic (Müller).

More fundamentally, one could examine the language of intrinsic evil against the background of our understanding of the moral act itself. The traditional textbook approach to the discipline emphasized the performance of prohibited acts or the omission of clear obligations as the focal point of identifying sins. The goal of the discipline was to train the priest-confessor to identify and evaluate the gravity of sins being reported in the confessional.

When moral theology began being done in vernacular languages, no attention was given to distinguishing between words like good and evil, right and wrong. Under the presumption that intention and circumstances were only of secondary importance, the concept of intrinsic evil insufficiently distinguished the descriptive and evaluative meaning of "evil" so that every moral act had to be purely good or indifferent (Selling). Reexamining the structure of the moral act must admit that any adequate description of human moral activity necessarily involves a consideration of circumstances. The "object" that one chooses can be considered the material element of that activity which should be right for the given circumstances, while the commitment one makes to achieving a goal through that activity is the formal element that should always be good. An important reason why these distinctions were neglected in traditional moral theology was because the textbook approach was all about a retrospective view of morality—what has already taken place—while an examination of the process of moral living and decision-making is a prospective view that begins with personal convictions and commitments (Wolbert).

Raising these questions brings us closer to what some would call the level of metaethics, an attempt to go beyond the controversies raised by ethicists using different ethical theories. If one takes a step back from the arguments, it becomes apparent that one's theoretical perspective has a direct influence on how they interpret the concept of intrinsic evil. In a normative context, the expression does not really occupy a meaningful place since normative ethics is primarily about justifying various moral norms through argumentation, whereas referring to intrinsic evil is basically an attempt at shutting down discussion. While the expression could be used in explaining the doctrine of the sources of morality, perhaps its real place is functioning as a form of parenetic speech or moral exhortation (Weiß). Finally, there is another reflection on the "irregular situations" in which people find themselves after entering into another union after a previous marriage. While Pope Francis has literally been accused of heresy, he nonetheless attempts to find a pastoral solution for these persons without, in some situations, forcing them to commit yet another sin by abandoning their partner or their children. This calls for a reflection on the proper role of conscience which must be the practical guide for persons. Conscience is guided not simply by assimilating rules but also by a process of discernment. Simultaneously, one can only understand this pastoral application if one takes account of Francis's emphasis on mercy—not as a kind of "looking the other way," but as a genuine acceptance of persons living in very difficult circumstances (Vacek).

FROM AN ETHICS OF BEHAVIOR TOWARD
AN ETHICS OF RESPONSIBILITY

All the participants at the workshop on intrinsic evil are in agreement that Catholic teaching about morality cannot be separated from a belief in being able to speak about objective good and evil. Fundamentally, this belief is similar to the reasoning that was first invoked by Aquinas to affirm the concept of natural law; namely, that God created human persons with an intellectual capacity to recognize the real or potential presence of good and evil. Catholic theology accepts the idea that we are all affected by sin and subsequently suffer from ignorance as well as an inadequate ability to deal with all our passions. This is why we need to be attentive to our own limitations, to heed the wisdom of the community of believers, and to periodically examine our conscience and ask ourselves if we are living up to what we claim to be ethical responsibility.

Our belief in objective good and evil, however, is rather different from the way of thinking that is so frequently attributed to the traditional understanding of natural law. While the latter relied on simple observation of the "natural world" and the patterns of thinking that would evolve into the physical and biological sciences, coming to grips with good and evil in the contemporary world presupposes a familiarity with what have come to be known as the human sciences. What is ethically good is good for persons—not simply as individuals but as persons-in-relations with other persons, with God, and with God's creation. What is ethically evil is evil for persons in the same way. This is one of the reasons that our pursuit of understanding good and evil must always be done in the context of a community, both present and historical. For the wisdom that humankind needs to survive and to flourish is not simply broad and profound, but also in a continuous state of development.

An "objective" knowledge of good and evil does not mean that good and evil are merely objects, "things" to be examined. They can be relationships, states-of-affairs, even processes. The classification of good and evil only makes sense in a human environment. They are labels that depend upon an intelligent assessment about whether things are beneficial or harmful to human persons. That assessment can change over time and because of circumstances.

For instance, some things we once thought of as good we now see as evil (slavery, divine right of kings, etc.). Some things we once thought of as evil we now see as good (democracy, gender equality, etc.). Some things invoke a spectrum of opinion about good and evil (co-education, using fossil fuels, etc.). However, simply naming things good or evil is not the end of the exercise. We need to prioritize and arrange goods, evils, and mixtures of the two. The order is something that we create, maintain, and adjust when appropriate. It reveals what we consider to be more or less important, helpful, and beneficial for the community—or not.[3] This is largely the area of what is traditionally called social ethics.

The notion of good and evil is thus not something abstract or "ontological." It does not exist in some realm accessible only to a chosen few. But it *is* real, and we can work toward the affirmation of its objectivity by consulting our communities, our traditions, and our own experience. This is not a matter of individual, subjective feeling or determining what is good (and evil) by a majority vote. But it is something that is certainly as existential as it is traditional.

Gaudium et Spes, 26 defines the common good as "the sum of those conditions of social life which allow social groups and their individual members relatively thorough and ready access to their own fulfillment." Notice that it does not elaborate what those "conditions of social life" might be. This is because those "conditions" may vary from one society to another, from one time to another. The needs of people in less developed countries are rather different from those in well-developed and prosperous countries. Another example from a historical perspective is that in medieval times—and today still in some societies—a family had to achieve a relatively large number of conceptions in order to have a suitable number of children to survive and grow into adulthood, thus sustaining the family. Today, most countries seek to have lower birthrates because the survival rate of newborns and children is much higher than it used to be 50, 100, or 150 years ago (depending on where one lives).

What some would like to call an absolute good, such as human fecundity, makes little or no sense. Such labeling is a good example of an "abstract" good as opposed to a "real" good. Conceiving a child is not always a "good idea." Saying that every conception is a "gift from God" may contain a mysterious message, but it holds little meaning for the family that is already struggling to survive. Saying that preventing conception is an absolute evil, is equally meaningless. In fact, the evolved traditional teaching of the hierarchy has explicitly endorsed the reasonable goal of limiting the number of births.[4] When church teaching suggests that *any* form of "artificially preventing conception" is intrinsically evil, it is, in fact, sabotaging its own teaching: encouraging the goals but severely limiting the means for achieving those goals.

Using the primary words of ethical discourse, good and evil, is inescapable. But exaggerating their meaning, with qualifiers like "absolute" or "intrinsic," is unwarranted when we consider that the very definition of what is good and/or evil is a human[5] task and activity that is never finished. Furthermore, even when we might arrive at a consensus of what is deemed being labeled good or evil, we still need to prioritize and order those goods (and our efforts to avoid or at least diminish evils) to complete the picture of our ethical environment.

We believe that it is possible to affirm the reality and importance of an "objective moral order" without going to the extreme of freezing it into static construction. It is possible to affirm that some things will always be worthy of the label good, such as kindness, honesty, integrity, mercy, and so forth; and that other things will always be worthy of the label evil, such as cruelty, deceit, corruption, vengeance, and so forth. Simultaneously, we realize that there are other things that we may have come to judge as good rather than evil, or vice versa, even in the course of our own lives. This is why we find a correlation (not a causation) between aging and wisdom.

THINGS THAT SHOULD NEVER BE DONE

Avoiding the labels of absolute or intrinsic evil does not mean that we eliminate the need to say that some things should never be done. As pointed out above, ethicists were able to do this in our Western tradition right up until the fourteenth century, when the term "intrinsic evil" was first used (and largely rejected). In going about this task, Christian ethicists of the past engaged in what Jeffrey Stout calls "moral bricolage,"[6] that is, a selective retrieval of ideas from various traditions, coupled with the best insights from other "sciences" available to them and guided by the Scriptures. Great moral bricoleurs of the past were, thus, able to "stitch together" impressive ethical systems that included and developed credible accounts of good and evil, prioritizing these goods in some sort of hierarchical order and identifying not only evils, but also "things that should never be done."

At some point in the Catholic tradition there was an attempt to siphon the contents of this category of "things that should never be done" into the emerging term "intrinsic evil." The brilliance of this methodological invention needs no further proof beyond the fact that the term endured within Catholic theology for more than six hundred years. However, when compared to some contemporary terms such as "dividend" (in economics) or "psychogenic disorder" (in psychology) that organize knowledge in a given field, there is nothing particularly surprising about the introduction of the term "intrinsic evil" in order to designate "things that should never be done."

This process of invention of terms should, nevertheless, not lose sight of the purposes for which they were developed and the edifices of knowledge which they presuppose in order to make sense. However, when tectonic shifts in regard to these purposes or edifices of knowledge take place, it is reasonable to expect that the terms that presuppose them will also shift in meaning and, in some cases, become obsolete (like phlogiston in chemistry).[7]

Perhaps the best evidence that the term "intrinsic evil" might have become obsolete comes from studying its historical development and the spectrum of meanings that have been attached to it. From morally bad and contrary to (divine) right or human/rational nature, to a confirmation of intrinsic morality, the term "intrinsic evil" has been identified with an entire range of meanings without discrimination. Thus, it has more than tested the boundaries of coherent thought, insofar as it is associated with too many diverse meanings. Have we, therefore, reached the point at which shifts in meanings of the term "intrinsic evil" are not sufficient for maintaining a coherent concept and are in fact defeating the purpose for which it was coined, thus making it obsolete?

In the minds of some reflective Catholics, perhaps one of the largest obstacles to responding positively to this question is a too close association between the term "intrinsic evil" and its purpose, that is, to refer to the notion of an objective moral order as it pertains to those things that should never be done. Hence, the fear arises whether we are getting rid of the (notion of) objective moral order by jettisoning the term "intrinsic evil," subsequently being left with nothing but relativism?

We believe that this conclusion follows only if the objective moral order is identified with some very specific ethical judgments of the great moral bricoleurs of the past. Instead of following this path, many contemporary Catholic moral bricoleurs stand firmly in the tradition of their predecessors by engaging in the same task. They reflect on an objective moral order on the basis of a selective retrieval of ideas from various traditions, coupled with the best insights from other sciences available to them, and guided by the Scriptures. In going about that task, contemporary moral bricoleurs do not seem to find it difficult to form judgments about "things that should never be done" without using the label "intrinsic evil." Furthermore, this methodological decision hardly makes them relativists, or, if it does, then they share this classification with theologians like Augustine, Thomas Aquinas, and every other pre-fourteenth-century theologian. Consequently, the association between the two—avoidance of the term "intrinsic evil" and "relativism"—is unfounded and reasons for the controversy surrounding the term ought to be searched for elsewhere.

Indicative of these reasons is the fact that there was an upsurge in the use of the term "intrinsic evil" and its derivatives in theological writings and documents of the teaching office in the second half of the twentieth century. This is the period in which the Catholic Church had convened the Second Vatican Council and took a more open and reconciliatory stance toward the world, becoming, in effect, the Church *in* the world, as opposed to the Church *above* the world. Consequently, the Church realized that despite its deposit of faith based on Scripture and Tradition, it cannot simply assume that it knows all the answers; that its role is not only to teach the world, but also to listen to and learn from different voices within the world.[8] Perhaps more consciously than ever before, the Church realized that it stands under a dual obligation of fidelity to its own tradition and contemporaneity.[9] Furthermore, these two obligations are not only generating their own demands, but are also in a dialectical relationship in the sense that failing to meet one also means betraying the other. This is why the "teaching office" of the Church today cannot be separated from its "learning office" without raising a doubt of being inauthentic and retreating back to the understanding of the Church above the world.

Due to the new developments in just about every sphere of life in modern societies, one of the issues that emerged through this dialogue with the world is precisely how to define the human good. While there is not much hope that a reasonable degree of consensus can be reached on this point in the near future, the sheer amount of voices that demand a hearing within this discussion can seem intimidating. This, in turn, encourages the fear of relativism that questions "the established truth" of what the human good is as it relates to more specific issues. On top of that, as the late Gareth Moore once pointed out: "Things which have meanings, like words and symbols, have an importance to people; they often don't like it when the words and symbols to which they are accustomed lose their meaning, or when others use them in different ways and therefore attach to them a different meaning."[10]

Seen against this background of questioning the established notions of the human good, the increase in the use of the term "intrinsic evil" does not seem very surprising. Insofar as one of its functions was to stop further discussion on certain ethical issues and to affirm previously established conclusions as an expression of the objective moral order, the employment of the term is a strategy born out of fear that things will get out of control. In other words, those who promote or harbor such fear seem to believe that such discussions on the human good need to be controlled not by arguments but by authority. In such endeavors, another function or meaning of the term "intrinsic evil," a confirmation of intrinsic morality, that is, morality that emerges through continuous discernment and reflection on sources of (moral) knowledge, is pushed to the side.

Hence, the struggle over what constitutes the human good (and evil) seems to be the core issue underlying discussions in contemporary theological ethics and the interpretative angle from which one ought to assess the term "intrinsic evil." In this perspective, the use of the term within these discussions is, at best, a rhetorical strategy and, at worst, an instance of not getting the point; that is, of imagining oneself as being part of some other struggle (for instance, defending the doctrine). This evaluation could hardly be cushioned by invoking other meanings of the term "intrinsic evil" (such as contrary to divine right or human nature), since the discussion on what constitutes the human good makes all of these meanings (concepts) a part of and a hoped-for outcome of the discussion, and not its starting point.

NOTES

1. It is not always immediately clear which principle(s) are indicated by specific commandments. Thus, the command "not to kill" becomes extended to the causation of any form of bodily, mental, or spiritual harm; while at the same time it admits of exceptions, such as a need to protect oneself or others or to safeguard the integrity of a just social structure.

2. Margaret Farley, *Just Love. A Framework for Christian Sexual Ethics* (New York/London: Continuum, 2006).

3. The process of prioritizing goods (and evils in something of a reverse sense) can also be seen as valuing the goods we identify. Valuing means the extent to which we are willing to expend our resources, time, and energy to achieve, hold on to, and promote these goods. We should remember that valuing is an activity, "to value" is a verb. When we strongly value a good, we tend to classify it as "a value," giving it a status that may not be experienced by all persons in all contexts. For instance, higher education is considered a value in highly literate and technological societies, but it would not enjoy the same status in a subsistence society.

4. Paul VI, "Humanae vitae," accessed July 17, 2018, http://w2.vatican.va/content/paul-vi/en/encyclicals/documents/hf_p-vi_enc_25071968_humanae-vitae.html, 24 states: "It is supremely desirable, and this was also the mind of Pius XII, that medical science should by the study of natural rhythms succeed in determining a sufficiently secure basis for the chaste limitation of offspring."

5. We imagine that some will object that it is not humankind but God who determines what is good and evil, perhaps by quoting some lines from Genesis to the effect that "God saw that it was good." This clearly states something of a message about the human community respecting God's creation, but it does not hamper the human community declaring that some aspects of that creation, like disease-causing viruses and bacteria, are harmful to human beings and thus considered to be evil.

6. Jeffrey Stout, *Ethics after Babel: The Language of Morals and Their Discontents* (Boston, MA: Beacon Press, 1988), 293–94.

7. Before the discovery of oxidation, the phlogiston theory was used to explain processes like combustion and rusting. The theory postulated that bodies contain a firelike element ("phlogiston"), which is released during combustion/rusting.

8. "Let the layman not imagine that his pastors are always such experts, that to every problem which arises, however complicated, they can readily give him a concrete solution, or even that such is their mission. Rather, enlightened by Christian wisdom and giving close attention to the teaching authority of the Church, let the layman take on his own distinctive role." Second Vatican Council, "Gaudium et Spes," accessed July 17, 2018, http://www.vatican.va/archive/hist_councils/ii_vatican_council/documents/vat-ii_const_19651207_gaudium-et-spes_en.html, 43.

9. In terms of this dual obligation, Joseph Monti argues: "Christian morality will certainly not affirm all that it finds in any given time and age, but if it is to be faithful, the Church must constructively engage its own contemporary worlds. Christianity is defined and identified as much by its present as its past, cast always upon the horizon of the future" (*Arguing about Sex: The Rhetoric of Christian Sexual Morality* [Albany: State University of New York Press, 1995], 6).

10. Gareth Moore, *A Question of Truth: Christianity and Homosexuality* (London: Continuum, 2003), 278.

REFERENCES

Farley, Margaret. *Just Love: A Framework for Christian Sexual Ethics*. New York/London: Continuum, 2006.

Monti, Joseph. *Arguing about Sex: The Rhetoric of Christian Sexual Morality*. Albany: State University of New York Press, 1995.

Moore, Gareth. *A Question of Truth: Christianity and Homosexuality*. London: Continuum, 2003.

Paul VI. "Humanae vitae." Accessed July 17, 2018. http://w2.vatican.va/content/paul-vi/en/encyclicals/documents/hf_p-vi_enc_25071968_humanae-vitae.html.

Second Vatican Council. "Gaudium et Spes." Accessed July 17, 2018. http://www.vatican.va/archive/hist_councils/ii_vatican_council/documents/vat-ii_const_19651207_gaudium-et-spes_en.html.

Stout, Jeffrey. *Ethics after Babel: The Language of Morals and Their Discontents*. Boston, MA: Beacon Press, 1988.

Index

About the Contributors

James T. Bretzke, S.J., earned his doctorate and taught at the Pontifical Gregorian University before returning to America in 1993 where he has taught at Jesuit institutions in Berkeley, San Francisco, Boston, and now at Marquette University in his native Milwaukee, Wisconsin. He also has taught regularly in Seoul, Korea, and in Manila, Philippines. His primary areas of research interest are cross-cultural Christian ethics and moral methodology. Most recently he has published the *Handbook of Roman Catholic Moral Terms* (Washington, DC: Georgetown University Press, 2013), *Consecrated Phrases: A Latin Theological Dictionary* (Collegeville, MN: Liturgical Press, 2003), and *A Morally Complex World* (Collegeville, MN: Liturgical Press, 2004), as well as more than one hundred scholarly articles.

Stephan Herzberg is professor of history of philosophy and ethics at the Philosophisch-Theologische Hochschule Sankt Georgen. His research interests are Aristotle, Thomas Aquinas, ethics, *intrinsece malum*. His main publications include *Wahrnehmung und Wissen bei Aristoteles* (Berlin/New York: De Gruyter, 2011); *Menschliche und göttliche Kontemplation* (Heidelberg: Universitätsverlag Winter GmbH, 2013); (coedited with Johannes Brachtendorf) *Vergebung. Philosophische Perspektiven auf ein Problemfeld der Ethik* (Münster, Mentis, 2014); and (coedited with Heinrich Watzka) *Transzendenzlos glücklich?* (Münster: Aschendorff, 2016).

Sigrid Müller is professor of theological ethics at the Catholic Theological Faculty of the University of Vienna since 2007. Her research interests cover the history of theological ethics, technology and ethics, and fundamental questions of theological ethics. She has written about late medieval philosophy and theological ethics and coedited volumes on bodiliness, medical ethics, and interdisciplinary bioethical questions. Among her most recent publications are (coedited with Konrad Hilpert) *Humanae vitae—die anstößige Enzyklika* (Freiburg i. Br: Herder, 2018) and *Philosophie und Theologie im Spätmittelalter* (Münster: Aschendorff, 2018). Together with Kerstin Schlögl-Flierl, she is currently working on *A Short History of Moral Theology*.

Nenad Polgar obtained his doctorate in theological ethics at the Catholic University Leuven (Belgium). He is assistant professor at the University of Zagreb (Croatia) and post-doctoral assistant at the University of Vienna (Austria). His research interests and publications are in the area of fundamental theological ethics, sexual ethics, and bioethics. He is currently working on a systematic study of the concept of intrinsic evil (as a habilitation project) entitled *The Origins, Meaning, and Relevance of the Concept of Intrinsic Evil*.

Stephen J. Pope is professor of theological ethics at Boston College. His research interests are the virtues and law, charity and justice, restorative justice, theology and the sciences. His recent publications include "Does Cosmic Evolution Have a Purpose? William Stoeger's Account of 'Nested Directionality,'" *Theological Studies*, 78 (2017): 462–82 and *A Step along the Way: Models of Christian Service* (Maryknoll, NY: Orbis Press, 2015). He is currently working on a book entitled *The Fullness of Life: The Science of Well-Being and the Ethics of Virtue*.

Gunter Prüller-Jagenteufel is associate professor of theological ethics at the Catholic Theological Faculty of the University of Vienna. His main research interests are the theology of Dietrich Bonhoeffer, ethics in political theology, and theology of liberation. As a member of the Board of the International Network of Societies for Catholic Theology (INSeCT—Connecting Theology Worldwide) he recently organized and edited several international conferences on the INSeCT Research Programs. The proceedings have been published in Gunter Prüller-Jagenteufel, Sharon Bong, and Rita Perintfalvi, eds., *Towards Just Gender Relations: Rethinking the Role of Women in Church and Society. The Asian and European Conferences of the INSeCT Research Project 201–7*(Göttingen: VandR Unipress, 2018). One of his most recent publications deals with the theme of confession and reconciliation: Gunter Prüller-Jagenteufel, Christine Schliesser, and Ralf K. Wüstenberg, eds., *Beichte neu entdecken. Ein ökumenisches Kompendium für die Praxis* (Göttingen: Edition Ruprecht, 2016).

Joseph A. Selling is emeritus professor of theological ethics in the Faculty of Theology at the Katholieke Universiteit Leuven, in Leuven, Belgium. His research interests are fundamental and sexual ethics. His recent publications include, "Is Lived Experience a Source of Morality?" *Intams* 20 (2014): 217–25, "Some Psychological Aspects of Religious Ethics: Virtue and Motivation," *Journal of Religion and Society*, Supplement 11 (2015), and *Reframing Catholic Theological Ethics* (Oxford: Oxford University Press, 2016).

Edward C. Vacek, S.J., has since 2012 held the Stephen J. Duffy Chair in Catholic Studies at Loyola University in New Orleans. For the thirty-five years before that, he taught in the Jesuit theologates in Chicago and Cambridge/Boston. He is the author of *Love, Human and Divine: The Heart of Christian Ethics* (Washington, DC: Georgetown University Press, 1996). He has authored more than seventy articles, most recently in *Horizons*, *Theological Studies*, and the *Journal of Moral Theology*. His past writing has been chiefly in the area of fundamental moral theology and sexuality. He is currently writing a book on *Emotions in the Christian Life*.

Andreas M. Weiß is assistant professor of theological ethics at the Department of Practical Theology and the Center for Ethics and Poverty Research, University of Salzburg, Austria. His research interests are ethical theory, virtue ethics, medical ethics, and environmental ethics. He is the author of *Sittlicher Wert und nichtsittliche Werte: Zur Relevanz der Unterscheidung in der moraltheologischen Diskussion um deontologische Normen* (Freiburg i. Ue.: Universitätsverlag; Freiburg i. Br.: Herder, 1996); "Deontologie und Teleologie. Einige Definitionen und Klärungen," in *Deontologie—Teleologie. Normtheoretische Grundlagen in der Diskussion*, eds. Adrian Holderegger and Werner Wolbert (Freiburg: Academic Press, 2012) 15–44; "Nachhaltige Entwicklung als ethisches Prinzip," in *Der gesellschaftliche Mensch und menschliche Gesellschaft. Gedenkschrift für Franz Martin Schmölz*, eds. Elisabeth Kapferer et al. (Innsbruck/Wien: Tyrolia, 2014), 297–322; and "Die Ehe als Freundschaft. Zur Deutung der ehelichen Liebe als Freundschaft in Amoris laetitia," in *"Freundschaft" im interdisziplinären Dialog*, ed. Angelika Walser (Innsbruck/Wien: Tyrolia, 2017), 139–55.

Werner Wolbert is professor *emeritus*. He taught theological ethics at the Theological Faculty Paderborn (Germany) and at the Theological Faculty in Salzburg (Austria). His research interests are ethical theory, bioethics, and social ethics. Recent publications include *Was sollen wir tun? Biblische Weisung und ethische Reflexion* (Freiburg i.Ue./Freiburg i.Br.: Academic Press Fribourg, 2005), *Gewissen und Verantwortung. Gesammelte Studien* (Freiburg i.Ue./Freiburg i.Br.: Academic Press Fribourg, 2009), and (coedited with Adrian Holderegger), *Deontologie – Teleologie. Normtheoretische Grundlagen in der Diskussion* (Freiburg i. Ue./Freiburg i. Br., Academic Press Fribourg, 2012).